Schizophrenic Germany

THE MACMILLAN COMPANY
NEW YORK · CHICAGO
DALLAS · ATLANTA · SAN FRANCISCO
LONDON · MANILA
IN CANADA
BRETT-MACMILLAN LTD.
GALT, ONTARIO

Schizophrenic Germany

by
John
Dornberg

71741

New York
THE MACMILLAN COMPANY
1961

DD259.2
.D71

First Printing

The Macmillan Company, New York
Brett-Macmillan Ltd., Galt, Ontario

Printed in the United States of America

Library of Congress catalog card number: 61–6582

For
Ulla and Stephan

The Author—

JOHN DORNBERG was born in Germany shortly before the first convulsive stirrings of the Third Reich. In 1939, when he was only seven years old, he and his parents fled their native country and settled in Denver. After studying journalism at Denver University, he returned to Germany in 1954 with the U.S. Army. Since his discharge, he has remained in that country as News Editor of *Overseas Weekly,* an American-owned publication for American servicemen abroad. He is the author of many articles on the postwar climate in Germany.

Preface

In this book I have endeavored to approach impersonally that which has affected me personally most of my life. I have tried to view objectively the postwar aftermath of the Nazi state whose existence affected me so closely.

I was born in Germany, the only son of Jewish parents who were forced to flee their native country in 1939, leaving behind most of what they owned, their friends, and a great number of close and distant relatives. Although I was only seven years old at the time, I still remember clearly most of the circumstances surrounding that flight and the events that led up to it. I can still visualize the Crystal Night of 1938 when my father was arrested and taken—in nothing more than his pajamas—to Buchenwald concentration camp. I can still recall the fearful and hectic months before his arrest. I still can see the burning synagogue in our town, the storm troopers at our door, the ravaged shops, and I still hear my mother saying, the morning after, that I would not be permitted to go to school any more. It hurt me, and I could not understand it, for I liked school. I still recall vividly my father's homecoming: he was wearing tattered, borrowed clothes, his head was shaven clean, he looked emaciated, and he smelled because there had been no soap or water.

I also remember being jeered and stoned on the streets by other children because I was a Jew.

Even more clearly, I remember our flight from Germany, the empty apartment, the tearful farewell to my grandmother, and the strange new experiences in the United States which, for us, was almost a different world.

There was the language to learn and the task of overcoming economic crises brought on by my father's illness, incurred during service with the German Army in World War I but aggravated by his internment at Buchenwald, and which eventuated in his untimely death.

Naturally, these are all a child's memories, dramatized and made more vivid over the years, and they should have no bearing on a book such as this. However, these experiences are part of the background which eventually compelled me to set out on this effort.

Throughout the war years I heard little good about the Germans. Occasionally my parents would say "they weren't all bad," but no one would ever detail for me what was good about them. Occasionally my father would become emotional about the country he had been forced to leave, such as the time when he gave me his World War I medals to donate to a "scrap for bullets" drive in 1943. But otherwise Germany, as I remembered it and as I was told about it, was all negative, and when the war ended I gave little thought to its peacetime future.

Actually, my return to Germany was purely accidental, coming at the courtesy of the United States Army. But what I found there was surprising. In contrast to all the prejudiced tales I had heard at home, it appeared as if the Germans were completely changed. I was amazed at all the reconstruction, the economic well-being, and more than anything else the spirit of freedom and democracy which seemed to prevail among the people I met.

I also learned of the other side of the German problem from my non-Jewish German wife and her friends and relatives who had seen the Nazi régime from a completely different point of view. Above all, I learned from them and other Germans that many of the crimes committed by the Nazis, many of the régime's actions, had been committed and carried out in secrecy. It was not until the war was over that many Germans learned the truth. I also met members of the anti-Nazi resistance movement, the existence of which I had even doubted. I began to dig deeper and I found many of the first impressions disappearing again. There were still Nazis, it seemed; there was a new army, and there were, once more, nationalistic trends. Yet so many people were opposed to these trends and fighting them, that I was no longer certain whether Germany had, or had not, changed.

Eventually I realized that postwar Germany, geographically ripped asunder, economically powerful, emotionally unstable, respected and feared simultaneously by its neighbors and allies, was neither changed, nor unchanged, but that it was in a puzzling state of betwixt-and-between which continues to prevail today. It is this fluctuating enigma which I have tried to analyze in these pages, and in so doing have tried to unravel for myself.

In accomplishing this I owe a great deal to my German friends and colleagues, with whom I have discussed these problems and who have provided me with helpful suggestions, background information and research material. Above all, I am indebted to the German press, in particular the *Frankfurter Rundschau* and *Der Spiegel*, for information and the permission to quote extensively. Portions of the sixth chapter appeared in articles I wrote for *The Nation* and *The Denver Post*, and I should like to express my appreciation to the editors of these publications for release of the rights.

My thanks also go to Mrs. Johanna Prym for her frequent help and to Dr. R. M. Kempner for his title suggestion.

I hope I have sufficiently acknowledged other debts in the notes.

J. D.

Frankfurt am Main
West Germany

Contents

Schizophrenic Germany

Chapter I

The Great Dilemma

For ten years, from 1949 until well into 1959, Western Germany has been pictured as a solidly democratic, economically successful partner of our Western community of nations. Chancellor Konrad Adenauer has been held up to the American people, the German voters, and the people of Western Europe as an Abe Lincoln, George Washington, and Methuselah, all poured into one wrinkled old skin. It was a flattering picture which the aging chancellor and his supporters have helped to popularize.

If there was anything to criticize about this new Germany it was its occasional embarrassing reluctance to compromise in the cold war between East and West and its failure to rearm as quickly and completely as it had promised to do.

Although there were voices within Germany and the United States that attempted to qualify this picture of a revived, radiant Germany with warnings that the issue of nationalism and militarism were still not settled, these voices were dismissed as those of vengeful alarmists. Despite occasional reports that hatemongers, militarists, and imperialists were still in power, or returning to power, it was generally agreed—in the United States at least—that our occupation of Germany had been successful.

1

But on Christmas Eve, 1959, an incident occurred which has changed all that. The reconsecrated Jewish synagogue in Cologne was smeared with swastikas and anti-Semitic slogans. Two young Germans, Paul Schoenen and Arnold Strunk, both members of an extreme right-wing nationalistic party, confessed to the act. Their wall scribbling was followed by a wave of anti-Semitic and neo-Nazi outbursts that soon spread around the entire world. In all, between Christmas Eve, 1959, and January 28, 1960, German authorities registered 685 such incidents. They ranged from swastikas painted in chalk on a sidewalk, to an attempt at burning up a synagogue near Nuremberg. More than a hundred individuals, most of them under twenty-one years old, were apprehended as suspects.

Although German officials, in the majority of cases, moved swiftly to punish those responsible, the luster of the democratic new Germany showed a sudden tarnish. German government agencies presented the world with a confusing dossier of causes and explanations. Chancellor Adenauer insisted the chain of incidents was being steered centrally, implying, but not stating directly, that he thought the Communists were behind the wheel. Others maintained that right-radical organizations were the motivators, while still others claimed the series of outbursts had no central relationship and that the incidents had caught fire among young people just as clothes and dance fads do.

In both the United Kingdom and the United States there were demonstrations of indignant protest against what was called a "revival of Nazism." Those who had previously expressed fear that all was not watertight in the German ship of state soon found a vast and receptive audience. In a few days, with the help of anti-German special interests groups, the German reputation was not just tarnished, it was badly blemished.

The basic questions posed by most Americans were:

"Is the new Germany really as democratic, really as reliable a partner as we have been led to believe, or is it true that Nazism still smolders underneath the German skin—that militarism, nationalism, and racism hide behind the front of Germany's miraculous economic recovery?

"Was our occupation toward reeducating and reorientating the

Germans successful or a sham that gave way to the exigencies of the cold war?"

These are black-and-white questions to which there are no black-and-white answers. The answers about Germany, instead, are a complicated, multifaceted set of gray shades. The problem can be understood more clearly by dealing momentarily with the question which has been asked frequently even during the Allied honeymoon with the Federal Republic: "Has the German analyzed the immediate past, the period of the Third Reich and World War II, with all its terror and horror? Is he aware of what part he personally played during the Nazi Reich or was it more convenient just to forget and thus be spared a bad conscience?"

The answer is that he hasn't really forgotten, but what he is trying to do is to shake off the collective blame imposed upon him in the early occupation days. It is natural for him to do this. Unfortunately, the process of becoming blameless, yet not forgetting, is as difficult as it sounds. Thus, the responsible German feels it essential to the rehabilitation of Germany that the Germans no longer be blamed collectively, but that, at the same time, they be reminded of what really happened. This is the great dilemma. For it is only in understanding the past that the Germans can prevent history from repeating itself. Simultaneously, however, remembering is inexorably intertwined with blame. And the German shies away from blame. What he seeks and cannot find is the objective and unemotional viewpoint.

Fascism, anti-Semitism, militarism, cartelism: these are elements that are neither dead nor alive in Germany today. Their status is difficult to determine because in certain instances there have been appearances of these elements in both a revived, not yet fully alive, as well as a dying, not yet completely dead form. Meanwhile, forces for and against these elements are grasping desperately for attention among a public that is well fed, well satisfied and, for the most part, politically apathetic.

Hans Schmidt, the Teutonic counterpart of John Smith, complacent in the "miracle economy," has suppressed or is trying to suppress in the darkest caverns of his mind all memories of the Hitler tyranny and Nazi crimes, the miseries of the war and the immediate postwar period. But all around him there are forces trying to re-awaken the good and the bad aspects of the Thousand-Year Reich. On the level of the movie and magazine industry alone there are so many forces at work, some so cleverly, others so blunderingly, that even non-Germans with no past to forget and no blame to evade are troubled. On one side Hans faces a concerted attempt by some pub-lishers and producers to reawaken the concept of collective guilt. On the other hand there are those who are trying to minimize the crimes and errors of the Nazis and glorify the war, especially the role of the common soldier who fought it.

Confronted with a Cinderella-like rise to power and recovery, Al-lied demands for rearmament on the one hand and demands for self-flagellation for militaristic crimes on the other, who can really blame Hans for being confused? Moreover, with installments to meet on his bug-sized car, his refrigerator, his television set, and his house, it is easy to see why he is apathetic. Hans was not a real Nazi and would not be a Nazi in the future. That does not mean, though, that he didn't go along or would not go along again. He probably voted for the Nazis, he hailed the leaders and reveled in their glories. Hans knows there were concentration camps, but he didn't start them, he didn't run them, and he wouldn't have anything to do with them in the future. Time has healed the wounds of the war and the occupation, and if he thinks about that at all today he does so with a smile. The hatred he felt for his Prussian drill sergeant has, in the years since the war, been transformed into a symbol for Hans of his own "resistance" to Nazi authority. The fear of the battle-fields has been replaced in his mind by the memory of comradeship which kept him alive under the pressure of fear. Today Hans calls himself a democrat and is proud of it. But he understands little of the workings of a democracy and his responsibilities in and to it. The problem which faces the democratic leaders of Western Ger-many, which presents itself to the Western world, and which ought to confront each and every Hans Schmidt is whether Hans will know which way to go if he ever stands at the crossroads again.

Postwar Germany, as it confronts Hans, is a perplexing and be-wildering society of contradictions. Ex-victims and terrorists of the Nazi régime now sit next to each other in city councils, state legislatures, and government agencies. Not infrequently, they are even members of the same political parties. Whereas the East Germans once had a monopoly on the political parlor game of accusing the Bonn government of harboring and supporting ex-Nazis, the Pankow régime lately has been getting a taste of its own medicine.

All around him, Hans Schmidt sees and hears the past relived. Over his midday *Knackwurst* and beer he can skim through the paper and find dozens of stories in which the years of the Nazi régime and its problems are still discussed and very much alive. While one of the country's numerous illustrated magazines will feature a serial on the Nuremberg war crimes trials, a competing magazine will run a popularized "documentary report" on the Nazi navy in which submarine commanders are shown as heroes. Bookshops display documentary reports on concentration camps on the same shelf with memoirs by former Nazi field marshals and admirals. Competing movie houses advertise pro- and anti-Nazi films in flickering lights.

Faced with all this, faced with the natural desire to absolve himself of personal blame for the wrongs of a system which he actively or passively supported, is it any wonder that Hans Schmidt will try to avoid the subject like a plague? Is it any wonder that if he can't avoid it he will search for the more pleasant, the more glorious aspects of it?

The men who lead him, those men whom he respects, are equally contradictory. There is, for instance, Chancellor Adenauer, who once said he was proud of the fact that he had never been in the army or worn a uniform. Yet an album of pictures of the new German army, presented to the chancellor on his eighty-fourth birthday, called him "the father of the *Bundeswehr*." Adenauer looked at the dedication, smiled, and said, "It's true."

Adenauer, once famed for his pan-European ideas, shocked his countrymen during a speech in July, 1960, when he said that Germany lacked in nationalistic spirit.

There is Defense Minister Franz-Josef Strauss, who said in a 1947 election campaign, "Any man who takes up a gun in his hand again ought to lose his arm." That same defense minister is spearheading a campaign to expand the Germany army, draft more men, draft them at an earlier age and for longer periods.

Dwight D. Eisenhower once said in 1945, when he was still a victorious general, that militarism and Nazism must be destroyed in Germany, that militaristic thinking should be eradicated from the German mind. When he was President, that same Dwight D. Eisenhower said that the German military potential would add substantially to the strength of the North Atlantic Treaty Organization.

Told to be one thing one day, something else on another, is it any wonder that Hans Schmidt would rather think about his installment payments?

No one could sum up the situation better than a middle-aged German woman, a journalist who is known for her stanch opposition to the Nazi régime and her equally strong rejection of any criticism of Germany in general. She fought the Nazis in every way she could, was arrested twice by the Gestapo for helping Jews to flee to freedom, tried, but acquitted for lack of evidence.

You Americans always go into extremes [she said]. Of course there are still Nazis. There are also neo-Nazis. It would be as foolish to deny that as to say that all Germans were Nazis when, in fact, thousands of them died and suffered torture in concentration camps or lived in fear of death and torture for their anti-Nazi efforts.

When the war ended, posters went up in German towns and cities proclaiming haughtily that you Americans had come, not as liberators, but as conquerors. We were told—and many of us had not known it—that we Germans committed more crimes against humanity than any other nation in history. You told us flatly that we'd never have an army again, that the forces of militarism, fascism, nationalism, racism, and cartelism, all those evil forces of our history which plunged the world into two terrible wars, would be doomed and outlawed for all time. Our surrender, don't forget, was an unconditional one, on your terms.

But it wasn't long before you had differences with your wartime allies. The differences soon developed into open antagonism. Soon, in order to support the Western cause, you turned to us. The German monopolists were given the nod to rebuild their industries. Soon you told us to start a new army. When we didn't build it fast enough, you told us to speed up. When some of us expressed doubts about the advisability of rearming at all, especially with atomic weapons, we were called "anti-American" and many other unpleasant things. You pardoned some of the same war criminals you told us you were going to hang. Some of them have gained top positions in German political and industrial life today while others draw fat pensions at the taxpayers' expense.

And thus we come to the present, a present where you Americans are helping to keep Berlin from being gobbled up by the Russian bear, that same Berlin in which you and the Russians are still keeping Rudolf Hess, Albert Speer, and Baldur von Schirach confined in Spandau war crimes prison. You are urging us to build up our army faster and faster, but at the same time we are still making reparations payments for the damage our last army did. Some of you still accuse us of horrible crimes, while others of you do business with the criminals and hobnob with them at parties. We're still paying out millions each year in reparations and restitution to Jews and other victims of the Nazi terror, but the terrorists are collecting other millions in the form of pensions.

Just what do you expect? [she asked].

All this tears and drags on Hans Schmidt and he tries to go into mental hiding. What Hans has to be made to realize is that one day soon he will have to meet the issues squarely, settle them, and compartmentalize them in his own mind, and go on from there using the bitter, unpleasant lessons of the past to prevent the promise of the future from turning into a new chaos.

What is Germany like today? How did all this come about? How do Germans feel and what are they doing about the situation?

The best point of departure is to examine first, in careful chronological order, the progress of West Germany's accounting with its own past. As a first step one must trace the history of German jurisdiction over war criminals and what the Germans have done and plan to do about the murderers and tyrants still on the loose today.

These are cases where German defendants appear before German judges in German courts. They are tried for violation of existing German laws—such as murder, assault, larceny, and arson—not "crimes against humanity" or "war crimes" which served as the foundation for the Allied tribunals. For the most part, the defendants are those overlooked by the Allied courts. But there are also those men on trial whose penalties, at the hands of the Allies, were too lenient in the eyes of German justice.

These trials, of course, are nothing new. They have been going on in a limited and haphazard fashion since 1946, full scale since the

1950's. Instead of decreasing, though, they are becoming more numerous. Each case, as testimony is unveiled, seems to produce new cases, like an amoeba propagating itself. For in each case witnesses implicate other, until then unheard-of individuals, who subsequently are brought to trial. This has resulted in what appears to be an unending chain reaction of trials.

The avalanche has become so overwhelming that German judicial officials established a central board to investigate Nazi crimes in late 1958, in the hope that as many people as possible could be brought to trial before the statute of limitations runs out. After one year of work, the board announced that charges had been preferred against some two hundred individuals, all of whom had committed crimes and atrocities against non-Germans outside Germany. Most of them have never faced a judge before.

Chapter II

The Germans Face Germany— In Court

Both Germans and non-Germans have criticized the Allied war-crimes trials, calling them "nothing more than acts of vengeance." The most frequent charge is that there was no legal basis for either the international or national tribunals and that the prosecution of war criminals was motivated by the fury of hatred.

The war-crimes program was, without a doubt, one of the most controversial aspects of the occupation, and as early as 1945 there were isolated demands that the Germans themselves be given jurisdiction over Nazis accused of "crimes against humanity and the peace." The first semblance of that jurisdiction came with the organization of so-called "de-Nazification" boards. Although the program was a dismal failure, it set the stage for later German prosecution of war criminals. In 1949, with the establishment of the German Federal Republic, the local authorities gained virtually complete jurisdiction and took over where the Allies had left off. Since then the German courts have had a field day trying Nazis for crimes they committed in and outside the country. Although the Adenauer government admits frankly that it does not know just how many such trials have been held, officials assume there must have been thousands. In just

9

one state, Bavaria, 5,958 persons have been brought to court since 1945 and some 60 cases are still on the docket.

The basic difference between the German trials and those conducted by the Allies is one of legal principle. While the Allied tribunals tried Nazis for "war crimes," "crimes against the peace," and "crimes against humanity," the Germans, frequently with equal zeal, have been prosecuting their own countrymen for violations of existing statutes against murder or manslaughter. While the recent rash of such trials gives the appearance that they will never end, in reality, German prosecutors are merely racing against time. The statute of limitations for manslaughter offenses took effect in 1960, that for murder will be implemented in 1965.[1]

These cases, which have received relatively little notice abroad, can be classified into four major groups. First and foremost are the concentration camp and extermination squad trials in which former SS men, camp guards, police officials, security service (SD) members, and civil servants are prosecuted for ordering or carrying out atrocities in established Nazi camps, occupied countries, or ghettos.

The second major group, the one over which the Germans have had jurisdiction the longest, comprises the so-called "war-end" crimes against German civilians. These are the cases of *Wehrmacht, Luftwaffe,* SS, SA (Storm Trooper), Nazi party and police officials who ordered the execution of their own citizens toward the end of the war because they had hoisted white surrender flags, refused to join the "people's storm movement," or had committed similar transgressions of what was then a rather twisted form of patriotism.

In the majority of these cases, community leaders, anti-Nazi resistance fighters, and sometimes "just plain Hans Schmidts" were haled before summary courts called on moment's notice, "convicted" of "treason" or "resisting the war effort," and ordered hanged or shot. The entire procedure, from "filing of charges" until execution, rarely lasted more than one hour. Today German prosecutors still have a backlog of such cases.

The third group, also involving war-end killings, comprises *Luftwaffe* or *Wehrmacht* officers who violated military law by ordering

[1] On March 23, 1960, the opposition Social Democratic party (Socialists) in the *Bundestag* introduced a bill extending the time four years in both cases to 1964 and 1969. The bill was defeated on May 24, 1960.

executions without trial of subordinates who had shown "cowardice before the enemy." In many instances "cowardice" had far-reaching meanings. Commanders who ordered their men to retreat in the face of overwhelming odds and soldiers who had fallen asleep at their posts from sheer exhaustion were labeled cowards and shot on the spot without the benefit of court martial or any other formal hearing.

Included in the fourth group are those accused of "purge killings." Among them are former high-ranking Nazi officials who have faced postwar prosecution for their parts in the bloody 1934 party inquisition of the SA storm troopers.[2]

The development of both Allied and German jurisdiction over war criminals is a somewhat complicated one. Actually, the same military government edict, Allied Control Council Law No. 10, serves as the legal basis for both. This ruling, which went into effect on December 20, 1945, called for the creation of tribunals to prosecute the war criminals. It was a product of joint United States, British, French, and Russian action. Although the intent of the law was mainly to establish Allied courts, it did provide for German jurisdiction "in the case of crimes committed by persons of German citizenship or nationality against other persons of German citizenship or nationality, or stateless persons . . . if authorized by the occupying powers."

Just how little this meant, however, became evident the day the law went into effect, when one of the first German petitions for jurisdiction was flatly rejected. It was an unusual case, which not only would have set postwar legal precedents had the Germans been permitted to prosecute, but which also provided a preview of German thinking along war-crimes lines in the years to come. The petition which American military government authorities rejected was one from the mayor of Aschaffenburg, Dr. Arthur Stock, who had asked permission to try two Nazis on charges of "causing the city's destruction." The two, Dr. Stock explained, had insisted on defending Aschaffenburg against advancing American troops at a time when any defense had already become useless. Their actions, he contended, had caused needless wreckage in the city.

Despite the flat denial of their petition to try this case, Germans in

[2] See pages 34–37.

the American zone of occupation had to wait only three months until they were suddenly given an opportunity to follow through on their demands for jurisdiction. A United States-sponsored law of March 5, 1946, called for the establishment of de-Nazification boards whose purpose was to "try" *all* Nazis in Germany and punish them for their roles and crimes, both major and minor, during the Hitler régime. This program, established in the four German states then under United States occupation, provided for the appointment of "ministers for reconstruction and political liberation" to serve as members of the recently created state government cabinets. These special cabinet members were to supervise the de-Nazification program.

The law prescribed that all Germans, eighteen years or older, would have to register and fill out lengthy questionnaires about their past political activities. By means of special hearings the boards were to classify all adult Germans into five groups: "major offenders, offenders, minor offenders, followers, and exonerated persons," against whom a variety of sanctions and punishments could be levied.

The "major offender" group included persons guilty of crimes against victims or opponents of National Socialism; pillaging, deporting, or other acts of violence; mistreating prisoners of war, and those who had held leading positions in the Nazi party or any Nazi or militaristic organization. The group also encompassed those individuals whose positions in government had been so important that only leading Nazis could have held them, as well as persons who had lent great support to the Nazi régime or had profited from its support. Automatically classified as major offenders were all active members of the Gestapo, SD (security service), SS (elite guard), secret military police, border police, and those who had participated in concentration camp, hospital, or insane asylum atrocities.

Punishments prescribed for them included work camp sentences up to ten years and confiscation of all property and wealth except that needed for their daily minimum requirements. The proceeds from such property, the de-Nazification law decreed, would be used to make reparations payments to victims of the Hitler régime.

Other possible penalties were permanent ineligibility to hold public office, loss of any legal claim to pensions, and the right to vote or be elected. Major offenders were barred from active participation in political parties. In addition to these sanctions, they could also be denied membership in a labor union or professional organization and barred, for at least ten years, from undertaking an independent economic effort, owning shares, or holding any type of employment other than that of a laborer. They could be banned from teaching, preaching, writing, editing, or commenting on the radio. They were subject to recruitment for labor to the public benefit.

Furthermore, major offenders could be deprived of all concessions and other licenses, including the right to own or drive an automobile.

For the next group, the "offenders," the punishments were essentially the same except that labor camp internment was limited to five years and economic restrictions were slated for a period of at least five, instead of ten, years. This second group, which included many more people than the first, of course, was divided into three classifications: "activists, militarists, and profiteers."

The "activists" included those who had taught Nazism, had been judges, had agitated against the churches, had written for or spoken publicly in behalf of the Nazi régime, had spied or informed on their fellow citizens, or had been active in the destruction of the trade union movement.

"Militarists" had attempted to bring German life in line with a policy of militaristic force, had advocated or been responsible for the domination of foreign people, their exploitation or displacement, or had promoted armament for these purposes. The group also included individuals who had participated in the bombardment of dwelling areas.

A "profiteer" was described as anyone who had obtained an office or important position because of his membership in the Nazi party, had received substantial donations from the party, or had profited from the political, religious, and racial persecution of others. Also classified as profiteers were persons who had made disproportionately high profits from the arms industry, had enriched themselves in an unfair manner in connection with the administration of occupied territories, or had escaped military service because of membership in the Nazi party.

According to the law, "minor offenders" were those who "belonged" to the first two groups but could be expected to fulfill their duties as citizens of a peaceful and democratic state. They were usually placed on two- to three-year probationary periods during which they were not allowed to operate business enterprises of more than ten employees and frequently were ordered to work as common laborers.

"Followers" were defined as "insignificant supporters of Nazism," including particularly those who had belonged to party organizations but had paid only membership dues and participated in such meetings at which attendance was obligatory.

People who had resisted the Nazi régime and suffered disadvantages as a result of it were classified by the boards as "exonerated."

Although this de-Nazification program was at first a unilateral action initiated by the United States Military Government in its zone, Allied Control Council Law No. 38, passed on October 12, 1946, standardized the procedures throughout the rest of occupied Germany, including the Soviet area. The four-power law encompassed the provisions of the United States measure, but stiffened the maximum penalties in such a manner that major offenders, guilty of a specific war crime, could be sentenced to death, life imprisonment, or from five to fifteen years in jail.

But the de-Nazification program was a failure. Before the responsibility was turned over to the Germans, that is, before March 5, 1946, they had criticized Allied de-Nazification methods as being too severe. When the Germans themselves took over, it soon became apparent that they weren't following through. The program was variously called "the great purge," the "big internal inquisition," and "the great cover-up."

Within a few months, Allied occupation authorities were forced to step in with severe criticism and sharp reprimands to recently established local and state governments for the manner in which the program was being handled.

De-Nazification is proving a slow and difficult process [a 1946 State Department progress report[3] on the occupation stated]. Certain Nazi elements remain entrenched in various sectors of public life and constitute a continuing threat to the attainment of the objectives of the occupa-

[3] Occupation of Germany 1945–1946. State Department Publication No. 2783.

tion. The application of the law in the U.S. Zone has been handicapped by the acute shortage of qualified and politically reliable personnel. The wide scope of the law, affecting directly or indirectly some 40 per cent of the population, creates fear and opposition. There is a wide-spread feeling among the Germans that the law is arbitrary in its application and that nominal or minor Nazis should be excluded. Local sentiment often obstructs effective enforcement. There is fear of Nazi reprisal if the law is rigidly enforced, due often to doubt concerning the length of the occupation.

Matters reached a critical stage in Bavaria in July 1946 when the Ministry for de-Nazification was reorganized and many prosecutors and members of the purge chambers were dismissed. All completed cases [had] to be re-examined. Courts throughout the Zone were found to have been unduly lenient in their findings, after reversing earlier military government verdicts relating to major offenders.

By the fall of 1946, the slowness of the court procedure and the leniency of the decisions caused general fear of a breakdown of the operation of the law. At a special session of the Council of Minister Presidents [governors] on Nov. 5, 1946, General [Lucius D.] Clay rebuked German officials for the lax enforcement . . . and declared that its operation in the hands of the German authorities was a vital test of democracy. He warned that military government would take necessary steps to eliminate Nazi influence if the Germans proved unwilling or unable to do so. He declared that thereafter, no person once removed from office by military authorities could be reinstated by the German courts.

De-Nazification remains one of the most difficult tasks of the occupation. It is essential to eliminate the most arbitrary features of the law, to deal more intelligently with individual cases so as to avoid patent injustice and to secure qualified personnel, not only to man the tribunals, but to replace dismissed Nazis in all essential posts. And a most serious difficulty arises from the tendency of ex-Nazis to coalesce into a dissident group and thus form the hard core of a neo-Nazi resistance to the occupation authorities. No adequte methods have yet been found to assimilate this group into German civic life or to prevent it from becoming a dangerous focus of unrest and opposition.

Despite the early danger signs and the remedial action initiated, de-Nazification never did become any more effective. State Department figures of May, 1949, reveal that less than 10 per cent of those individuals originally registered had been tried in de-Nazification courts. And of this small minority, only 1,600 had been classified as

major offenders and 22,000 as offenders. The minor offender and fol-
lower category included more than 600,000.

The sentences—and they duplicate themselves in many instances
—included 9,600 labor camp terms, 569,000 fines, 124,000 employment restrictions, 28,500 confiscations of property, and 23,000 ban-
nings from public office. Appeals had reduced the sanctions in approximately 10 per cent of the cases. Many Germans still feel today
that important Nazis were allowed to go free or were sentenced to
insignificant financial disadvantages or fines while thousands of unim-
portant fellow travelers were treated too severely.

But regardless of the criticism and the injustices, de-Nazification,
while failing in its own aims, paved the way for the Germans to settle
their own scores. For out of the de-Nazification program came the
seemingly endless chain of German trials which today symbolize Germany's accounting with its past. Strange as it may seem, German
courts trying their own countrymen for Nazi crimes have generally
been much more severe in their sentences and verdicts than the de-
Nazification tribunals were. Yet there has been only a minimum of
criticism of these trials, most of the objections coming from die-hard
or neo-Nazis. The explanation for this may be the fact that a wide
cross section of the community saw in the de-Nazification tribunals
an instrument of the occupation authorities which had been sugar-
coated to make it appear German. Local courts, however, were unquestionably "home-grown." It would have been illogical to accuse
them of conducting a "purge" or "inquisition."

One of the first such cases on record dates back to 1946 when a
municipal court in Ansbach convicted *Luftwaffe* Colonel Ernst
Meyer, city police Captain Georg Hauenstein and police Lieutenant
Johann Zippold of manslaughter for the execution of Robert Limpert,
a young student active in the anti-Nazi resistance movement. The
essence of the case was that on April 18, 1945, as United States forces
approached the Ansbach city limits, Limpert had cut the telephone
wires to Meyer's headquarters. He was detected and arrested. Meyer
convened a summary court martial which Limpert was not even permitted to attend. The youth was sentenced to death and hanged
a short time later in front of the Ansbach city hall. Meyer received a

ten-year prison term. The police captain was sentenced to one-and-a-half years, the lieutenant to a year in jail.

Although there were repeated requests during 1947 to turn jurisdiction of all war criminals over to the Germans, the prospects for this remained slim. For instance, when U.S. Brigadier General Telford Taylor, chief attorney for the war crimes court in Nuremberg, discussed the question of German jurisdiction at a press conference in May of that year, he told newsmen that he doubted very much whether the Germans would get jurisdiction over cases other than crimes against their own citizens in the forseeable future. Although the Germans were being permitted to handle more and more such cases of crimes against their own citizens, the high-ranking Nazis accused of similar transgressions remained within the exclusive domain of the Allies.

General Taylor's predictions held true until May, 1949, when the first real German war-crimes trial took place at a municipal court in Munich. The defendant, Max Raettig, was charged with committing forty-two murders in the Polish ghetto of Thomaszow. Raettig had gone "underground" after the war, but by chance a former woman inmate of the ghetto had spotted him in March, 1948, while riding a Munich streetcar. She had remembered him, she told the court, because Raettig had beaten to death her three-year-old child.

The Munich court convicted him on two counts of murder and two specifications of manslaughter. He was sentenced to death just a few months before the ratification of West Germany's new constitution which outlawed the death penalty. Later, after the Federal Republic was established, Raettig appealed and the death sentence was commuted to life imprisonment.

By the beginning of 1950, German jurisdiction over war criminals was an accepted fact. During the spring of that year a number of minor officials came to trial on murder and manslaughter charges and several life sentences were imposed. One of the more sensational trials during this period was the case of Dr. Walter Huppenkothen, a colonel in the SS and an official of the *Reichssicherheitshauptamt* (Reich Security Agency), who was charged with aiding and abetting the murder of Admiral Wilhelm Canaris and Major General Hans Oster. Canaris, the chief, and Oster, deputy head of all German intelligence operations, had participated in the abortive July 20, 1944, assassination plot against Hitler. They were hanged at Floessenburg concentration camp after a kangaroo trial at which Huppenkothen had appeared as a chief prosecution witness.

Even as hearings such as Huppenkothen's made headlines, prosecution officials in Augsburg were busy on the most unusual war crimes case ever held in a German court: the trial of Ilse Koch, infamously known as "The Witch of Buchenwald." Her case marked a milestone in German jurisdiction, for not only was she the most notorious Nazi to come before a German court since the war, but when the hearing was ended the Germans had successfully completed a job the Americans had failed to do.

Frau Koch, wife of the commandant of Buchenwald concentration camp,[4] had originally been sentenced to life imprisonment by an American war-crimes tribunal. However, she was released by American authorities after serving only four years of her term because of irregularities in the trial. The German court in Augsburg subsequently sentenced her to another life term and today, ten years later, she is still in prison. But in addition to this strange development in postwar German justice, her trial late in 1950 presented still more unusual paradoxes. While witnesses in Augsburg gave blood-curdling testimony about lamps of human skin and bones which had been made for the Koch family, hundreds of Germans marched on Landsberg war-crimes prison not far away and demanded clemency for two dozen convicted Nazis scheduled to be hanged. While crowds of Germans stood outside the Augsburg courtroom eager to lynch Ilse Koch, other crowds demonstrated outside the walls of Landsberg to save the necks of twenty-four condemned men.

Those who conclude that the demonstrators in Augsburg were anti-Nazis and those at Landsberg, pro-Nazis, are mistaken. The demonstrators in both cases crossed all demarcation lines of political background or belief. Pastors, schoolteachers, Social Democrats, Christian Democrats, and even some victims of Nazi terror were among the crowd outside the prison. The basic motivation was the fact that the Federal Republic's new constitution had outlawed the

---

[4] Her husband had been executed by his own SS colleagues in the wake of an investigation of corruption and graft at the concentration camp. She had been acquitted at the time.

death penalty and no executions, they felt, should be carried out on German soil.

It was a strange situation, indeed, where Germans cheered the commutations granted by U.S. High Commissioner John J. McCloy for Landsberg's condemned men and jeered Ilse Koch as she was again sentenced to life in jail. But as the years passed, the situation became even stranger and more complex. The prosecution of war criminals has continued, the number of trials increasing year by year instead of decreasing, for from each trial new cases issue forth.

Seventeen major war-crimes trials took place or started in the Federal Republic in 1958. Of these, a half dozen cases brought out testimony that implicated—and eventually brought to court—nearly a dozen new defendants. The complexity and incongruity of Germany's accounting with its own past is demonstrated most effectively and dramatically by three of these cases: the trial of SS guard Martin Sommer, the concentration camp case of Gustav Sorge and Wilhelm Schubert, and the hearing of ten former "extermination squad" members.

Sommer's trial resulted in sensational testimony about a sadistic concentration camp doctor who had established a successful practice after the war with the help of government grants and prisoner-of-war compensation. When the doctor's role was made public, he escaped to Egypt where he now holds an important position at a hospital.

The months-long trial of Schubert and Sorge was significant because it raised anew the possibility of a Nazi underground organization.

The "extermination squad" trial, at which ten former Nazi officials were convicted for the murder of thousands of Jews in Lithuania, was noteworthy because it was the first postwar case in which German authorities had staged a mass trial, involving all the defendants in a single criminal action. Furthermore, although the final sentences in the case were widely criticized as too lenient, the successful prosecution of several defendants simultaneously paved the way for the establishment of a central agency to investigate all still unpunished Nazi crimes.

Martin Sommer was brought into a Bayreuth district courtroom in a wheel chair amid the jeers of hundreds of spectators who stood outside the courthouse. Sommer, gray and emaciated, looked like the personification of death. Seeing this feeble, ailing man, no one would have believed that he could ever have harmed anyone. But Sommer entered that courtroom accused of murdering fifty-three inmates of notorious Buchenwald concentration camp where he had been an SS guard. In fact, the fifty-three murders with which he had been charged, reflected only a fraction of the crimes for which the Bayreuth district attorney could easily have obtained convictions. Some hundred and fifty other counts of murder had been dropped in deference to Sommer's critical physical condition and his inability to stand the strain of a longer trial.

Sommer had been chief of the concentration camp's guardhouse and had committed countless cruel and sadistic acts, ostensibly to stay in the good graces of Ilse Koch and her husband. On the charge sheet against him were listed the names of twenty-five camp inmates whom he had killed personally with poison or air injections, as well as the names of twenty-one whom he had selected for execution on November 9, 1939, a day after an alleged assassination attempt on Hitler.

Other allegations against Sommer were that he had once used two inmates as live targets for pistol practice, that he had killed one prisoner by scrubbing him for hours with a disinfecting brush, then held his head under water to drown him, and that he had lured another prisoner outside the camp boundaries to pick up a cap that had been thrown there, then had the man shot by a tower guard. Sommer was also accused of having invented an infamous whipping rack, a homemade model of which he introduced as evidence in court, saying it was, in fact, a more humane way of administering corporal punishment than other systems. He also admitted candidly that he had been in the habit of storing the corpses of his victims underneath his bunk in the guardhouse orderly room.

Even other guards had been appalled at Sommer's brutality and some of them came to court to testify against him, telling of his sadism and his lust for torture. Sommer, they explained, used to visit the camp on his days off just to watch or participate in the mistreatment of prisoners.

The trial, which lasted nearly a month, resulted in Sommer's conviction on twenty-five counts of murder. He was sentenced to life imprisonment, the maximum penalty. The charges against him had been in the draft stages for eight years, but he could not be tried because of his ill health.[5] Judicial officials ruled that he was healthy enough to go to court when he married his nurse at a local veterans' hospital and fathered a child.

This affair with the nurse, seventeen years his junior, gave Germans almost as much to talk about as the trial itself, for she had given up a handsome young intern in preference to the cold-blooded, sadistic SS guard. It must have been real love, because when the Henchman of Buchenwald, as the press had nicknamed him, was taken to jail for pretrial confinement, his tearful wife ran down the street after the police ambulance until she collapsed from exhaustion.

"I believe in my husband," she told newsmen. "I am sure he never did what he is accused of having done. He never tortured anyone and never killed anyone. He is a good man. For me, he's the best man in the world."

Her loyalty cost her her nursing job. She was fired from the Bayreuth hospital after officials there had received a flood of protest letters and cables from all over the country.

All these aspects—Sommer's extreme brutality, his years of avoiding prosecution, his involvement with the SS investigation of corruption at Buchenwald, and his strange affair with an attractive young nurse—were enough to spotlight his trial in Bayreuth. But Sommer's month in court would have gone into the record as just another concentration camp case had it not been for the startling testimony of one witness who said: "The wrong defendant is sitting here. There ought to be someone who will file charges against Dr. Hans Eisele. He killed more people in one week than Sommer murdered in his entire lifetime.

"Imagine," said the witness, Wilhelm Jellineck, for years a political prisoner at Buchenwald, "this doctor now has a practice in Munich.

[5] Sommer had been wounded during the final days of the war. His right leg is amputated almost at the hip, his left leg is completely crippled, and he has many shrapnel wounds. His war injuries are an indirect result of his extreme cruelty, for Sommer had been sent to a combat SS unit in 1944 when even the Buchenwald administration had found his methods too brutal for them. He was arrested a short time later in connection with the corruption scandal at the camp (see note, page 18) and returned to Buchenwald as an inmate. After the Koch trial, shortly before the end of the war, Sommer went back to the front in a probationary unit and was wounded.

Women—mothers, sisters, daughters, and wives—go to him in confidence, unaware that perhaps it was he who murdered their brothers, husbands, sons, or fathers."

This testimony, typical of the manner in which many other Nazi sadists have been exposed and eventually brought to trial as the result of evidence at someone else's hearing, hit Germany with tornadolike impact. Newsmen investigated immediately and discovered that Dr. Hans Eisele really did have a prosperous practice in the Munich suburb of Pasing.

Eisele, it turned out, had been given a 4,000 DM cash settlement and an interest-free 25,000 DM loan with which to launch his postwar career upon his release from Landsberg where he had served a war-crimes term imposed by an American tribunal. Originally, Eisele had been sentenced to death, then his penalty was reduced to life imprisonment. In 1952, after having served seven years, he was paroled.

When Eisele was brought before a German de-Nazification board after his release from Landsberg, there was insufficient available evidence on which to impose further sanctions or punishments on him, allegedly because American authories had refused to release the record on the case. Eisele was exonerated, restored to all his rights, including those of a war veteran, and his term in Landsberg was considered POW internment. This entitled him to handsome indemnities.

When the story of Dr. Eisele's mysterious return to medical practice broke in the German press, the doctor disappeared. He turned up again in Egypt.[6]

Of all German war-crimes trials, none caused as much talk, received as much German press coverage, ran as long, or cost the German taxpayers as much money as did the joint trial of Gustav Sorge and Wilhelm Schubert, two former SS sergeants from Sachsenhausen concentration camp. Neither had there ever before been a war-crimes case which was prepared with such thoroughness, such painstaking detail, and effort to prove every last charge. One reason may well be that the trial was held in the district court of Bonn, West Germany's capital.

6 See Chapter V, page 52.

Schubert and Sorge went to court on October 13, 1958, accused of 11,200 counts of murder. Of these specifications, 10,800 involved Russian prisoners of war who had been liquidated in specially constructed "shower rooms" at Sachsenhausen. As the Russians stood in the shower stalls, expecting to wash, from the outside SS guards aimed a bullet at each prisoner's head through special holes in the wall. This activity not only won Schubert a medal, but also the nickname of "Pistol Packin' Schubert." After each shooting session, other camp prisoners had to cart out the corpses to the crematorium and wash out the shower stalls so they'd be ready for more Russians.

Schubert and Sorge were also charged with four hundred other specifications of murder, most of them involving fatal beatings and maltreatment of political and religious prisoners at the camp.

On February 6, 1959, nearly four months after the prosecution had opened its case, with the courtroom filled to capacity nearly every day, the two were convicted on 141 charges of murder and aiding and abetting murder. Both men were sentenced to life imprisonment.

The long hearing had been highlighted by records and tape recordings from a Soviet tribunal which once had sentenced Schubert and Sorge to life imprisonment.

Witnesses had come from countries all over the world. Some of them had even set up a "Sachsenhausen committee" in a Bonn hotel to advise others on how to testify. The committee not only served as a center of reunion for former Sachsenhausen inmates, but also brought up new evidence against other men involved in brutalities and atrocities at the infamous camp. Thus the trial of Schubert and Sorge, like so many others, also resulted in new investigations and new charges.

Most German newspapers, even the conservative ones, reported the proceedings day by day, thus aiding effectively in impregnating the somewhat lethargic German conscience with its collective guilt, and the entire country, it seemed, expressed indignation when one day Schubert got up in court and blatantly accused the jury of conducting a rigged hearing in which he had been convicted before the proceedings had even started.

However, what made the case so significant was not the day-to-day testimony on the mass extermination program at Sachsenhausen, but a number of news stories and developments during the course of the trial which spotlighted unusually unorthodox pretrial confinement practices and gave rise to the possibility of an organized Nazi underground movement. The Associated Press reported at the start of the trial that Schubert, while in prison, had been permitted to carry around a portrait of Hitler until a few days before he went to court. AP also said that Schubert had greeted his Bonn county jail guards and fellow prisoners with the Nazi salute from time to time.

In addition to the report on the Hitler photo, another news story of unusual behind-the-scenes activities just at the start of the trial revealed that the Bonn branch of a neo-Nazi organization had provided Schubert with an extra tailor-made suit to wear in court. The Bonn representative of the group allegedly had promised Schubert's court-appointed defense counsel to arrange for "good press coverage" of the trial.

When, in the last days of the hearing, Schubert suddenly admitted most of the murders with which he had been charged, the presiding judge asked him why he had not made such a confession previously. Schubert told the judge he had been advised against confessing by a pretrial defense lawyer. Both Schubert and Sorge admitted that this lawyer had himself once been an SS man. Sorge explained that when he and Schubert arrived in Germany after their release from Russian internment, they had been approached by "certain legal officials" who advised them not to admit anything about conditions at Sachsenhausen. One of these "legal officials," Sorge said, had given him a list of "approved" defense counsels. On it was the name of the former SS man. This admission resulted in an investigation of reception practices at the border camps where the Soviets released POW's.

Of all the trials held in the significant postwar legal year of 1958, one stands out as most important in terms of its later impact on German attitudes toward the war-crimes problem. This was the "extermination squad" case in Ulm. It not only was the first German hearing in which there were a number of defendants, all linked to the same act, but it also set the stage for a new, more methodical approach in war-crimes prosecution.

Actually, the mass trial was the result of a bit of legal luck. Bernhard Fischer-Schweder, one of the SS men convicted in the case, had succeeded in "going underground" after the war to avoid prosecution.

He would probably never have been detected had he not filed a suit in a labor court under his real name. This resulted in several news stories about his past and eventually his arrest and indictment in May, 1956.

Even then, all thirteen defendants would never have been arraigned had it not been for the systematic sleuthing on the part of Stuttgart prosecutor Erich Nellmann who was determined in his efforts to unearth all the circumstances. When Nellmann had completed his investigations, Fischer-Schweder wasn't even the chief defendant anymore. The result of his snooping had turned up most of the Gestapo, SS, and SD agents who, together with Fischer-Schweder, had taken part in the mass murder of 5,502 Lithuanian Jews in the occupied country. Their squad, in turn, had been part of a larger special unit responsible for the liquidation of Jews and Communists in the Baltic countries. The area covered by the Tilsit squad was a border strip only twenty-five miles wide.

By the time the trial opened, only ten defendants remained to go to court. Three others had committed suicide after their arrests. The hearings lasted sixty days. The sentences, however, totaled only seventy years imprisonment, far below the demands of the prosecution. In fact, the prosecutor had asked for life terms for a number of the defendants and the court's maximum of fifteen years was criticized widely in and outside Germany.

The stiffest terms—fifteen years in the penitentiary—went to two men: Hans Joachim Boehme, director of the state police office in Tilsit, and Werner Hersmann, former SD (Security Service) chief in Tilsit. Fischer-Schweder, who had been chief of police in Memel, was sentenced to ten years. Branas Lukys, a Lithuanian police official, got seven years.[7] Franz Berendt and Werner Kreuzmann, the latter a Gestapo agent in Tilsit, were sentenced to five years each, and Gerhard Carsten received a four-year term.

In explaining the verdicts and sentences, the presiding judge excused the light terms by saying they had been handed down in recognition of the collective guilt of the entire German people. But the main defendants, he said, "were really Hitler and his stooges Himmler

[7] Lukys appealed and on February 23, 1960, an appeals court ordered a retrial.
Werner Schmidt-Hammer, a police lieutenant who had been sentenced to a three-year term, also appealed and was granted a rehearing on February 23.

and Heydrich who carried out the mass slaying of thousands of innocent people with premeditation and planning."

"Wherever absolute power reigns, absolute injustice is usually
right there, too," the judge said. He added that the real importance
of the trial lay in driving that point home to Germany's youth which,
he hoped, would never again be led into temptation by such a "front
man" as Hitler.

But despite the disappointments which the trial brought for Stuttgart's district attorney, the case proved conclusively that even after
fifteen years it was still possible to gather reliable evidence with
which Nazi crimes could be punished. For Erich Nellmann this was
an important realization that eventually led to his public plea for
establishment of a central board for the investigation of unsolved,
unpunished war crimes. As a matter of fact, the Ulm trial was, more
or less, the trigger for this sorely needed coordinating board which
seeks to bring order into the chaos of postwar handling of Third
Reich atrocities.

There has been considerable criticism of these trials in Germany,
however. Conservative and right-radical elements have demanded that
there be a final and general amnesty for the criminals of the Hitler
régime. Much of this pressure comes from so-called "victims of de-
Nazification and Allied internment," ultranationalistic veterans'
groups, associations of former SS men, and neo-Nazi political groups.

Fortunately, their pleas have fallen generally on deaf ears. Instead,
victims of Nazi persecution, associations of former resistance fighters,
labor unions, individual politicians, some of the political parties, the
churches, and democratic youth and student organizations, supported
by most of the press, have clamored for more investigations and
trials. This, in itself, is a welcome development. When the Allies
marched in and set up their war-crimes tribunals, millions of Germans refused to believe the atrocities reports. They rejected as "victor's propaganda" the fact that an international blood bath had been
tapped by Germans in the name of all Germans. The conscience, although presented with irrefutable evidence, simply had not yet begun to function. The facts brought out in Allied controlled newspapers, at Nuremberg, at de-Nazification proceedings, and at later
trials were just too gruesome to believe.

But after a few years, even the most incredulous Germans began to realize that the crimes, atrocities, and brutalities ascribed to them were not merely a "pack of lies." The individual conscience, however, was not properly jarred until German officials, operating under German laws, undertook prosecution. It was an almost foreseeable development. There is bound to be a basic difference in attitude toward a trial conducted by occupation authorities and one being held downtown at the municipal courthouse with a local jury and a judge everyone knows presiding. Instead of meeting the demands for a general amnesty, many Germans listened, instead, to warning voices that the war-crimes program should be coordinated, organized, and accelerated. The need for this seemed pressing in view of the fact that many of the crimes would no longer be punishable after 1960, and none of them would be subject to prosecution after 1965. There were repeated suggestions for the establishment of some type of central clearing board to sift out the cases and prepare charges.

There had been the virtual chain reaction of cases in 1958, new suspects popping up at almost every trial. The federal government had no figures on how many such hearings had been held in the thirteen years since the end of the war. Wasn't it possible, many Germans asked themselves, that hundreds of Nazis could hide out and escape prosecution until time had expired for the filing of new charges?

The first "official" demands for such a board or agency were made in September, 1958, by Stuttgart's district attorney Nellmann. His suggestions appeared in a signed article in the *Stuttgarter Zeitung,* the city's largest daily newspaper. Nellmann suggested that this proposed agency be headed by a responsible district attorney and that it come under the auspices of the federal attorney general's office. According to Nellmann's proposal, prosecutors and police officials from every German state should be detailed on a temporary duty basis to this bureau. As the investigations progressed, allegations should be turned over to these assistants from the various states who then could file charges against the individuals involved.

Nellmann based his suggestions on the belief that there was no excuse for "letting murderers and their helpers go free and unpunished," and in some cases, permitting them to assume positions "as servants of the state, and even the police," when it was possible to ferret them out with systematic and planned efforts.

One month later, at a conference of the various state ministers of justice, the proposal for such a central agency was made by Nellmann's superior, the Baden-Wuerttemberg minister of justice, Dr. Wolfgang Haussmann. When the meeting ended, the project was under way. Dr. Haussmann promised to take over responsibility for organizing the agency and establishing it as well as laying out the principles under which it would operate. Its basic purpose would be to seek out those individuals who had committed crimes as Nazis but had not yet been prosecuted. The emphasis, Haussmann decreed, would be on crimes committed by Germans in occupied territories during the war. The agency was to operate with a relatively small staff. It was not designed to be a prosecuting instrument or a special judicial institution, but merely a central investigative body which would pass the results of its research on to district attorneys responsible for the individual cases.

On December 1, 1958, the agency, officially called "Center for Preparation and Coordination for the Prosecution of Concentration Camp and War Crimes," took up its work in the little city of Ludwigsburg, not far from Stuttgart.

District attorney Erwin Schuele, chief of the prosecution team in the Tilsit extermination squad case, was appointed to head the project. In addition to passing evidence to local law enforcement authorities, the agency was also established to serve as a central clearing board for Nazi trials. Local prosecutors have been instructed to submit information to the center on cases already being processed. A central index of all such cases has been set up at Ludwigsburg.

At a press conference following the opening of the center, Justice Minister Haussmann answered questions on why it had taken so long to establish such an agency. Haussmann explained that the occupation powers had retained jurisdiction over these cases for a good many years and when the Germans finally assumed responsibility, it was the general belief throughout Germany that practically all the cases had come to trial. Local prosecutors, Haussmann explained, just weren't in a position to obtain an over-all picture of the situation. It was not until the major trials of 1958, that is, Schubert and Sorge, Sommer and Ulm, that German judicial authorities realized how much work remained to be done.

The center started as little more than a "one-man operation." In addition to two assistants, Schuele employed two secretaries.

Asked by newsmen how he planned to operate, he said, "Leave that up to me. Give me a half year's time to get organized, and by then, I'm sure you'll be hearing plenty from and about us."

Less than a year after he "went into business," Schuele produced results. On October 21, 1959—by then the agency had quadrupled in size—he announced that his investigations had led to the filing of charges against some two hundred individuals. They are expected to go to court during 1960 and 1961 in a series of twenty to twenty-five trials.

Most of the cases involve special extermination squads or concentration camp atrocities. The majority of defendants, the agency reported, are former high-ranking Nazis who were responsible for the crimes. Less influential SS and Security Service members who carried out liquidation and execution orders will not be included so as to rule out the possibility of defendants claiming they had been "forced" to carry out orders under threat to their own lives.

Some of the principal results were: The arrest of Georg Haeussler, state police chief in the Rhineland-Palatinate, who was accused of ordering the mass extermination of Russians and Jews on the Eastern Front; the filing of charges against a former SS lieutenant colonel and captain, both living in Berlin, who are considered responsible for the execution of twenty thousand Russians in a six-month period in Wilna, Witebsk, Wjasma, and Smolensk, and filing of charges against nearly a dozen SS officers who had been members of the Auschwitz concentration camp staff. The Auschwitz case is expected to be the longest and most extensive war-crimes trial ever held by German authorities.

The agency sees no immediate end to its work, and as it continues to plod through reams of evidence one is reminded of the underlying principle which the Baden-Wuerttemberg justice minister established for it in 1958. "The criminal code, which provides severe penalties for murder, existed during the Third Reich, too," Haussmann said. Although murder was carried out en masse in the most horrible and inhuman fashion during that régime, the murderers were not prosecuted because those responsible for upholding law and order had themselves given the command to kill, he added. But this is no excuse for letting those crimes go unpunished during a more enlightened period of Germany's history in which law and order are once more in force.

Chapter III   *The Courts Settle a Score*

The crimes committed in concentration camps, in the ghettos of Eastern Europe, and in the occupied territories are so monstrous that the sufferings of the German people at the hands of their own masters are usually ignored or belittled. But there was nothing insignificant about them. Unleashed terror reigned within the Reich just as it did in the conquered lands. Even passive, trivial resistance to the régime was punishable by death or lengthy imprisonment, and thousands of Germans experienced the bestiality of Nazi leaders (sometimes their own friends and neighbors) for virtually trivial opposition. It is no wonder that when the war ended Germans sought and were afforded the opportunity to settle their own scores first.

Out of this grew Germany's jurisdiction over the war criminals. Although this second stage still dominates the judicial scene, the outrages against the German people have not passed into oblivion. Courts all over the country still have a backlog of such cases to try.

They fall into three main categories.

There are the murder, manslaughter, and assault cases involving those fanatics who, acting either on their own initiative or on orders from higher authorities, hanged, shot, and tortured hundreds of German citizens who wanted to surrender themselves or their towns and villages to the advancing Allied armies. Anyone caught hoisting a white flag, any schoolboy or old-age pensioner who refused to march to the edge of town to stop tanks with Molotov cocktails and anti-tank grenades, any mayor or municipal official who wanted to surrender instead of ordering the citizens to fight until the last man faced a similar fate: hanging or shooting.

There are also the cases involving former high-ranking *Wehrmacht* officers who usurped military law to order the execution of subordinates who had failed to carry out "last-ditch" commands, had been what the Nazis interpreted as "cowards before the enemy," or had merely raised the ire of a commander who considered himself above the law.

The third category comprises the crimes of Nazis against Nazis, that is, those who acting either on the *Führer*'s orders or on their own initiative purged members of the party for their own personal aggrandizement. Dominant among these cases are the trials that have arisen from the 1934 "blood purge" of the SA (Storm Troop) leaders.

To most Germans today such court hearings are a more vivid reminder of the Nazi terror than anything else. This is when the dictatorship, the ogre which they themselves had created, boomeranged in all its fury. Usually these trials are held right in the communities where the shootings or hangings took place. The survivors, together with prominent local citizens, become prosecution witnesses. There have been hundreds of such trials, and most likely there will continue to be more. There is hardly a German community where some Nazi atrocity was not committed toward the end of the war. The basic defense raised in all such hearings is a blanket order issued by Hitler which called for the immediate execution of anyone who "resisted the war effort." "Resistance" was given a very wide interpretation.

One recent trial, typical of many, is that of former German air force Major Erich Stenzel and Captain Alfred Banholzer, who were tried for the manslaughter of a Bavarian miller and setting fire to the mill. Stenzel was sentenced to three and one half years in prison; Banholzer was acquitted.

Testimony revealed that the two, both thirty-three years old at the time, were making a motorcycle reconnaissance patrol near the isolated mill in Uffenheim county, Franconia, on April 12, 1945. The mill was located in no man's land between the German and American fronts. Stenzel and Banholzer stopped to question the miller, David Guggenberger, about military activities he had noticed. Searching around the house, the two officers discovered that Guggenberger had displayed a white towel in one of the windows facing the American lines. Guggenberger explained that United States troops had been at the mill the preceding day and had told him that, if he raised the white flag, they would not shell his place. Stenzel wouldn't accept the explanation and arrested Guggenberger. He ordered the miller's wife and three small children to leave the house, then led Guggenberger behind the barn and shot him. Stenzel and Banholzer set fire to the mill.

During their trial the two accused each other of firing the fatal shots and setting fire to the buildings. After a month-long hearing the charges against Banholzer were dropped. Stenzel was convicted of manslaughter and arson. At one point during the trial, Banholzer told the court that he and Stenzel got back on the motorcycle after the shooting and headed toward their own lines. They were intercepted by a patrol of Americans who had opened fire on them. "We waved white handkerchiefs and surrendered," Banholzer admitted.

When the trial, which was held in a district courtroom in Ansbach, moved to the Uffenheim county courthouse for on-the-scene hearings, hundreds of local farmers crowded the chamber to hear the proceedings. Most of them had been close personal friends of Guggenberger. His widow still lives in the community and came to court as one of the chief prosecution witnesses.

Trials such as these, more than anything else, provide a great mass of Germans with insight into the madness that characterized the Nazi régime. Usually they take place in small communities, towns and villages that did not suffer from air raids, and in which there was still enough to eat when the rest of the country was starving.

Of similar importance are the cases involving army, air force, and navy officers who took military justice into their own hands, rationalizing their actions by saying that they had to "maintain discipline" or that they were compelled to act under "orders and decrees of the *Führer*." Of all such trials, none generated as much public interest as that of ex-Field Marshal Ferdinand Schoerner, nicknamed the "Infantryman's Terror" by World War II German soldiers. The last field marshal to be appointed by Hitler, Schoerner commanded forty German divisions on the Russian front. He spent nearly ten years in a Soviet POW camp, and when he was repatriated in 1954, German law enforcement agencies all over the country suddenly were bombarded with accusations against him. Schoerner, dubbed by his subordinates as "the devil's own field marshal," was one of the most hated men in the German army. Even loyal Hitler generals and marshals who appeared as character witnesses at his sensational manslaughter trial in Munich had difficulty making complimentary remarks about him.

At one time after his repatriation, thirty accusations alleging murder, manslaughter, and attempted murder were on file against Schoerner. There were twenty more allegations that he had ordered executions without court-martial. The complaints and charges came from all over the country. Germans ranking from private to colonel during the war were among Schoerner's accusers. When he finally went to court in October, 1957, only three charges were left. Lack of evidence had forced Bavarian district attorney officials to drop the rest.

Schoerner stood trial on one count of manslaughter and two specifications of attempted manslaughter. On the first charge, he was accused of having ordered the execution without court-martial of Private Walter Arndt, whom Schoerner had spotted asleep behind the wheel of an army truck on the Russian front. Arndt's vehicle had blocked part of the road on which Schoerner was beating a hasty retreat in a staff car. On the attempt counts, Schoerner was alleged to have ordered the execution without court-martial of Colonel Rudolf Sparre, commandant of the city of Neisse, and Major Walter Juengling, Sparre's executive officer. The reason? Sparre and Juengling had surrendered the city in the face of overwhelming Soviet odds. The intervention of another general under Schoerner's command, however, saved their lives. Both Sparre and Juengling came to Munich to testify against their former superior.

While Schoerner was on trial for these crimes, which finally resulted in a four-and-one-half-year jail sentence,[1] the general himself had a couple of suits running against the German government. For

---

[1] He was released after two years because of ill health.

one thing, Schoerner had demanded the customary cash payment of 6,000 DM due a late returnee from prisoner of war internment. He had also filed suit with the German federal government for payment of his military retirement pension.

Once during the lengthy trial a German war veteran stepped up to Schoerner in the Munich courtroom and slapped him in the face. Schoerner filed assault charges against the former soldier. An inferior court sentenced the vet to a 100-DM fine.

Although Schoerner lost his appeal against the manslaughter and attempted manslaughter conviction and had to go to jail, he did get his returnee pay. His pension demands are still tied up in a disciplinary procedure with the federal government. If, as a former officer, he is found guilty of misconduct by a government board, the monthly pension of 2,600 DM will be denied.

Another legal hassle involving Schoerner resulted from the City of Munich's refusal to pay him the customary 100 DM which it gives as a "welcome home greeting" to late repatriates from Soviet POW camps. The city council voted to deprive Schoerner of this gratuity. Schoerner consequently sent a fiery letter to the city administration threatening an insult and slander suit in a civil court. What angered Schoerner in particular was a remark by a Social Democratic council member (Albert Bayerle). "If we had been able to prevent Schoerner's return from Russia, we would have done so," Bayerle had said.

At a press conference, Schoerner dismissed the councilman's remarks as "vulgar."

Bayerle, himself a German war veteran, said Schoerner could not be identified with other German soldiers, "most of whom were brave." He said he knew of a number of commanders who had stayed with their units even after Germany's capitulation instead of fleeing by plane from their area of battle. When the heat was on and the war almost over Schoerner had cleared out. This, even more than Schoerner's cold-bloodedness, aroused public opinion against him.

Some of the most extraordinary postwar cases deal with crimes committed in the Nazi régime's infancy. These trials stem from the great purge of the Hitler SA (Storm Troop) organization which took place in June and July of 1934.

The most important was the one in which ex-SS Lieutenant General Josef (Sepp) Dietrich and former SS Colonel Michael Lippert were tried for the slaying of seven of their Nazi comrades during the bloody party purge. Dietrich, now sixty-eight, was charged with ordering the execution of two lieutenant generals, three major generals, and one colonel, all SA storm troopers, the rowdy bunch of brownshirts who had helped vault Hitler into office. At the time Dietrich ordered the executions, he was head of Hitler's SS bodyguard. Lippert, one-time commandant of Dachau concentration camp, was charged with manslaughter for the assassination of General Ernst Roehm, SA chief of staff and a member of Hitler's cabinet.

Roehm, a ruthless homosexual brawler and murderer, had been one of the organizers of the National Socialist German Workers Party and had fought his way to party prominence with a marauding private army that staged beerhall fights, beat up rivals, carried out assassinations, patrolled flag-waving mass rallies, and terrorized opponents. From scanty beginnings he turned the brownshirts into Hitler's private force, three hundred thousand strong. Out of it grew the even more elite SS guard, which originated as Hitler's personal bodyguard, became a special police force, and later an actual combat arm with many divisions.

Dissension between the SA and the SS was not long in coming. There had always been serious tensions between Hitler and Roehm, whose perverse excesses had caused a rift with the *Führer* as early as 1927. However, they had managed to patch things up once more. After Hitler came to power, Roehm wanted to become war minister, incorporate the army into his storm troop outfit, and mastermind Germany's military planning. The army staff was shocked at the idea and several generals won Hitler to their side. He made a pact with the *Reichswehr*. He would support them against Roehm if they would support him for the German presidency. At that time Hitler was chancellor. Reich President Paul von Hindenburg, eighty-seven, was expected to die in a matter of weeks. Hitler promised to denude the SA of all its powers and subject the organization to military control. Until then the storm troopers had had their hands in everything. For weeks the army and Hitler's more popular personal SS collected evidence against the SA, some true, some trumped up. Roehm had no idea of what was happening behind his back.

But Hitler had collected enough information to make it appear as if Roehm had planned a *Putsch*. During the night of June 29 to June 30, 1934, Hitler ordered all SA officers apprehended. Roehm and six other principal officers, arrested by Hitler personally, were imprisoned in Munich. Later during that day Lippert and SS Brigadier General Theodor Eicke,[2] Lippert's predecessor at Dachau, sent a pistol into Roehm's cell and ordered him to commit suicide within ten minutes. When Roehm refused, Lippert and Eicke allegedly entered the cell and both fired their revolvers at the storm troop boss. Lippert, the charges against him in Munich read, had fired the *coup de grâce*.

Sepp Dietrich, the Bavarian prosecutor's charges said, had been ordered by Hitler to take a firing squad to the prison and shoot the other six. The *Führer* gave Dietrich a list of names of the men he wanted executed. In his own defense, Dietrich said that he had not stayed around at the prison long enough for all six to be shot. By late afternoon of July 1, 1934, the entire SA leadership had been purged, hundreds of Hitler's opponents who had nothing to do with the storm troopers or any of the Nazi party organizations had also been arrested. One month later Hindenburg died and Hitler became *Führer*. Although the homosexuality of the leading SA men was known to the police as early as 1924 and to all the party leaders no later than 1927, Hitler, Goebbels, and Goering had consistently denied the reports. But after the purge Hitler and Goebbels suddenly made a major issue of the SA leadership's perversion.

The unusual postwar trial in which all these events of 1934 were discussed again took place in May, 1957, in Munich. Until a few months before the investigations had started, Dietrich was still serving a war-crimes sentence at Landsberg. He had been convicted in the Malmédy massacre of American soldiers during the Battle of the Bulge. Originally slated to die, his sentence later was commuted to a life term. After an extensive investigation by the United States Senate into the interrogation and trial methods used at the Malmédy hearings, Dietrich was finally released in December, 1955.

Hundreds of policemen cordoned off the courthouse where Lippert and Dietrich pleaded innocent to the manslaughter charges.

---

[2] Killed in action in World War II.

The indictment was an eighty-eight-page document. The two were defended by Dr. Alfred Seidel, Rudolf Hess's lawyer at the Nuremberg International War Crimes tribunal.

The most amazing piece of evidence in the week-long case was the original piece of paper with the names of the SA officers to be arrested. Check marks in the margin indicated the six whom Dietrich was ordered to kill. The list was signed by Hitler. Throughout the trial, which drew hundreds of spectators, newspapermen, and photographers from all over Europe, Dietrich referred to Hitler as *"der Führer."* He called the SS men under him a "decent, clean and faithful bunch." Dietrich admitted that he'd gotten the orders to shoot the six from Hitler directly but insisted that "the *Führer* would not have given me an order to shoot these traitors if he didn't think it was justified." Besides, he added, he himself would never have left Munich alive had he refused to carry out the orders.

Lippert, dressed in a smart brown suit with a maroon tie, looked more like a successful businessman than the Nazi henchman he had once been. He categorically denied the manslaughter charge. He told the Munich jury that he had been ordered to keep watch outside Roehm's prison cell while Eicke went inside. Lippert claimed he never even heard a shot fired. Returning to the cell a short time later, Lippert told the court, he found Roehm's body and assumed that the storm troop leader had committed suicide. Both men were convicted. Dietrich got a one-and-one-half-year term on a charge of aiding and abetting manslaughter and spent most of it right in Landsberg prison where he had served ten years for the Malmédy murders. He was released in February, 1959, because of a serious heart and circulatory ailment.

Not all the sentences passed in purge killings were as light as those levied against Lippert and Dietrich, however. In Osnabrueck, for example, there was former SS Lieutenant General Udo von Woyrsch, sentenced to ten years in prison on eight counts of assisting manslaughter.

Chapter
IV
*Pity
the
Taxpayer*

Germany's squaring of accounts with its own conscience doesn't stop in the courtroom. A major share of it requires cold cash. But it is particularly in this form of settling the moral and physical debts that one of the strangest paradoxes in postwar German political life has developed.

Determined to make restitution to anyone who suffered damages in the war, the German government today pays billions in reparations to individuals and countries that were victims of the Nazi terror; to citizens bombed out of their homes in Allied air raids; to German war veterans or their widows; to soldiers interned in POW camps; to refugees from the Soviet zone and the Eastern territories, and, strangely enough, to some of the biggest shots in the Nazi hierarchy. And, while all this occurs, there is still an active de-Nazification chamber in Berlin which levies fines and confiscates the property of some of the same ex-Nazis who are already back on the public dole. The German taxpayer foots the entire bill.

In the center of the controversy are the postwar restitution, compensation, and reparations programs for victims of the Nazi régime, and a law for the rehabilitation of former civil servants and professional soldiers. Compensation for victims of Nazi persecution was a haphazard affair until April 1, 1956, when the present law went into effect. Until 1949, when the Federal Republic was founded, settlement of claims was left to the individual states in the various zones of occupation. There was no West German coordination whatsoever.

The first effort at codifying the various state regulations into a national law took from 1949 until 1953 when the "Supplementary Federal Law for the Compensation of Victims of National-Socialist Persecution" was enacted. Under this bill, restitution and compensation provisions were considerably more stringent than they are today. Eligible for payments were those who had suffered actual physical damages and handicaps; loss of property, both real and financial; those who had been retarded in their economic progress and had been confined by any of the organs of the Nazi police state. Excluded entirely from provisions of the bill were those thousands who had lived in that part of Germany now under Polish or Soviet control. There was dissatisfaction with this measure right after it was enacted and the new *Bundestag*, which took office in September, 1953, following the general elections, set about drafting a new bill.

The new law calls for compensation not only to those who had been jailed or confined by the Nazis, but also those whose freedom had been curtailed, had been forced to live under circumstances "similar to confinement," or under conditions "degrading to human dignity."

Original estimates were that the more generous new regulations would cost the federal government approximately 7 billion DM (about $1.7 billion). The law in its more liberal interpretation opened the door for thousands of victims of Nazi oppression who previously had considered the restitution and compensation standards of the individual states too stringent to venture a claim for which they might have to pay high attorney fees if they lost. The new program also enabled thousands of victims who had lived in the territory now comprising the Soviet zone to file claims which previously would not have been honored. But, in addition to these legal claims, the law also made it possible for a number of swindlers to file and receive payment for injuries and oppression they never experienced.

Bitter attacks against the law were launched in early 1958 following a speech by German Finance Minister Fritz Schaeffer.[1] Schaeffer estimated that by the time all claims had been met some 29 billion DM would have been paid out. Twenty per cent of this, he said, would end up in the pockets of foreign attorneys. On the heels of Schaeffer's speech, the Rhineland-Palatinate restitution and compensation bureau announced an estimate that some 25 billion DM would be needed. The federal finance ministry, by that time under the guidance of Franz Etzel, set the figure at about 18 billion DM. Organizations of Nazi victims fired back by saying that in actuality barely 3 billion DM had been paid out and the majority of claimants, some of them in dire financial need, had been waiting for years for at least a partial settlement. Schaeffer's speech, at any rate, set off a wave of protests in Germany. Old hatreds, nurtured during the Third Reich, were reawakened. Not long after that mysterious rubber stamp slogans were seen on walls, streetcars, in public rest-rooms, and on trains denouncing the entire restitution program.

In addition to these payments to individuals, the federal government has passed a law calling for restitution and reparations payments in the amount of approximately 3.5 billion DM to Israel, a law for restitution of "determinable property losses"[2] in the amount of 1.5 billion DM; another program provides payments of 61,500,000 DM for former employees of Jewish congregations; there is an estimate that payments to persecuted public officials has already cost more than 1 billion DM and there is a regulation calling for maintenance and repair of damaged Jewish cemeteries, which costs many thousand marks a year.

The West German government is also negotiating with six countries for the payment of compensation and restitution to their victims of Nazi persecution. Agreements with five other nations have already been made. These provide for payments of 400 million marks to France, 60 million DM to Norway, 18 million to Luxembourg, 16 million to Denmark, 100 million for Holland, and 115 million for

---

[1] At that time and still minister of justice.
[2] The 1956 law provides for payments for losses of property which can no longer be accurately substantiated because of the circumstances at the time.

Greece. Negotiations are still under way with Great Britain, Belgium, Italy, Austria, and Switzerland.

That's part of the ledger. But the financial story has other facets. There are laws which provide for "equalization of war burdens" suffered by the German population. There are laws calling for payments to repatriates from prisoner-of-war camps, to Germans interned for political reasons in the East zone, and to POW's and internees of the occupation forces. Under these provisions, for example, a POW can collect up to 60 DM a month for every month he spent in confinement. He is entitled to long-term loans for the establishment of a business or the purchase of a home and furniture.

But what makes the entire situation so incongruous is a law which provides for reemployment or pensions and social security benefits for former civil servants and professional soldiers. Popularly called the "131 Law," [3] it affects former civil servants, government officials, and government-employed laborers who were ousted from their jobs after the war, either because of formal membership in the Nazi party or because the government bureaus for which they had worked were dissolved. Also included are professional soldiers, especially officers, who have not reenlisted or been recalled to the *Bundeswehr*.

In particular, the law covers those civil servants who worked for a government bureau or office which since has been dissolved; those who were employed in government bureaus outside the territorial limits of the Federal Republic; those in the state or local administration of the Protectorat of Bohemia and Moravia, employed in the state or local administration of a foreign country who were expelled because of their German origin; retired and inactive civil servants who were unable to receive their pensions and retirement benefits after May 8, 1945; professional soldiers of the former *Wehermacht* who were still on active duty or already retired and entitled to their pensions; the professional employees of the Reich Labor Service, and the dependents of individuals in all these groups and classifications.

This law has made it possible for thousands of ex-Nazis to reenter

[3] So named because it is a law passed under the provisions of Article 131 of the German Federal Constitution of 1949. Its exact title is *Gesetz zur Regelung der Rechtsverhältnisse der unter Artikel 131 des Grundgesetzes fallenden Personen vom 11. Mai 1951 in der Fassung vom 11. September 1957.*

government service, the military, and other branches of public endeavor which fall under civil service regulations in Germany. Among them are teachers, judges, public prosecutors, policemen, sanitation experts, tax collectors, railroad and postal officials. Those who have not been reemployed have been permitted to retire with the benefits they accrued during the Third Reich.

Despite the fact that there are control provisions in the "131 Law" as well as in the compensation and aid laws for prisoners of war, internees, and returnees, Germany today is faced with the strange dilemma of having to shell out millions annually, not only to the victims of Nazi persecution but to the persecutors as well. Those ex-Nazis who have failed to regain their civil service positions or to get on the retirement and pension dole have established powerful lobby groups with which they hope to change the "131 Law" so that they, too, will be included in its provisions. One of the most powerful of these is the "HIAG der Waffen SS" ("Self-Help Organization" of former members of the Army SS). Their basic objective is to have the fighting SS, that is, those SS units which actually saw front duty, considered part of the German army. If that were to happen, professional SS men who later led fighting SS units in battle would be entitled to pension and retirement benefits. Other groups are also pressuring for the inclusion of former Gestapo members, civil servants who "violated the principles of humanity and justice" during the Nazi régime, and those who lost their civil service positions through legal de-Nazification proceedings.

Although there are distinct safety controls in the law, hundreds of big and small Nazis have successfully obtained pensions, returnee payments, POW compensation, and long-term loans under the provisions of the various programs. Generally it is up to the local courts and civil service disciplinary boards to make the decision. But if the circumstances are right, if an applicant has a good lawyer, he's as good as on the payroll.

Several cases illustrate just what can happen. The widow of Alex Piorowski, former SS lieutenant colonel and for two years commandant of infamous Dachau concentration camp, fought a bitter battle over her claim for a war widow's pension. Her husband had been executed in 1948 at Landsberg war crimes prison by a United

States Army firing squad. Mrs. Piorowski's suit charged that records of the American war crimes trial had failed to establish or elaborate which specific crimes her husband had committed. Thus, she and her lawyer argued, his execution had been unjustified and his death could be classified as something akin to being killed in action or in an enemy POW camp. Fortunately German authorities did not agree with her. The claim was rejected and Mrs. Piorowski didn't get her pension.

But there is another lady who did get paid. Her name is Mrs. Reinhard Heydrich, classified a "war widow" in 1958 and granted 60 per cent of a major general's pension, retroactive to September, 1950. Heydrich was an SS major general who headed the SD (Security Service) from 1931 to 1934; became chief of the Security Police in addition to the SD in 1934; was named boss of the Gestapo and the *Reichssicherheitshauptamt* (National Security Agency) in 1939, and while holding that job, became Reich Protector of Bohemia and Moravia in September, 1941. A Czech patriot assassinated him in 1942, and in retaliation the Nazis massacred the village of Lidice. In granting her a monthly 1,000 DM pension, a court decided that Heydrich's assassination had been the "direct result of war," not a political act.

Franz von Papen, Germany's chancellor before Hitler, afterward vice chancellor in Hitler's first cabinet, has filed a claim for a pension. It was denied. Papen was acquitted of crimes against the peace at the Nuremberg International War Crimes tribunal. But Hitler's valet, Heinz Linge, a major in the SS, was granted a lump sum indemnity payment for the twelve years he spent in a Russian POW camp. The presiding judge said that Linge's memoirs, published in England, had proved clearly that the valet took care of all Hitler's personal matters but had had no part in political or military decisions. The judge decided Linge couldn't be considered as one of the "supporters or advocates" of the Nazi régime.

Figures for early 1960 indicate that twelve former state secretaries [4] and ambassadors and twenty-two widows in this category receive pensions under provisions of the "131 Law." In addition, seven government presidents or their widows and fifty-nine ministry directors

[4] Highest civil service title.

or their survivors are receiving benefits. There are 1,036 generals and admirals who receive retirements pensions. For a general the amount is 2,600 DM ($650) per month. Widows receive 60 per cent of the total.

In late summer of 1958 the Lower-Saxony council of the German Federation of Labor Unions published a shocking report about former high-ranking Nazis who had received pensions, government loans, or subsidies, or were back in public life.[5] Publication of the list set off a wave of protests, in and out of Germany, but with little result. More than a year after its publication, most of the bigwigs are still getting their money. In only a few isolated cases have steps been taken to reevaluate early court decisions or verdicts on claims. The union's list included:

Admiral Karl Doenitz, submarine chief, German chancellor during the few days between Hitler's death and Germany's capitulation, sentenced to a life term at Nuremberg but released early from Spandau because of his age and ill health, has been granted the pension of a rear admiral for the rest of his natural life.

Hjalmar Schacht, predecessor of Walther Funk as German economics minister under Hitler, tried but acquitted at Nuremberg of crimes against humanity, receives a monthly retirement pension of 2,800 DM ($700).

Grand Admiral Erich Raeder, convicted at Nuremberg, received a monthly pension of 2,246 DM since his release in 1953 from Spandau war crimes prison until his death November 6, 1960.

Dr. Rudolf Diels, founder of the Gestapo, active in right-radical circles from 1945 until his death in 1957, received a monthly pension of 600 DM.

Dr. Ernst Lautz, chief prosecutor at the special *Volksgerichtshof* (People's Court) in Berlin, originally sentenced to ten years at Landsberg, then released, received a monthly pension of 1,692 DM from April 1, 1951 (shortly after he left prison) until 1953. From

[5] The *Deutsche Gewerkschaftsbund* (German Federation of Trade Unions) is Germany's largest organization of labor unions. Its state council in Lower Saxony has publishd for several years a periodic news letter service entitled *Feinde der Demokratie (Enemies of Democracy)* which is aimed at radical elements of both the left and the right. The list appeared in three special issues in 1958: Vol. VII No. 9, 9A, and 9B.

1953 until April 1, 1958, he received 1,342 DM monthly. Since April, 1958, Lautz has received a monthly pension of 786 DM.

Field Marshal Erhard Milch, Hermann Goering's deputy, state secretary at the air ministry, convicted by a United States court for his part in the plans involving slave labor of the civilian population of countries and territories occupied by Germany, receives a monthly pension of 1,300 DM. Milch was originally sentenced to a life term in Landsberg which later was reduced to fifteen years.

SS Major General Eggert Reeder, deportation specialist for Belgium, Nazi government chief of Cologne, received 26,000 DM in support and loans and draws a 1,400 DM monthly pension.

Alexander Andrae, former general, a right-wing agitator since 1945, gets the pension of a retired general.

Goering's personal advisor, Dr. Erich Gritzbach, the press chief of the Prussian State Ministry after the Nazis came to power, and an SS brigadier general, draws 1,293 DM monthly.

Dr. Martin Hellinger, an SS doctor, considered a specialist in the removal of gold teeth from concentration camp victims, received a special 10,000 DM grant with which he reestablished a dental practice.

Dr. Hans von Helms, who joined the Nazi party in 1922, then became a major general in the SA storm troops and an official in the Reich Ministry of Interior, is retired on the pension of a high-ranking civil servant.

Rudolf Jordan, Nazi *Gauleiter* of Saxony-Anhalt, was paid 6,000 DM as POW indemnity.

SS Colonel Anton Kaessler, commandant of infamous Sachsenhausen concentration camp, also received 6,000 DM POW compensation.

Paul Koerner, Goering's adjutant and co-worker who advanced from 1931 through 1942 to the rank of SS lieutenant general, receives a monthly pension estimated at between 1,500 DM and 2,000 DM. Koerner was Goering's assistant in the economics program and a ranking civil servant. At Nuremberg he was sentenced to fifteen years' imprisonment of which he served only six.

Dr. Kurt Matthaei, Nazi police commissioner in Schaumburg-Lippe, a district government president under the Nazi régime, receives a 795 DM pension. Matthaei was a functionary of the neo-Nazi Socialist Reich party until it was outlawed and has been active in right-wing radical groups since then.

Otto Andres, former assistant *Gauleiter* in Danzig, was awarded the pension of a county commissioner after his release from internment in Poland.

Hans Hinkel, former director of the special anti-Semitic propaganda department in Goebbels' propaganda ministry and vice president of the Reich Chamber of Culture, an SS brigadier general, is paid the pension of a high civil servant.

Dr. Johannes Krohn, former state secretary in the Reich ministry of labor, then transferred to the Reich justice ministry in 1941, receives the 2,700 DM pension of a state secretary in accordance with the "131 Law."

SS Lieutenant Colonel Hermann Krumey, trained at Dachau concentration camp and an assistant to SS Lieutenant Colonel Adolf Eichmann, received special long-term credits after 1945 in the amount of 12,000 DM. Krumey has been accused of taking part in the massacre of Lidice, Czechoslovakia.

Kurt Rothenberger, former state secretary in the Reich justice ministry, receives the standard pension of a district court judge amounting to 1,300 DM monthly.

Jochen Peiper, former SS colonel and colonel in the Army SS, originally sentenced to death in the Malmédy trial, then granted clemency and released from Landsberg in 1956, received 6,000 POW indemnity.

SS Brigadier General Dr. Helmuth Poppendieck, former chief doctor in the SS Race and Resettlement office, sentenced to ten years' imprisonment by a United States war crimes tribunal in Nuremberg, then released in 1951, received internment indemnity as a "returnee."

Bernhard Ramcke, former paratroop general and active in right-radical organizations after 1945, receives a general's pension.

Otto Ernst Remer, former major general, accused of participating in the murder of the July 20, 1944, resistance fighters, receives a pension as a major general.

Manfred Roeder, former air force judge advocate general, accused of having passed many death sentences against opponents of the régime, receives a pension as a general.

Hans Joachim Sieber, former SA lieutenant general and director of the storm troop athletic schools, receives the pension of a colonel.

Walter Schroeder, former Nazi police chief of Luebeck, and SS brigadier, receives a monthly pension of 1,200 DM.

Harald Schnuhr, former civil servant and district inspector, receives a 450 DM monthly pension.

Dr. Erich Stolleis, ex-mayor of Ludwigshafen, receives a pension of 900 DM.

Dr. Hans Widgassen, former Nazi mayor of Osnabrueck, gets a monthly pension of 950 DM.

Alexander von Woedtke, former SS colonel, draws the pension of a police chief.

The publication of the list by the trade union is the first and only concerted effort to draw public attention to these payments. Until then, most Germans had no idea that the "131 Law" was being applied for such purposes. But when the list was published, some action was taken. In the case of Dr. Ernst Lautz, for example, German authorities launched an immediate investigation into his past and initiated a civil service disciplinary proceeding to discontinue his pension. Nevertheless, by the time the list had appeared Lautz, referred to in the press as "the devil's own prosecutor," had cost the German taxpayer more than 125,000 DM.

A great many injustices can be attributed to the fact that former Nazis are again sitting on the benches of jurisdictional courts and in minor civil service positions where they can render decisions in favor of their old comrades.

Yet while all this occurs Berlin still has a de-Nazification board which actively levies fines against former Nazis. The board has successfully confiscated the property of many high-ranking officials although they no longer live in Berlin. This is because most of the party leaders had houses, bank accounts, or other valuables deposited in the city. Thus, when aging ex-economics minister Walther Funk was released from the four-power Spandau war crimes prison in 1957, the Berlin board went into action. Although Funk moved to Frankfurt, he still had 17,000 DM worth of property in Berlin. The de-Nazification board confiscated 10,900 DM. Funk had been sentenced to a life term by the Nuremberg international tribunal but was released in 1957 because of ill health.

Similar sentences have been passed against other Third Reich officials. The Berlin chamber fined Dr. Wolfgang Muenstermann, once a judge on special Nazi courts, a total of 50,000 DM for advocating and advancing the National Socialist régime. Muenstermann was charged with passing fifty political death sentences. He was also receiving a 950 DM monthly pension. Berlin authorities filed a disciplinary proceeding to prevent further payments.

In other decisions, the Berlin chamber confiscated the 25,000 DM worth of property belonging to the heirs of Phillipp Bouhler, former special advisor to Hitler on the Jewish question. The chamber sentenced SS Brigadier General Heinz Jost to a 15,000 DM fine.

Many Germans who are appalled at this Nazi line-up for the public dole are concerned about the fact that more and more organizations and lobby groups composed of former Nazis are being organized to obtain indemnity and payments for those few who are still left out. One of their goals is to establish a restitution and compensation program for "persecution by the Allies" similar to that created for victims of the Nazi régime. The organizations generally form fronts for the rightist fanatics who believe that some day they can return to power.

Chapter V

The Mysterious Route to Africa

"Will the Nazis go underground? Will Hitler, Goebbels, and Goering be able to escape to friendly neutral countries such as Spain or Argentina?" These were vital and frequent questions during the last few months of World War II, after an Allied victory had become a certainty. In part they were inspired by the fact that a number of important Nazis already had succeeded in escaping and winning political asylum abroad. To a far greater extent they were prompted by Nazi propaganda and rumors that plans had been laid for the establishment of resistance cells in Bavaria, each equipped with liberal caches of food, arms, ammunition, money, treasure, and medical supplies. Small groups of fanatics, based in the German Alps, according to the reports, were to try to fight the Allied occupation armies for years to come. There were also numerous stories that elaborate arrangements had been made to spirit Hitler, Goering, Goebbels, Himmler, Rosenberg, and other leaders out of Germany in specially equipped submarines. The destination of their flight was variously reported as Spain, Argentina, and Antartica.

Of course, when the war ended only a fraction of these plans—both the real and the imagined ones—materialized. True, there were

49

small bands of fanatics who held out for a while in the Alps. Caches of Nazi treasure and supplies have been found, there are still treasure hunts, and there are bizarre reports of cave-dwelling Nazis who guard mountain hide-outs in which vast deposits of gold, cash, and other valuables are stored. Anyone who dares come near these strongholds, the rumors say, is a marked man. Strangely enough, some official and unofficial treasure hunters have been murdered. Many important Nazis did go "underground" by assuming aliases. Some are still "missing," others have "reappeared" on their own initiative, and a few have been "discovered" and "unearthed."

There are still arguments about whether Martin Bormann, Hitler's right-hand man, is at large, or whether he died during a Russian artillery barrage on Berlin. Nevertheless, a warrant for his arrest was issued to Brazilian federal police on May 30, 1960, following reports that he might be hiding in the state of Santa Catarina in southern Brazil where numerous Germans live. For years there were best-selling stories that Hitler had escaped, that he was selling rugs in the Orient, that he had been hidden away by Argentinian dictator Juan Perón, or that he had finally frozen to death at the South Pole. Today, however, there is little doubt that Hitler shot himself and was cremated by his aides in his Berlin bunker.

The really important leaders of the Third Reich did not escape, although there is evidence that many "second string" Nazis fled to Spain, Argentina, other Latin American states, and to sympathetic Arab countries following the fall of Perón. Unofficial sources report that four German submarines carrying nearly two hundred crew members and Nazi officials reached Argentina during a two-month period in the summer of 1945.

The ease with which Nazi criminals disappeared in the chaotic postwar days has recently been demonstrated dramatically by the capture of former SS Lieutenant Colonel Adolf Eichmann, charged with responsibility for mapping out the "final solution to the Jewish problem" which took the lives of six million people.

Although there are still many loopholes in the chronology of Eichmann's flight from justice, the following story seems to be reasonably accurate.

Eichmann left his Berlin headquarters on the 1st or 2d of May, 1945, and headed south to Austria and Bavaria, hoping to find refuge with party comrades there. On May 3, he showed up at the hide-out of Dr. Ernst Kaltenbrunner, Heinrich Himmler's deputy. Kaltenbrunner, captured in a fortified chalet on May 15, turned down Eichmann's plea for refuge. Some reports have it that he was afraid Eichmann would hurt his own position with the Americans, others indicate that Kaltenbrunner gave Eichmann well meaning advice to head for Spain.

Whatever the case, on May 8, 1945, Eichmann was captured near Salzburg, but his captors didn't know who he was. Eichmann was wearing a *Luftwaffe* private's uniform and went under an assumed name, Hirtl. He claimed he had destroyed his identity papers, and the Americans apparently believed him. Later, to account for his SS blood group tattoo, he changed his identity to that of an SS lieutenant.

Eichmann managed to escape from the camp and made his way north to seek sanctuary with an SS comrade's brother who gave him work as a woodcutter. For five years, apparently, Eichmann lived incognito in Germany, not even looking up his wife and their three children in Linz, Austria, or his girl friend. It is believed that he fled to Argentina—by what means is not yet clear—in 1950. At any rate, in 1952, police in the Argentinian province of Tucuman provided Eichmann with identity papers under the name of Ricardo Clement.

His wife and the three boys, Klaus, Adolf, and Dieter, disappeared from Austria in 1952. Frau Eichmann, who had previously petitioned for a declaration of her husband's death, suddenly pulled the boys out of school, took out a passport in her maiden name, and dropped from sight.

Eichmann, it has been reported, first worked for an estimating firm run by an ex-SS officer. The company, which later went bankrupt, had been set up allegedly to provide work for former SS men. It did market research and estimates for industrial firms planning to set up branch plants in Argentina. Eichmann apparently fitted in well because he had studied engineering. When Israeli agents nabbed him in May, 1960, he was working for Mercedes-Benz-Argentina.

Eichmann's case certainly is not singular. It stands out mainly because of his dramatic capture and the fact that, along with Bormann, he was the most hunted Nazi criminal still unaccounted for. Although his rank in the SS hierarchy was not high, Eichmann is responsible for the technical follow-through on most of the Jewish pogroms and he is the initiator of the mass extermination policy.

There are many "little Eichmanns" still at large. Many of them are known to be in South America or the Arab countries, but authorities there have either refused to extradite them or are themselves at a loss to find them, such as the case of Dr. Josef Mengele, experimenter with concentration camp inmates, allegedly hiding out from Argentinian authorities. Others, such as Nazi propagandist Johannes von Leers, spent years in Argentina, then escaped to the Near and Middle East when Perón fell. Von Leers today is an active anti-Semite in the United Arab Republic.

But the postwar escapes are only a part of the story, and a part that seemed to be fading from the realm of current events to history until Eichmann was captured. By the time the Federal Republic was founded in 1949, discussions about a Nazi underground or an organized Nazi resistance movement had pretty much subsided and the subject had passed into near oblivion. It was revived suddenly in the summer of 1958, some thirteen years after Germany's capitulation in the wake of the mysterious disappearance and subsequent Egyptian reappearance of concentration camp doctor Hans Eisele and schoolteacher Ludwig Zind.

Eisele was the man who had been tabbed as a mass murderer during the trial of Martin Sommer. When the allegations against him appeared in the press, the doctor vanished. A few weeks later he turned up in Cairo. Zind was a high-school teacher in the Black Forest town of Offenburg who had been convicted of making anti-Semitic remarks. He appealed his case and when a higher court upheld the sentence and it came time for him to report to jail, Zind also disappeared. Several weeks later he too showed up in Cairo. The two cases, following each other so closely, sparked speculation that a Nazi or a neo-Nazi underground organization was at work. There were several similar factors involved in both disappearances, and the fact that the two had escaped to Egypt and been received there with unusual cordiality hinted at a possible connection with the underground and former Nazis living in the Nasser realm.

The news of Eisele's escape, after he had been accused by a witness in the Sommer trial, completely overshadowed the remainder of the concentration-camp hearing. The first inevitable questions: How did

Eisele evade de-Nazification? Why was he allowed, even helped, to reestablish his medical practice? Wasn't there anyone who knew his real background? Who had helped him collect 4,000 DM prisoner-of-war indemnity and how had he been able to obtain a 25,000 DM long-term loan?

By the time any of these questions could be properly considered, the doctor was gone. Initial reports indicated that he was in Italy on vacation. This conclusion was based on the fact that he had sent picture postcards from there. But it wasn't long before he was spotted in Egypt, hiding safely behind the dunes of Gamel Abdel Nasser's anything-but-anti-Nazi government.

German attempts to persuade Egypt to extradite Eisele ran against a solid wall of Arab stubbornness. At first the Egyptian authorities admitted the doctor was in their country. Then they denied it. Finally they acknowledged the doctor's presence and announced that he had been given a position of considerable responsibility in a provincial hospital. Throughout the storm, Eisele's wife repeatedly disclaimed that she had known of her husband's plans to flee. But in September, while Egyptian officials were still acknowledging one day, denying the next that they'd ever heard of or seen Eisele, the doctor's wife put the family home in Munich-Pasing up for sale. The asking price: 85,000 DM. In early December, 1958, Mrs. Eisele, her two sons, and her daughter departed from Munich and were seen next in Cairo where they joined the doctor.

Just how did he escape? No one really knows, but there are plenty of theories and rumors. Most German newspapers charged outright —or at least implied—that an underground organization of former SS men had a hand in the matter. Suspiciously quick to repudiate the allegation was Kurt Meyer, an ex-SS major general who serves as "federal speaker" of the "HIAG der Waffen SS," the self-help organization of former "Army SS" men whose avowed purpose is to help members of "SS families" find their missing husbands, brothers, and fathers and obtain social benefits for members of the élite guard organization.

A slip on the part of Mrs. Eisele, shortly after the doctor disappeared, indicated that he had outside help in effecting his escape. Questioned by newsmen, Mrs. Eisele said she had no idea where her husband had gone but admitted that she had received an anonymous letter "in which I was informed that he is no longer in Germany and that, perhaps, I would get more news from him at a later date."

The United Arab Republic's strange treatment of the Eisele case deserves closer scrutiny. The Egyptians first entered the picture on July 12, 1958, with the announcement that Eisele had been arrested in Cairo by police and turned over to Interpol (International Police) authorities who had brought the doctor to a jail for foreigners on the outskirts of the city. The Germans prepared extradition papers, being careful also to charge Eisele with fraud (for drawing his P.O.W. compensation and interest-free loan on false pretenses) so as to rule out all possibilities that the Egyptians might consider him a political refugee and grant him asylum.

The German Foreign Office contacted U.A.R. authorities on July 29. On August 5, an official of the German Embassy in Cairo disclosed that Eisele's extradition would be just a matter of days, and that the only legal snags remaining were the transportation arrangements. Suddenly, on August 10, Egyptian officials said Eisele was not in the jail, had never been there, and as far as they were concerned they had no idea where he was. German Embassy authorities expressed "surprise" at the statement, but added that Egypt had not responded to the extradition demand. On August 18, more than a month after a wire service photograph had shown Eisele flanked by two Egyptian policemen, Cairo authorities denied having any knowledge of the case. When confronted with the photographs, the police officials retorted bluntly: "Are you sure that's Eisele?"

On November 3, 1958, the German Foreign Office reported that its efforts to extradite Eisele had failed. A spokesman explained the negotiations had run aground on the legal technicality concerning the difference in the German and Egyptian statute of limitations. Whereas Germany has a twenty-year limit, Egypt's is only ten. By U.A.R. standards, Eisele could no longer be tried.

The Egyptians found a legal loophole. No one can deny that. But it is doubtful whether this alone caused the sudden about-face by the U.A.R. authorities. After all, in the early stage of the negotiations there seemed to be no question that Eisele would be extradited. Cairo seemed willing and helpful. What had caused the sudden reversal? It must have been influenced extensively by the many ex-

Nazis in the Nasser entourage. It was obvious that Nasser was persuaded to change his mind about the extradition proceedings by domestic forces too important to ignore.

The Eisele case also had its legal repercussions on the German home front. Shortly after the doctor's disappearance there were extensive investigations into why Eisele had not been arrested immediately after the allegations were made against him in the Sommer trial. Bewildered state officials discovered that Bavaria's chief prosecutor, Dr. Max von Decker, had received information implicating Eisele in concentration camp crimes as early as 1954. Decker, however, had taken no action. Further probing revealed that Decker himself had been a member of the National Socialist party from 1931 until the end of the war. The prosecutor was suspended from his post pending the outcome of a more complete investigation.

Then the spotlight turned on Munich's police force. Police chief Anton Heigl, detective chief Andreas Grasmueller, and two plainclothesmen were accused of dereliction of duty for failing to act promptly in issuing a warrant for Eisele's arrest. The allegations against the police officials had been made by Dr. Hugo Freund, a Social Democratic member of the Munich city council. Freund charged that Munich police had launched an investigation into Eisele's background two months previous to the damaging testimony at the Sommer trial, but that they had failed to file a complaint against the doctor despite statements and depositions from numerous witnesses to Eisele's crimes at Buchenwald.

Freund claimed that he had approached Chief Heigl twice on the Eisele matter, the last time on June 24, 1958, less than two weeks before the doctor's escape. "When I asked Heigl whether it might not be better to issue a warrant for Eisele's arrest," Freund stated, "Heigl brushed me off, asking, 'Where could he go?' "

At a press conference, Heigl described Freund's assertions as unjustified. He emphasized that inquiries into Eisele's past had progressed slowly because witnesses were hard to find. When they were located, the police chief explained, their statements proved to be too vague to support the filing of a criminal charge or issuing a warrant for the doctor's arrest. Besides, said Heigl, Eisele was believed to be on vacation and there was no reason to suspect he might escape.

After weeks of probes, detective chief Grasmueller and the two policemen were reprimanded. Heigl, ill at the time, received his reprimand some time later.

State Prosecutor von Decker, amid protests from former Buchenwald inmates, was reinstated in office. He was also reprimanded and fined 300 DM by a civil service disciplinary board for failure to "follow through" on the allegations made to him in 1954.

Eisele was still making sporadic news when suddenly the case of Ludwig Zind burst into the headlines.

Zind, fifty-two at the time, was an Offenburg high-school teacher accused of making slanderous anti-Semitic remarks and condoning war crimes. The trial, a sensation in itself, was held in April, 1958. Zind, a former storm trooper, went on trial for insulting Kurt Lieser, a half-Jewish textile wholesaler; defaming the dead (Jews executed in concentration camps); and approving of a crime (the mass execution of Jews). The charges stemmed from a heated argument between Lieser and Zind in an Offenburg restaurant the night of April 23, 1957. During the argument, Zind, who sports a Hitler-type mustache and has a face crisscrossed with dueling scars, said he approved of the Nazi tactics and shouted that all too few Jews had been liquidated in the gas chambers. Under cross-examination at the trial, attended by newsmen from all over Europe and abroad, Zind defended the Nazi régime's policies and made additional anti-Semitic remarks. Sentenced to a year in jail, he appealed to the German Supreme Court. On November 28, 1958, the court upheld the conviction.

From the time he was first charged until the high court made its decision, Zind was free on his own recognizance. He was suspended from his teaching job and worked as a chemist in a factory. When police came to arrest him on Saturday, November 29, the teacher had disappeared. They were told that Zind had gone out of town to visit a wartime buddy. Then police went to the town where the friend lived. They were informed that the man in question had been dead for a year. Another day passed and authorities faced the unpleasant fact that Zind had escaped. Speculation ran wild as to where the teacher might be and how he had gotten there. Allegations and counterallegations bounced back and forth from one government agency to the other. Police and district attorney officials, in their own defense, explained they had not issued a warrant for Zind's arrest because they assumed there was no danger of his fleeing. After all, they contended, Zind had his family and a house in Offenburg, and there appeared to be no reason to hold him in jail.[2]

Then a spokesman for the German Federal Ministry of Justice declared, to everyone's amazement, that if Zind had fled the country he had done so without a passport, which, the spokesman revealed, had been confiscated. But that would have been only a trivial obstacle in the teacher's plans, since most European countries have simplified border crossings to such an extent that only national identification cards are required.

On Thursday, December 4, 1958, a number of Zind's friends and acquaintances received picture postcards from him, stamped in Italy. Suspecting that Zind might head for Argentina, the German foreign ministry flashed a request to the Argentinian government that he be held as a fugitive from the law. But Zind wasn't on his way to Argentina. By December 7, it appeared certain that he was headed toward Egypt. Passengers on a Greek liner talked of a fellow German traveler "from Offenburg" with scars in his face. The mysterious passenger had refused to reveal his name, however. The following day newspapers reported that Zind was living in a pension called "Hotel Nasser" under the name of Helmut Vollmer. One of the first visitors he received there was Mrs. Eisele, wife of the Buchenwald doctor.

How did Zind manage his escape? After a little detective work, German officials realized it had been simple. Zind used the passport of a niece's brother-in-law, Helmut Vollmer, who had died earlier in 1958. By merely exchanging the pictures in the passport, substituting his own for Vollmer's, Zind had "become" Helmut Vollmer.

After receiving Mrs. Eisele's call, it was alleged, Zind took up contact with an organization called the "Islamic Congress," headed by a former German named Hans Appler, alias Salah Gaafar. Another contact he made, according to reliable reports, was with Dr. Johannes von Leers, the former Goebbels propagandist who went from Argentina to Egypt and now busily supports Nasser while, at the same time, contributing frequently to anti-Semitic and right-radical publications in Germany.

---

[2] Germany has only very limited provisions for release on bail.

From the start German judicial authorities ruled out the possibility that Egypt would extradite Zind. The crimes of which he was convicted aren't recognized as such in the UAR, so that the Egyptians probably wouldn't even consider an extradition request, authorities theorized.

At last report, Zind was teaching geology at the *American-sponsored* University of Libya. In July, 1960, he mysteriously returned to Germany for a visit with his relatives. While in the country he audaciously wrote postal cards to newspapers, magazines, and government officials, chatted with a policeman in front of the parliamentary buildings in Bonn without being recognized, and had himself photographed at will by Ernest Zaugg, a Boston newspaperman who operates the "Hometown Feature Agency" in Munich.

By the time Zaugg's pictures, showing Zind at a Bonn carnival, in a Bonn park, and various other places, appeared in one of the German illustrated magazines, Zind had skipped the country again. However, apparently Israeli intelligence agents were on the search for him and several days after the magazine published the pictures, Zind's name was discovered on the passenger list of a steamer, the *Citta di Tunesi*, docked in Naples. He was arrested by Italian police. It is believed that he was planning to attend the Olympic games in Rome.

German authorities immediately started extradition proceedings. Zind, when arrested, had an Egyptian "stateless person" passport.

Had someone helped Zind make his initial escape? There seems to be very little doubt according to one German, Walter Krause, Baden-Wuerttemberg state legislator, who maintained that Eisele and Zind had been aided by the same organization. The extraordinary similarity between the two flights lends support to this theory. Both men left Germany via Italy, both men went to Egypt. In both cases law enforcement agencies either had been asleep or had deliberately failed to act. One bitter charge came from *Die Welt der Arbeit*, the official publication of the German Federation of Trade Unions (DGB). Its theory was that an underground organization, equipped with submarines, was at work. Such an organization, the article alleged, had been active in spiriting many Nazis to Argentina at the end of World War II. Today, the same organization is still at work, the paper said, only the place of refuge has been changed to Egypt.

In the midst of the upheaval came the trial of Robert Kremer, accused of helping a well known Nazi escape to Syria. Kremer was publisher of a magazine called *Die Anklage (The Indictment)*, an unofficial publication of neo-Nazi groups pressuring for compensation and indemnity for interned and de-Nazified leaders. He was charged with aiding Franz Rademacher, a former legation secretary in Hitler's foreign ministry, escape confinement. Rademacher had been sentenced to three years and five months imprisonment for aiding and abetting in the manslaughter of thirteen hundred Yugoslavian Jews. After his conviction, Rademacher, just like Zind, was released from custody pending the appeal. When a new warrant was issued for his arrest, the Nazi diplomat had disappeared.

Rademacher apparently stayed in hiding in Germany for several weeks, then used a Spanish passport to flee the country. Kremer was accused of having driven Rademacher to Marseille from where the ex-diplomat sailed for Damascus. At his trial in December, 1958, Kremer admitted the allegations but denied he had any knowledge of Rademacher's conviction and appeal.

"I heard the Allies were after him," Kremer told the court. "As an upstanding German, I felt I ought to help him."

Asked by the judge whether he hadn't read any newspapers, all of which covered the Rademacher case, Kremer replied bluntly that he wasn't in the habit of reading postwar papers because "they make me regurgitate."

Kremer was sentenced to five months in jail for aiding the escape of and harboring a criminal. The incident would have little meaning were it not for the fact that Kremer had a long record as a neo-Facist, that his magazine *Die Anklage* has been banned by the German government for espousing pro-Nazi and antidemocratic sentiments, and that he was closely associated with neo-Nazi groups. One frequent contributor to *Die Anklage* was Johannes von Leers. There certainly was more than just "sympathy for an old friend" involved when Kremer helped Rademacher escape.

The escapes of Eisele and Zind put German law enforcement and judicial authorities on the alert. When Dr. Otto Schweinsberger, Frankfurt deputy prosecutor, was accused of war crimes in December, 1958, a warrant for his arrest was issued almost immediately. Nevertheless, even before police had closed in on Schweinsberger, a ticket to Cairo had been booked in his name at an airline office in Munich. Schweinsberger himself insisted he had made no plans to flee the country. Although the war-crimes allegations against him were later dropped, Frankfurt authorities undertook an extensive investigation into the strange circumstances surrounding his arrest. They made futile attempts to check out reports that a room had been reserved for him at a first-class hotel in Cairo. The airline booking had been made by telephone and weeks of investigations failed to turn up a single clue. The call to the Munich airline office could have come from any number of places, as most German cities are connected by a long-distance direct-dial service.

An unparalleled case is that of Professor Werner Heyde, alias Dr. Fritz Sawade, a German doctor who had a major part in the Nazi euthanasia program during which some seventy thousand mentally ill persons were killed in insane asylums throughout Germany. Heyde, an officer in the SS, escaped from Allied custody in 1947. A warrant was issued for his arrest. He had been on the "wanted list" for years. His wife, living in Munich, had him declared legally dead. Between 1952 and 1959 she drew nearly 65,000 DM in pension money. In reality, Heyde had gone underground. Friends helped him to live incognito as a gardener and caretaker in Ploen, Holstein. He succeeded in getting false identification papers and surfaced again with the name of Dr. Fritz Sawade. Under this alias he obtained employment as a doctor with the city administration of Flensburg and soon advanced rapidly to become a medical authority and medical investigator for the Schleswig-Holstein state insurance administration, the Schleswig-Holstein State Court for Social Welfare Disputes, and other Flensburg courts.

Although there is reliable evidence that earlier complaints had been filed against him and that state officials had been informed several times that Sawade was in reality a fugitive from justice, no action was taken until November, 1959, when state authorities decided to arrest Sawade. On November 5, the day the arrest plans were made, but forty-eight hours before the actual arrest was to take place, the doctor disappeared.

When the story broke in German newspapers, it was generally assumed that he had escaped to Egypt. But this time events took a different course. On November 11, Heyde suddenly surrendered in Frankfurt. By that time, however, it was public knowledge that high officials in Germany's northernmost state had been tipped off several times in preceding years about the doctor's real identity. Nothing had been done about it despite that fact that Sawade-Heyde was listed as a wanted criminal.

In December, 1959, a subcommittee was formed in the Schleswig-Holstein legislature to investigate state officials who had protected the euthanasia doctor. At present, nearly a dozen judges and civil servants have been suspended from their posts and are awaiting trial for harboring a fugitive. Schleswig-Holstein's minister president, Kai-Uwe von Hassel, announced in January, 1960, that as many as twenty prominent state officials would be implicated by the time the investigations into the matter are completed. The officials, according to Hassel, will probably fall into three categories: those who knew that Sawade was really someone else but weren't sure who; another group which knew his identity but had no knowledge of the criminal allegations against him, and a small group which had been cognizant of the role Heyde had played in the Third Reich. Members of the legislative subcommittee probing the case expressed surprise at Hassel's statement. According to their preliminary calculations, many more than twenty state officials would be incriminated.

Of course, none of these examples could give conclusive evidence to support the theory that there is an underground organization at work which helps ex-Nazis escape German justice. In each of the cases cited, there is too great a margin of conjecture to permit such a generalization. What evidence is available indicates that, although there is a great similarity between the Eisele, Zind, and Rademacher escapes, a certain amount of ingenuity was used by each which, in turn, raises the possibility that each case was a unilateral action that can be linked only by the coincidence of timing and final destination.

It took no underground organization to advise Zind how to paste his own picture into a dead relative's passport. Schweinsberger denied steadfastly that he made any attempts to fly to Egypt. Rademacher and Kremer, despite their mutual neo-Nazi associations, had been acquaintances, if not outright friends. Although Dr. Heyde disappeared for a week to no-one-knows-where, no evidence has ever been presented that he even considered fleeing to Egypt or some other

Arab country. But one cannot evade the fact that Eisele and Zind were cordially received in the Middle East, that German efforts to obtain their extradition were blatantly thwarted and ignored by Egyptian officials, and that there is a large, although not exactly determinable number of ex-Nazis who live and work in the Arab countries, usually in the service of Arab nationalist politicians.

The close journalistic association between such men as Leers and right radical and nationalistic publications in the Federal Republic is indicative of at least an ideological bond between the Nazi expatriates in the Arab countries and the budding neo-Nazi movements in Western Germany. A physical link would be difficult to verify. It is probably still in the developmental stage and its realization will depend on many external factors, such as the alliances which the Arab countries make in future years, what steps the West Germans take to counteract the right radical movement in the Federal Republic, and what future services the ex-Nazis will render the nationalist governments of the Middle East.

If a neo-Nazi underground movement ever gains sufficient momentum to endanger German democracy, doubtlessly it will be connected in some way with the Nazi expatriates in the Arab countries. But the danger at present is not very great. Nevertheless, it is sufficiently apparent so that German government leaders should remain alert.

Chapter VI

The Ghost of the Goosestep

To people throughout the world, be they in the Western camp or on the other side of the Iron Curtain, fear of a reincarnated German nationalism and imperialism is closely interwoven with mistrust of Germany's new military power.

Despite the strategic benefits which the West hopes to derive from a new armed force, there are widespread feelings that remilitarization will boomerang. A generation may have to pass before all the qualms and anxieties are allayed, for the imprint of German boots is just too indelible in the minds of both our allies and our potential enemies to let them forget or forgive more quickly. The most inexplicable development, however, was the reaction of the Germans themselves. Although rearmament plans collided with a wall of resistance, most people refused to believe they would ever materialize. When they did, and the *Bundeswehr* was started in 1955, it met with violent opposition. Protest demonstrations were held all over the country and Germany's new soldiers were beaten on the streets. But despite these spontaneous, at times organized outbursts of enmity, the *Bundeswehr* grew. Finally, the active resistance subsided. Although a new display of antiarmy sentiments followed in 1959, when World War II veterans had to register for the draft, this eruption, though fierce and intensive, was brief. While the Germans may have become accustomed to the concept of a new army, they haven't gotten used to the sight of the uniform. The *Bundeswehr*, after five years, numbers nearly a quarter of a million men but even in garrison cities German civilians still stop on the streets, twist their necks, and gape after one of their own soldiers out for a stroll. The uniform evokes a sea of unhappy memories.

The frantic opposition to rearmament and the unbridled antagonism which the Germans displayed toward the first volunteers struck observers as one of the most unusual phenomena of the postwar years. Some of the most vehement outbursts took place in Bavaria which once was considered a hotbed of Nazism and militarism.

In Munich, for example, uniformed *Bundeswehr* soldiers were banned from entering restaurants, cafés, and bars. Within a few weeks after the first German troop units were stationed there, proprietors posted signs reading: "Men in uniform not wanted." Because there had been a large contingent of American troops since 1945 and the placards were written in German, it was obvious at whom they were directed.

Most of the incidents occurred during September and early October, 1956. One of the first involved a scuffle between a twenty-year-old Munich youth and a group of *Bundeswehr* soldiers on a crowded streetcar. The young man had been asked to move to the rear of the trolley by the conductor. "The army ought to make way first," he said, referring to the German soldiers. A brawl resulted and police were called to restore order.

A few days later, two German soldiers were attacked on the street by a group of twenty teen-agers. The soldiers were severely beaten and stripped of their insignia. At the famous Munich *Oktoberfest* in 1956, five German soldiers were jeered and forcibly driven off the carnival grounds by a group of civilians. Several days later, residents living near one of the military posts filed breach-of-the-peace charges against a young *Bundeswehr* lieutenant because he had ordered his platoon to sing marching songs at six o'clock in the morning, thus disturbing their sleep. A municipal court ordered the post commander to limit singing from the period between 8 A.M. to 8 P.M. and fined the lieutenant 150 DM ($35).

Then the demonstrations and wave of incidents spread northward, finally gaining momentum all over the country. In Giessen, a small university town in northern Hesse, a group of returnees from Russian prisoner-of-war camps held a reunion. One of their members had joined the *Bundeswehr* as a captain. When he arrived at the meeting, the others refused to sit at the same table with him.

On a Hamburg street, eighteen German teen-agers attacked six *Bundeswehr* noncoms. One of the soldiers was hospitalized with a broken jaw. A few days later, again in Hamburg, thirteen civilians jumped three German soldiers and beat them up.

When recruiting teams for the new army set out to drum up business, they ran into considerable trouble. In Freudenstadt in the Black Forest, for instance, when they tried to show movies and slides in a public square, they were chased away by civilians. The recruiters had set up their display right next to a memorial for World War II dead. Veterans' organizations assembled and heckled the *Bundeswehr* men, then forced them to leave. In Wiesbaden, capital of the state of Hesse, two hundred teen-agers milled in front of the army's recruiting office and peered and shouted at the *Bundeswehr* men until police arrived and arrested seventy youths.

There were dozens of incidents and the defense ministry was sufficiently concerned to conduct a survey of attitudes toward the new army. The highest rating, in Northern Germany, was only "good to fair." Gradually the manifestations subsided until later in October when the initial draft registration of nineteen-year-olds was to take place.

In Dortmund, fifteen city employees, who had been transferred from other bureaus to the draft board, went on strike the morning the first registrations were scheduled. "We're not going to send our kids into the army," they declared. "Our conscience would bother us if we had to register these boys."

Most other cities also reported difficulties in the program which prescribed the registration of all nineteen-year-olds between October 25 and November 5, 1956. By deadline, only a fraction of eligible youths had shown up. The biggest fiasco occurred in the Hessian town of Hanau, where only one boy out of seventy-five eligibles appeared. He asked to be reclassified as "unavailable." In Munich, 15 per cent showed up, compelling the draft board to send out special letters in which the board warned that the registration law could be backed up by a court order and fines up to 1,000 DM. When Nuremberg's draft board completed its registration, only 25 per cent had reported.

It was during this period that Germany's conscientious objector movement made its greatest strides, winning widespread public support. It served as the fulcrum for the antirearmament agitation because the Federal Republic's 1949 constitution guarantees that "No one can be forced to perform military service with weapons against the dictates of his conscience."

They included not only the traditional groups such as Jehovah's Witnesses and the Quakers, but also nonreligious objectors who rallied behind a second constitutional guarantee that "conscience is an individual matter" which cannot be controlled by any law or any state. This paved the way for "political" conscientious objectors who disassociated themselves from traditional pacifist organizations.

What they believe was summarized most eloquently by one of the leading objectors, Werner Haak, when he wrote in a German trade union paper:

It is Germany's responsibility, the responsibility of German youth in particular, to prove to the world that militarism is not an inborn cancer of the German mind. We must prove to the world there are Germans who represent a creative, peaceful, and modern Germany. We must show that there are Germans who are ashamed of their generals and their landowners, ashamed of Kaiser Wilhelm, Ludendorff, Hindenburg, Hitler, and their bandit gangs. There are Germans who deplore Auschwitz, Buchenwald, Oradour, Lidice, Rotterdam, Coventry, and Sevastopol. There are Germans who hate weapons, uniforms, medals, and the phrases and lies of our history. We consider ourselves united with the tortured Jews, Russians, Czechs, Poles, and Norwegians. We are indignant because we see that the murderers of yesterday are already celebrating their resurrection. We no longer want this hell.

At the height of their success, in 1956 and 1957, there were a hundred thousand active, dues-paying members in three major conscientious objector organizations. The collected dues were used to pepper *Bundestag* members with letters and cables, and lobbyists to provide draft-eligible youths with free legal service and to stage anti-rearmament demonstrations.

The largest and most active is the *"Gruppe der Wehrdienstver-weigerer"* (Group of Defense Service Objectors). Under the slogan of "Neither a People's Police nor Federal Soldiers," it at one time maintained nearly seventy offices staffed with part-time attorneys who gave advice to draft-eligible Germans. Its membership forms include a pledge that the applicant will protect the association's independence from special-interest groups, in particular, the Communists and their front organizations.

One of its leaders, Hans A. Nikel, a young Frankfurt publishing house executive and former editorial staff member of a Frankfurt daily, summed up his reasons for being a conscientious objector.

I'm a product of your American reeducation program [Nikel once said]. I was drafted into the German army as a teenager and served until the Hitler régime collapsed. In 1945 you Americans told us that we should never again have an army. In 1950, your reeducation officers all packed their bags and went home. Coming in behind them were your generals and politicians who told us to get busy on rearmament. I'm sticking to the original lesson. It appeals to me and, besides, I'm getting tired of being reeducated.

One of the group's unaccomplished objectives was to prove the unconstitutionality of the German draft law, in particular a certain clause concerning conscientious objectors, which reads: "He who is opposed to every use of weapons between states on grounds of conscience, and thus objects to military service with weapons, must complete a term of service or civilian compensatory duty outside of the Federal Army. He can, on application, be admitted into the Federal Force for duty without the use of weapons." The objectors took exception to the phrase "every use of weapons."

What the government is trying to do [said Nikel], is limit conscientious objection to traditional pacifism. If you're a member of an established pacifist religious sect, you're covered. But if you object to military service on political grounds or in a particular situation, you're not protected by the law. We consider this unconstitutional, because the constitution states specifically that no one can be forced to perform military service against the dictates of his conscience. Everyone has his own conscience. The constitution guarantees the individual his right to follow its dictates. The government has tried to lay down a norm of conscience and we are convinced this is illegal."

Though the group never gained support in the courts for its contention, the special commissions, established to test the conscience of individual applicants for exclusion from military service, did take this principle into consideration.

There are many members in our organization who would gladly defend the constitution under which they seek protection [a *Gruppe* spokesman said]. They would defend Germany from attack, but only if they could be certain it was *really* an attack. The experience of the last decades teaches us that plain soldiers and the general public can never know for sure when a war is a defensive or an aggressive action. Take the 1956 Suez crisis. Even countries not directly affected did not really know who attacked whom. The Israelis called it retaliation and a war to bring peace. The Egyptians called it an invasion. And according to the French and the British it was a police action. We have even more classic examples in Germany. Turn back to 1938 or 1939. Every German believed that Czechoslovakia and Poland were attacking Germany, or at least planning an attack or suppressing "German minorities." Every German was convinced that England was waging an imperialistic war against us. What else could we believe? The German radio and newspapers screamed nothing but lies, and if you listened to BBC, you were arrested by the Gestapo.

The *Gruppe* took a lot of credit for the 1956 draft registration muddle. They explained, however, that it had never been their intention to persuade eligible German youths not to show up at all. The law required anyone who wanted to apply as an objector to register first with the draft board. But by the time draft registration took its course and was completed, after several months' delay, there remained very few registered objectors.

At the height of the antirearmament demonstrations in 1956, a German opinion poll revealed that 65 per cent of the German population was *opposed* to military service and the establishment of a new army. But by the summer of 1959, the same poll reflected that 53.5 per cent were *in favor* of the *Bundeswehr* and only a minority categorically opposed. It appears that a defense ministry spokesman was accurate in 1956 when he said, at the crest of the demonstration wave, "The job is difficult at the moment, but in due time, I am confident, the new army and Germany's remilitarization will become more acceptable to the German public."

Antiatomic campaigns continued, most of them guided and sponsored by the Social Democratic party, but they too fizzled out except in those areas where the SPD has a municipal or state majority. But the antiarmy sentiments, while dormant, were by no means completely dead. There was a tumultous revival in the summer of 1959 when the defense ministry decided to register for possible draft or recall as reservists all German men born in the year 1922, that is, World War II veterans who were then thirty-seven years old.

In early 1959 the defense ministry announced that it *"might be necessary"* to register all these men to determine their potential value to the *Bundeswehr*. The ministry explained that there existed a critical shortage of experienced personnel in certain fields and the only way to fill the gap *might be* by drafting a limited number of veterans. That first announcement raised protests, but nothing compared to the storm that was raised later in the year when registration actually began.

Germany's thirty-seven-year-olds were men with bitter memories of the war. They are the veterans of the most devastating battles. They are old enough to be reasonably settled in the postwar world and pursuing a career, raising a family, and looking forward to final success in life. The demonstrations against the registration of this group were virtually spontaneous. German rearmament to these men was no longer something to debate over a card game or a mug of beer at the corner tavern. For this time their own necks, their own careers, their own futures were at stake. Reestablishment of a German army was no longer a matter which concerned teen-agers or those few volunteers who had decided to reenlist. For the more than three hundred thousand Germans born in 1922 the government's registration program was a personal matter. And they didn't like it.

From the time of the ministry's first proclamative hint until mid-August when a formal announcement set up the program, there were general grumblings of discontent. On the first registration day, however, there was an eruption of opposition.

The initial center of resistance was in Constance where, on Monday morning, August 17, 1959, nearly a hundred of the city's eligible thirty-seven-year-olds marched on the town hall. They crowded into the room where the registration was to take place and handed the officials in charge a resolution which had been drafted over the weekend.

"We object to military service," it read. "We refuse to give any information about our former military duties." [1]

The officials tried to disperse the crowd, telling them, "We live in a democracy, not an anarchy."

"We aren't anarchists," the veterans replied. "We are former German soldiers who, after the last war, were defamed and degraded by our current allies. We are former German soldiers who were forced, both in American as well as Russian prisoner-of-war camps to sign declarations that we would never take up arms again."

Finally, toward noon, there was an armistice. They would be registered individually, but would not be required to give any information about their former military activities. "We don't want to break any laws with this demonstration," a spokesman for the group declared, "but only wish to emphasize that our generation, our age group, which was hit hardest by war, does not want to serve in the military, regardless what government demands it."

In Aschaffenburg a protest meeting held on the eve of the registration had the result that more than 40 per cent of the veterans in town signed a resolution calling for conscientious objection to service.

"I have drawn the consequences of the past. Never again will I point a weapon at someone who hasn't harmed me," said one of the leaders of the meeting.

He stressed the point that thousands of German soldiers who had served in Russian and American POW camps had been forced to sign promises that they would never take up arms again. Since Germany still has no peace treaty, he said, "every former POW—and the Russians and Americans registered them by name—could be shot for guerrilla warfare were he to serve in the *Bundeswehr*."

[1] One of the purposes of the registration because all military records had been destroyed after the war.

"We murdered and destroyed once," said another veteran. "We don't want to be guilty of that again. I'll never shoot at a human being again just because he speaks a different language, has a different color skin or is obsessed by a different ideology.

"We aren't Communists," he continued. "We're merely conscientious objectors. That's the least we can do for our dead buddies from the last war. Those who want to serve as volunteers, well, let them, but not us."

Once more, the protest and demonstration spirit caught on throughout Germany. "Action Committees 1922" were created, generally under the protection or sponsorship of already organized conscientious objectors. Newspapers published the consequences for not registering: 1,000 DM fines and arrest. The defense ministry made repeated announcements that registration did not *necessarily* mean draft. Despite the warnings and the assurances, the demonstration fever spread. In many communities no one at all appeared. One of these was Bensberg in North Rhine Westphalia, constituency of Housing Minister Paul Luecke. Of the town's 190 eligible thirty-seven-year-olds all 190 refused to register and demanded instead, that Luecke come to the community and explain the government's policies. Finally, attention again focused on Constance, where a double amputee sent his artificial legs by parcel post to the draft board with this note: "Here's all that's left of the generation of 1922."

In Rosenheim, Bavaria, the thirty-seven-year-olds staged a parade with a huge placard quoting one of Chancellor Adenauer's once famous election speeches in which he had said: "I'm proud of the fact that I never was a soldier."

While Defense Minister Franz-Josef Strauss continued to reel off assurances and explanations that only a few men would be drafted, the campaign gained momentum. Newspapers were flooded with letters from veterans such as these:

"The generation of 1922 was decimated in the last war as no other," wrote a man from Buedingen in Hesse. "Hardly a man in this age group escaped the war and combat. While Adenauer was raising roses and Heinrich von Brentano [2] sat out the war, the genera-

2 Foreign Minister.

tion of 1922 bled to death on the battlefields of Stalingrad, El Alamein, and Normandy. We'll never forget. Too many of us are alive today to serve as limping warnings.

"Anyone who was a soldier in the last war and wants to be one again today apparently slept through the battles and never experienced what war really meant," said an Augsburg veteran.

"Six years of my life were stolen from me by the war. That is enough for me. I won't let anyone steal another week," an Augsburg metalworker wrote.

"Defense Minister Strauss can take my place," said another vet. "And while he's learning how to take apart a gun he can give some thought to the election speech he made in 1947 when he expressed the opinion that 'anyone who takes up a gun in his hand again ought to lose his arm.'"

". . . And where are the Americans who 'promised' us in 1945 that none of us would ever soldier again?" asked still another Augsburg man.

"For three years I 'worked' on a machine gun, and you can bet your life I didn't shoot into the air. But they can cut my fingers off before I'll ever squeeze a trigger again. That's the decision I made after I was wounded eight times and taken prisoner," a vet from Munich proclaimed.

"My suggestion," one man said, "is that Defense Minister Strauss call up the generation of 1895 instead of 1922. They have lived through two wars and would have double the experience needed."

That which makes the "1922 Action" so unusual is the attitude reflected in all the protest activities and demonstrations: self-accusation and acknowledgment of personal and national guilt during the Third Reich.

Why was the *Bundeswehr* so insistent on the registration program when it was obviously so unpopular and posed a potential political danger for Adenauer and Strauss? The answer lies in the new army's development during the first four years and its desperate need for qualified and experienced personnel. The *Bundeswehr* simply cannot meet its commitments unless it gets a substantial boost in trained, mature officers and noncoms. As Strauss predicted, only a small percentage of the veterans will actually be drafted. They are tech-

nical specialists and combat-seasoned cadre men who will help fill
the gaps in the present personnel structure.

What sort of army faces the veterans when they do go back into
service? It is certainly a different type of military institution from
the one they served in the Third Reich. Attitudes and training
methods have changed radically. On the other hand, it is not the
army which Germans and the Western Allies had been promised
when rearmament was started. For, as active German resistance to
remilitarization has worn off, the character of the *Bundeswehr* itself
has changed. Unfortunately it is drifting away from many of the
democratic principles which it once championed.

When the proposal of a German armed force within the framework of a European Defense Community was first discussed, German
officials were reluctant. However, they assured the world, and their
own people, that any new army would be a "democratic one," based
upon Western military doctrines. None of the old Prussian military
spirit would be permitted. Only the beneficial attributes of German
soldiering would be incorporated.

The EDC never materialized. But plans progressed for German
sovereignty and a German army which would become part of the
North Atlantic Treaty Organization. The assurances still stood. Liberal leaders in Western Germany listened to the proposals skeptically.
They warned that if a new army evolved, no matter how attractive
the theories, how progressive the plans, it would eventually take on
its old appearance, driven along primarily by the momentum of
indefatigable and indestructible Prussianism.

To make sure this did not happen, a respected, Utopian-minded
military expert, Count Wolf von Baudissin, was made head of a
special "internal guidance division" in the "defense office."

When the Federal Republic joined NATO in 1955, the "defense
office," headed by Theodor Blank,[3] became the defense ministry.
Baudissin was commissioned as a colonel. His department's mission
was to direct the development of the new army along democratic
lines. It was not an easy task. To meet its NATO commitments as
fast as possible, the *Bundeswehr* was forced to rely immeasurably on
experienced, old-time professional soldiers. Although these men had

[3] Now Minister of Labor.

been selected on the basis of their political neutrality or opposition to the Hitler régime, they had all come up through the ranks of a traditional German militarism, quite different from that which Baudissin and his associates hoped to build. From the start there were two rival factions in the ministry, each battling for dominance.

Baudissin's concepts were wrapped up in a slogan which he envisioned would characterize the new mission and ideals of the *Bundeswehr:* "Citizens in Uniform." [4]

Whether consciously or unconsciously [he said,] military training in Germany has hitherto been patterned on the ideas of Frederick the Great. In this Prussian ruler's day, the individual soldier had to function like a machine if the troops were to be effective in battle, so that the most important aspect of military training was to drill them with an iron hand.

Today a soldier in battle often has to depend on himself. It is not only superfluous but even harmful to drill such individual combatants. On the contrary, it is necessary to develop their imagination and their initiative. Naturally, the handling of weapons must be second nature to them so that, even today, a certain amount of drill is necessary and has a point.

Neither the crews of airplanes nor tanks nor radio teams nor the operators of atomic guns are troops in the old sense of the term. Such men are highly trained specialists, each, in his place, an expert. They cannot be taught to cooperate by drilling procedures such as were Frederick the Great's grenadiers. They have to work hand-in-hand through reason, circumspection, and mental penetration.

The discipline of the modern fighting man must be self-discipline if he is to hold out on modern battlefields.

It cannot but follow that the relationship between the soldier and his superior must also be different from what it used to be. In Germany this relationship was for a long time determined by feudal principles, since even up to the nineteenth century most officers came from the aristocracy and, as the middle classes were generally excluded from military service, the mass of soldiers came from the lower classes of society. Military command obedience was often infused with an undertone of social tension.

After the downfall of the German Empire in 1918, the army found itself in what might be called a vacuum, since it was to the Kaiser that,

[4] From *The Bulletin,* Press and Information Office of the German Federal Government.

previously, each soldier had given his oath of allegiance individually. Many officers did not easily adjust themselves to recognizing as their master something as abstract as a democratic state or to serving this state with the same loyalty as they had felt for a monarch. For this reason, the army never succeeded in becoming an integral part of the Weimar Republic—a fact that hastened the deterioration of that republic and aided Hitler's rise to power.

Those were the principles upon which Baudissin based his plans for the new army. Uniforms, training methods, disciplinary measures, welfare, promotions, mess halls, recreation, housing, medical care, guard duty, ceremonies, the infusion of traditions, saluting—everything that could have a possible effect on the democratic development came under Baudissin's scrutiny.

Whereas in Kaiser and Hitler days the drill sergeant's responsibility was to degrade the individual and turn him into an automaton, Baudissin aimed toward the opposite pole: the dignity of the individual. Even kitchen police, still used widely in the United States Army, was abolished in the *Bundeswehr* as too humiliating for Germany's citizens in uniform. The uniform itself, an optical source of military glory, was radically changed from the style in use during the two world wars.

Soon it became apparent that the conservative professionals disagreed with Baudissin's concepts. As early as 1956 alert Germans expressed their public fears for the colonel's future and with it, for the future of his ideas. Defense Minister Blank was accused of reducing Baudissin's position to that of "parliamentary errand boy," because the colonel was popular with legislators but had a waning influence in the ministry.

One of the first to bring the problem to the attention of a large audience was Marcel Schulte, editor-in-chief of the conservative *Frankfurter Neue Presse*,[5] and a frequent commentator on radio. "Count von Baudissin has been deserted by his defense minister and he's fighting with his back to the wall, a sacrifice to the 'old-time-spirit' men," Schulte charged in an evening broadcast in September,

[5] Frankfurt daily with a 1959 circulation of 102,000.

1956. He told his audience, and his readers, that, by observing the rise or fall of Baudissin's influence, they would have a barometer for democratic trends in the *Bundeswehr*.

Schulte made much of the uniform. The appearance of an army's uniform may seem a trivial point, but in postwar Germany it was indicative of events behind the weather-beaten red brick walls of the defense ministry. At that time there were still rumors that the casual-looking *Bundeswehr* suit was due for a few alterations. While officials commented that "changes are being considered" for purposes of "practicality," insiders insisted that the changes reflected the wishes of the "Prussian" element in the new army.

The "modifications" called for a single-breasted, instead of a double-breasted jacket. Military-type flap pockets were planned in place of the slit pockets which, the ministry said, didn't provide soldiers with enough space to stow away their identification papers and personal belongings. Branch-of-service insignia (that is, infantry, armor, artillery, ordnance, and so on), patterned after the American style in the form of brass emblems pinned to the lapels, were to be replaced by the colored collar tabs in use in the *Wehrmacht*.

Colonel Peter Roewer, *Bundeswehr* public information chief, insisted the changes were merely "under consideration," and nowhere near to general adoption throughout the army. "An experimental unit will try out some changes . . . of a purely practical nature," he explained. One of the reasons for changing to a single-breasted blouse, he added, was that the double-breasted style "develops an ugly fold over the belt line when a man is seated."

"Since when do soldiers spend so much time sitting down that you have to change the uniform for that reason?" asked Marcel Schulte. "Bonn is trying to pass off the uniform change as purely routine when in reality it is a matter of *esprit de corps* and spit and polish.

". . . They promised us a uniform that would reflect the 'modern defender of a democratic Germany.' Now we're being told the uniform lacks 'snap.' When the East German People's Police was transformed into an army, our defense ministry prided itself on the fact that while the East Germans had kept to the old *Wehrmacht* uniform, we were 'democratic' and progressive and had changed to a new style. But now we too are trying out a new uniform, closer in appearance to the one we had (during World Wars I and II)."

Schulte's prophecies, unfortunately, turned out right. It was not long before the changes "under consideration" became sober reality. The jacket was changed, the pockets were altered, the emblems were replaced, and even the cap was reworked, giving it a shorter bill and a higher crown, similar to the type the *Wehrmacht* had worn.

After the public had digested that much, the old-style *Wehrmacht* boot was adopted. Defense ministry officials wasted no time in rationalizing publicly that the lace-up combat boot, modeled after the American style and used in numerous armies throughout the world, was too impractical in the case of alerts. German soldiers, a ministry official explained, wouldn't have sufficient time to lace up the boot. It would be simpler to have a boot (like that during Hitler days) which a soldier could slip into. Strong criticism from the German press and reminders that millions of soldiers in dozens of armies around the world had to wear laced boots fell on deaf ears in Bonn. The ministry emphasized that the slip-in boot "is not like the one in World War II." True, it had no hobnails—the exact number of which was a major inspection point in the *Wehrmacht*. But within two years its rubber soles had already been embellished with a metal cap that added snap to the sound of marching feet.

When, in addition to these changes, German soldiers were also permitted to wear the medals and decorations they had won during the two world wars,[6] the picture of the *Bundeswehr* soldier was quite different from what most Germans had hoped to see.

What about Count von Baudissin? What happened to him?

After Franz-Josef Strauss took over the ministry from Theodor Blank, Baudissin's position deteriorated rapidly and his influence became negligible. In early 1958 he held a press conference at which he announced that he would go into the "field" as a battle group commander in the *Bundeswehr*'s Second Grenadier Division. Baudissin told newsmen it would be a brief assignment, designed primarily to let him meet the men in the field for whom he had been writing directives and regulations. Then, he promised, he would return to Bonn.

[6] Swastikas have to be removed from all decorations worn publicly. Medal manufacturers have replaced the Hitler emblem with an oak leaf cluster.

Baudissin didn't elaborate on how brief the period would be. But by February, 1960, although promoted to brigadier general in the meantime, he was still in the field. On February 25, Strauss dampened all hopes for a Baudissin comeback by announcing that there were five candidates to replace the colonel's successor,[7] but that Baudissin was not one of them. Furthermore, Strauss also ruled out the count's two former subordinates as candidates for chief of the "internal guidance division." But within less than two months, the defense minister was forced to retreat on that point and named Colonel Werner Drews to head the department.[8] The reason for his sudden about-face was a critical report on the *Bundeswehr* by the special parliamentary commissioner for rearmament matters. Although in February, Strauss had still maintained adamantly that there was no need for Baudissin protégés, he gave no explanation for his changed attitude in April.

Although the *Bundeswehr* publicly still subscribes to the Baudissin concepts of "citizen in uniform," internally it is all too apparent that many Baudissin ideas have gone out of style. Nevertheless, they have left their mark. While Baudissin's opponents doubtless have been successful in lassoing the colonel's projects and branding them with their own interpretations, they have not as yet butchered them entirely.

When Germany's first draftees reported for duty in April, 1957,[9] the Baudissin philosophy showed through clearly and the training methods were very commendable. Three years later,[10] the *Bundeswehr*'s attitude toward "citizen soldiers" was less admirable. But, one cannot deny that, even then, the training methods, enforcement of discipline, and relations between officers and enlisted men were far more liberal and progressive than in the United States Army.

The 1957 recruits were trained in the best traditions of commando

[7] Baudissin's successor was promoted to brigadier general and took a field command January 1, 1960.

[8] See page 86.

[9] The author visited a basic training camp in the north Hessian town of Giessen a few days after the first postwar recruits had reported in. He went there with many misgivings but was more than favorably surprised.

[10] He returned to Giessen in July, 1960, visiting a new group of draftees and found the drill tone, the atmosphere, and the attitude more Prussian.

warfare. Virtually no drill was applied, and what little there was would have caused a Prussian drillmaster to twist uncomfortably in his grave. Training schedules called for no more than two hours of close-order drill a week. Instead, on their first day of training, the new recruits were tossed a rifle, told to tear it apart and put it together again. Draftees were given the basics of squad tactics during their first few days in camp—something the United States Army doesn't teach until the last few weeks of basic training.

"Our mission is to train an effective fighting force, capable of thinking for itself where each man can depend on the others. We aren't trying to establish a caste system of robots," said one company commander.

Some of the other policies would have made any American soldier's mouth water. For instance, there is no kitchen police, and even the rawest recruits are allowed out on pass every night, something an American basic trainee would give a month's pay for.

The company commander is also an adviser for his troops, and the captain explained that "any German soldier can come to see his commanding officer any time he feels like it. He doesn't have to ask the first sergeant for permission. I don't have any conference hours. I'm available any time."

Considerable emphasis was placed on the role of the citizen soldier in a democracy.

But how does the *Bundeswehr* look today? Although officers still give lip service to them, many of the Baudissin guidelines are becoming faint and dim with the passage of time. Formal drill has increased. While in the beginning soldiers were told they did not have to salute either officers or noncoms except their company superiors, today they are "advised" to salute everyone, and they do. The tone and attitude of officers and sergeants has changed, becoming increasingly severe and snappy over the years. The first sergeant, once dreaded in the *Wehrmacht*, has gained a much stronger position in the company structure than he had a few years ago. Everything has become more "military," snappier, one could say, more Prussian, particularily the marching.

Yet, the *Bundeswehr* is a far cry from the *Wehrmacht* insofar as formality, obedience, and discipline are concerned. Although German soldiers click their heels when they come to attention today and did not do so in 1955, 1956, or 1957, they click them much more democratically than in 1939.

One young recruit starting his year of service in Giessen in 1957 summed it up accurately.

"We'll make out all right this year. They'll stick to that slogan about citizens in uniform," he said. "But later, they'll fall back into the same rut they were in twenty years ago. That's the reason I volunteered for the draft. I'll take this year's duty to any in years to come."

He was right in many ways.

But, the army has had its share of troubles, too. Building an armed force out of a vacuum is not easy. Yet, that is what the Germans had to do. They were besieged with innumerable problems.

In addition to the general public attitude toward rearmament, there were a number of major incidents which rocked the already shaky confidence in the *Bundeswehr*. A purchasing scandal involved high *Bundeswehr* employees and officers at a procurement center in Coblenz. Defense Minister Strauss came under fire for the way he handled contracts with tank, airplane, and munitions suppliers, and some of his choices were severely criticized. During the wave of anti-Semitic outbursts following the desecration of the Cologne synagogue on Christmas Eve, 1959, a number of swastika smearers were found in the ranks of the *Bundeswehr*. The German negotiations with Spain in February, 1960, severely damaged domestic as well as foreign trust not only in the *Bundeswehr* but German foreign policy as a whole.

The *Bundeswehr* has also had its share of spies, troublemakers, and imposters, which results in a skeptical attitude toward the personnel make-up of the new armed force. From 1956 until mid-1960, the *Bundeswehr* registered 172 officers and men who defected to the East zone. In July, 1960, there were fourteen desertions, among them two officers with critical staff positions. One of the most shocking revelations was that an imposter by the name of Robert Schneider had become chief of the psychological screening program and psychological advisor to the *Bundeswehr* on personnel matters. Schneider, it turned out, had forged his own documents, "promoting" himself to psychologist. Since he had a hand in interviewing numerous officers and noncommissioned officers and had laid down the principles for the psychological qualifications which applicants would have to meet, it turned out that, for all practical purposes, eighty thousand officers and noncoms had been screened by a quack.

Moreover, there was considerable external pressure to accelerate the *Bundeswehr's* establishment. The Germans were taken to task by the West for not meeting their original commitments. In fact, when the new force is at full strength, it will number approximately 40 per cent less than the originally planned five hundred thousand men.

Recruitment of qualified cadre personnel has been one of the major problems. General public antipathy toward the entire rearmament program resulted in excruciatingly close control of manpower administration. The ministry as well as a parliamentary subcommittee scrutinized the background of all applicants with the object of excluding as many militarists and ex-Nazis as possible. As a result, many technically qualified applicants had to be rejected for political reasons. On the other hand, many veterans who satisfied both political and technical requirements rejected the idea of reentering military service. The experience of World War II and the humiliation they had suffered during the occupation when militarism was vilified, were memories too strong to overcome. For many others purely economic reasons prevented them from reenlisting. They had become prosperous in Germany's postwar economic miracle and the potential benefits of military life could never compare with the lucrative civilian advantages.

The consequence: to a considerable extent the defense ministry has been forced to rely on inexperienced and sometimes inferior personnel to fill the ranks.

At no time was this more apparent than when two tragic accidents struck the fledgling force. One of these occurred during a training exercise when fifteen recruits who couldn't swim were drowned because their platoon leader had urged them to wade through a flooded river. A subsequent court hearing put the essential blame on inexperienced leadership.

A few weeks later one German GI was killed and another seriously injured because a corporal had accidentally set off a dud tank grenade by slamming it against the side of an armored vehicle. The corporal, it was revealed later, had been warned to throw the grenade into an ammo dump. He had kept it, however, and was demonstrating how it would have to strike the armor plating of a tank to explode.

The problem is obvious to the Germans whenever they open one of their newspapers. There they will find, on a regular schedule, advertisements for new recruits, noncoms and officers. To the Germans, the concept of advertising for soldiers in the "help wanted" columns is a strange phenomenon indeed.

Just how desperate the personnel problem is, became evident in 1959 when the German navy got down to grass roots levels in its recruiting program. A trailer with marine displays was sent around the country to convince young men they should seek a life at sea.

Despite the close political screening of officers and noncom candidates—a parliamentary subcommittee examined the backgrounds of six hundred colonels and general officers, rejecting 10 per cent—it has, nevertheless, been possible for militarists and even ex-Nazis to gain a foothold in the *Bundeswehr*. Former members of the Army SS through the grade of lieutenant colonel have been accepted since 1956. Government officials admitted in November, 1959, that four to five hundred former SS Elite Guard members were in service, but emphasized that "the great majority" of these men were in the lower ranks.

Yet, and this must be reiterated, the *Bundeswehr*, despite deviation from original plans, is still, for all practical considerations, a much more "progressive" army than those of Germany's past.

Although Baudissin is no longer in Bonn and three years passed before one of his protégés finally took up the reins again, his concept of "citizens in uniform" has caught on with the German recruits, in particular the draftees. Thus Germans chuckled recently about the story of a basic trainee who had listened to a one-hour lecture by his company commander on the ground rules of military courtesy and etiquette.[11]

One of the captain's last remarks, before the lecture ended was: "A good soldier will never be seen with his hands in his pockets." One recruit raised his hand and asked to speak. "Captain," he said, "you emphasized to us that we should never be caught with our

[11] As reported in *Der Spiegel* Issue No. 10, 1960, Germany's leading news magazine.

hands in our pockets. Yet, during the talk—and I timed you with my watch—you kept your hands in your pockets for fourteen minutes." The captain replied with a grin, "That's a point for you." Such an interlude would have been impossible in the Kaiser or Hitler armies.

Naturally, not all officers would have reacted that way, and by far not all agree with such an approach. A veteran captain in Giessen lamented that "the first thing we're told to teach new recruits is what their rights are. Most of them know their rights already. What they never seem to learn is what their duties and obligations as soldiers are."

The captain and those who agree with him were shocked recently when a district court in Landsberg, Bavaria, upheld a German airman's right to complain to the newspapers about poor food in the mess hall. Private First Class Walter Krausser had gone on trial accused of threatening his commanding officer. A municipal court first found him guilty but an appeal, filed with the district court, reversed the ruling and upheld Krausser's position.

The soldier had complained about the food to his commander in a letter dated January 13, 1959.

"The food served in the enlisted men's mess has been so bad recently that I started wondering whether the 2.50 DM deducted from my daily pay is being spent properly," the letter read in part. "I would like to point out that I lost thirteen pounds in the past three weeks despite that fact that I spent 1 DM extra a day for additional food. If the food situation doesn't improve, within the near future, I will find myself forced to invite a representative of the press to a meal in our mess hall."

The commander saw a threat in this and filed charges against the airman with the local district attorney.[12]

"My intended invitation to a press representative was no threat to the commander or the military as alleged by the prosecution," Krausser retorted in testimony in his own behalf. "I had no intention whatsoever to present the press with a biased story. On the contrary, my invitation was intended to give the reporter a chance to get an objective impression of the food situation at Landsberg air base."

[12] There are no courts-martial in the *Bundeswehr* and violations of both civil and military law are tried in civilian courts.

Krausser's superior, a captain, told the court that the defendant was an average soldier, "but too critical and always eager to complain about alleged grievances."

The young airman's defense attorney argued that the "*Bundeswehr* is subject to public control and the public's representatives are the press media. Therefore, there can be no offense involved if Krausser appeals to the public which is authorized to control the armed forces."

In its verdict, the district court ruled that there had been no threat. "To notify someone of a possible press publication is no threat. If a soldier appeals to the public with the aim of gaining food in suitable quantity and quality, he is certainly within his constitutional rights," the court decreed.

One of the most important safeguards German soldiers have for their rights is a special parliamentary commissioner for military matters. Appointed by the *Bundestag*, his responsibility is to serve as liaison between the parliament and the defense ministry, receive complaints from members of the armed forces and investigate them, and keep the *Bundestag* informed on technical and political developments within the armed forces. The position is described in the German constitution as "the means of protecting the basic rights . . . and as an aid to the *Bundestag* in exercise of its legal control over the armed forces."

At present the post is filled by Helmut von Grolman, a former lieutenant general in the *Wehrmacht*. He took office in mid-April, 1959.

One of his principal missions is to listen to and act on complaints of German soldiers and to be on the watch for injustices and malpractices. During the first year in office, Grolman registered more than three thousand complaints from enlisted men. All of them were filed directly with his staff or with him personally in Bonn. None of them had come through the normal military channels.

His agency, located in an unobtrusive villa on a tree-lined street in Bonn, is open every day of the week, including Saturdays, to any German soldier, airman, sailor or member of his family. All German servicemen have to do to bend Grolman's ear is to write or go to the villa, ring the bell, and there will be a sympathetic listener.

Some of the cases recorded are unique, as for instance the complaint of one soldier that his company commander had reprimanded him for wearing civilian clothes in public places. Grolman saw to it that the captain was reprimanded in turn. Many complaints have involved mass punishment which has been specifically outlawed. The majority of grievances, however, are of a different nature, concerning inadequate support for dependents or hardships. Only 10 per cent involve transgressions by superiors.

In the first year, Grolman reported, there were only two instances where superiors attempted to revenge themselves on soldiers who had come to him and complained. In both cases the officers were tried and convicted, for the law which established Grolman's bureau expressly prohibits retributive action on men who go to him with their troubles.

It is also Grolman's responsibility to enforce the democratic principles which the *Bundestag* wants maintained in the *Bundeswehr*. He is, in a sense, the parliamentary arm for the enforcement of Baudissin's ideas, and in more than one way, the two men are very much alike in their beliefs.

"When I used to hear officers or sergeants shout and harass men," Grolman said in speaking to newsmen of the days when he was a general, "I always assumed they were incompetent and I treated them accordingly."

It took this parliamentary watchdog over the *Bundeswehr* a scant year to catapult himself into the center of a big controversy. His means of doing so were his first annual report.

In it Grolman charged that the *Bundeswehr* had been established too quickly, resulting in serious internal problems. He emphasized that the principle of "citizen in uniform" was not yet firmly entrenched and that many officers and noncoms still lacked trust in the democratic form of administration. The rapid build-up, Grolman said, not only had an effect on the "internal guidance and structure" aspirations, but also resulted in a lack of experienced officers, particularily company commanders. Grolman made a point of the small number of young officers and sergeants, limited training areas, overwork of officers and troop unit leaders, administrative problems, and too many changes in unit structures.

As soon as his report was published, Grolman was criticized by conservative elements in the parliament and cabinet for overstepping the boundaries of his responsibilities. Defense Minister Strauss suggested that in the future Grolman clear his reports with the ministry before making them public and giving them to the *Bundestag*. Yet, what he had to say must have hit close to home, for within days after the report was public, Strauss reversed his position on naming a new chief for the internal guidance division and appointed Colonel Drews, the Baudissin protégé.

Grolman, despite attacks from the Old Guard, is standing pat. He has admitted that certain "Prussianistic" officers and noncoms have been pulled back into service as a result of the shortage of qualified personnel and the accelerated build-up. He feels, however, that these incompetents are spotted soon enough.

One can only hope that the *Bundeswehr* minority which hopes to reestablish a state within a state will remain as ineffectual in the future as they have been in the past.

Chapter VII

Nazis: Coming or Going?

When Arnold Strunk and Paul Schoenen smeared swastikas and anti-Semitic slogans on Cologne's synagogue and a memorial to victims of Nazi persecution on Christmas Eve, 1959, they not only set off a chain reaction of similar incidents throughout Germany and most of the civilized world, but also focused long overdue official attention on the problem of a neo-Nazi movement in Western Germany.

Strunk and Schoenen were both members of the extreme right-wing German Reich party (DRP) and admitted, with considerable audacity, that they had been influenced extensively by the teachings of the "Movement of the House of Ludendorff," a wildly anti-Semitic organization. German authorities were already discussing possible steps to outlaw the German Reich party when, a few days after Christmas, a bizarre neo-Nazi rally, involving members of two extreme nationalist student and youth groups, took place in a Berlin park. As the wave of anti-Semitic incidents spread over Germany and eventually around the world, observers in and outside the Federal Republic theorized about the possibility of a neo-Nazi underground. And little wonder. For one month after Strunk and Schoenen

had fired the fuse, Germany alone had registered nearly 700 smearings or related acts.

Although plans to outlaw the German Reich party nationally
never materialized, one German state successfully put the party out
of commission for at least a while. In the meantime, the federal interior ministry prepared a study of the anti-Semitic and neo-Nazi
incidents. Published in the form of a white paper, it indicated there
was no discernible political relationship among all the church, synagogue, cemetery, and sidewalk smearings.

Be that as it may. The impression that has been left on both Germany's allies and its enemies, however, is that a Nazi movement of
considerable scope and influence is active and at least partially responsible for the tidal wave of anti-Semitic outbursts since Christmas,
1959. Of course, this is no new presumption. It has variously been
charged outright, implied guardedly, or alleged unofficially by "reliable sources" in the European and American press that there is such
a movement in Germany. Nor is it a completely new concept in
the Federal Republic where certain limited segments of the community, particularly the labor unions,[1] liberal political organizations,
and associations of victims of Third Reich persecution have warned
repeatedly that ex- and neo-Nazis are agitating actively behind thin
veils of democratic patriotism. But these warnings reach only a
small audience, and puzzling as it may seem, Bonn has remained
impassive to them.

There are, of course, no overt neo-Nazi organizations, simply
because they are illegal. Instead, there are many political parties,
pseudo parties, associations, leagues, federations, cultural societies,
study groups, and movements which, if they don't have the label,
drift ominously close to the principles. Few German observers would
go so far as to call them neo-Nazi or neo-Fascist. Instead they have
been described safely as "right radical," "militaristic," and "nationalistic." In fact, the various parties and associations, though competi-

[1] In particular the *Deutscher Gewerksachftsbund* (DGB—German Federation
of Trade Unions, closest equivalent to the AFL-CIO) which has sponsored a
regular newsletter entitled *Feinde der Demokratie* (*Enemies of Democracy*).
Published on a ten-times-a-year basis, it has for nearly nine years served as a
sharp-eyed watchdog over the activities of ex- and neo-Nazis as well as left-wing
radicals who endanger democracy in Western Germany.

tive and far from unified, refer to themselves as members of the "Nationalist Opposition." Mysterious, almost imperceptible ties bind and interlace these various organizations. However, their objectives are too divergent to enable them to establish any kind of united front. Although the number of groups has increased, their electoral results have diminished, leaving one to ask: Are the Nazis coming or going?

Whatever the answer, it is possible to categorize the variety of associations into five major classifications.

First there are the youth groups which, according to reliable estimates, encompass forty thousand members. Of these there are two subdivisions: nationalistic and militaristic.

Second are political parties and movements, including the German Reich party with sixteen thousand members, and such organizations as Mathilde Ludendorff's which are propagandistically active but do not participate directly in local, state, or federal elections.

Third are the leagues and federations of "victims of de-Nazification" and other "injustices of Allied occupation" which concentrate on lobbying for pensions and financial benefits while, at the same time, providing neo-Nazis with a sounding board for anti-Allied propaganda.

The professional military and "veterans" organizations, such as the *Stahlhelm,* the Navy League, and Federation of German Paratroopers form the *fourth* important category. They are active in influencing the *Bundeswehr* and German attitudes toward remilitarization.

Fifth are the organizations of refugees, expellees, and so-called ethnic Germans, representing nearly 15 per cent of the entire West German population.

All of them publish magazines and newspapers with varied circulation success. All of them present a tremendous potential danger to Germany's fledgling democracy. Their astonishing numerical strength is due primarily to the lack of publicity they have received outside their own sphere of interest and to the mystifying ostrichlike attitude of the federal government.

Not until the summer of 1959 was there any detailed, cohesive publication effort toward exposing these elements directed at a mass audience. In July of that year, the *Frankfurter Rundschau* [2] published the first in a series of articles about the neo-Nazi threat in Germany, baring the organizational links between neo-Fascist elements in the Federal Republic and allied organizations in other European and Western countries.

The author of the series, Thomas Gnielka, was spurred to action when, in June, 1959, seven of Germany's major right-radical youth groups merged forces to launch what they called the "German National Youth Movement." According to Gnielka's report, the fusion meeting had taken place at Idstein, a small mountain town outside Frankfurt. The leaders of the various groups had appeared in paramilitary uniforms, some of them resembling closely the dress of the Hitler Youth.

Gnielka estimated that there are twenty thousand German youths who belong to nationalistic organizations and that another twenty thousand are members of militaristic groups, most of which are associated with adult military and veterans' leagues such as the *Stahlhelm*. The nationalistic organizations are often linked with neo-Fascist, ultranationalist, or right-radical political movements.

One of the principles to which the leaders of the seven major groups had to subscribe before completion of the merger was this:

The Allied powers of the last world war destroyed the German Reich. They cannot be considered as friendly powers, but rather as forces whose aims are in direct opposition to the interests of the German people.

Among the seven organizations which fused into a national movement at Idstein was the *Nationaljugend Deutschlands* (National Youth of Germany) whose members are uniformed in gray shirts, black breeches, riding boots, Sam Browne belts, hunting knives, and black-white-red shoulder patches.[3] Headquartered in Berlin, this is one of the two neo-Fascist youth groups involved in the crackdown

[2] Independent Frankfurt daily with a circulation of 114,000. The series was later compiled and published in booklet form under the title of *Falschspiel mit der Vergangenheit*. Thomas Gnielka is the *Rundschau*'s correspondent in Wiesbaden, state capital of the state of Hesse.

[3] Black-white-red are the colors of Imperial as well as Hitler Germany, commonly used among all nationalistic and right-radical political groups.

on right-radical and Nazistic organizations in the four-power city following the January 3, 1960, rally.[4]

Bedside reading for members is Hitler's *Mein Kampf*. Some of the boys belong to a special "battle group," sometimes dubbed "security service" which is used for provocative gang fights with members of democratic youth clubs. During a search of *Nationaljugend* leader Peter Bernau's apartment, police found daggers, swastika flags and other Nazi emblems, and a stack of National Socialist literature. Members of the organization included students, high-school and junior-high-school pupils, apprentices, and young clerks.

One of Bernau's objectives had been to merge all right-radical youth groups in Berlin into one large federation or movement. Between the time he participated in the national fusion meeting in Idstein in June, 1959, and his arrest in January, 1960, Bernau's success toward that end was reflected partially in the emblems which he had added to his uniforms. During the six-month period he had apparently established "cordial" relations with several other organizations and had adopted some of their insignia.

Also represented at Idstein was the *Deutsch-Sozialistischer Jung-sturm* (German Socialist Youth Storm) which dresses its members in black shirts like those of the Italian Fascists. The organization is based in the Saarland. Its leader, a one-time Nazi functionary and former official of Otto Strasser's right-wing postwar party, is Werner Diehl.

The *Deutschwandervogel*, which in translation means something akin to "German Hiking Birds," is headed by a jungle-helmet-wearing night watchman named Alfred Zitzmann, alias Viking. Zitzmann was an SS man during the Third Reich. Among other activities, his organization celebrates heathen Germanic ceremonies. The uniform his followers wear is strangely reminiscent of that of the Hitler Youth.

The *Schillerjugend*, ruled by Hans Siebrenz, is pledged to upholding the "great cultural heritage of our fatherland."

---

[4] The youths were caught in Berlin's Glienecke Park at midnight, January 2 to 3, 1960, singing Nazi songs and waving swastika flags in a Teutonic solstice ceremony. Among those arrested were *Nationaljugend* leader Peter Bernau and members of the *Bund Nationaler Studenten* (League of National Students).

The *Jungdeutsche Freischar*, piloted by former Hitler Youth leader and SS man Guenter Hessler, is dedicated to the belief that "our greatest honor is loyalty to the fatherland, which extends, not from the Rhine to the Elbe, but stretches from the river Meuse [in France] to the Memel [in Lithuania]."

The *Wikingjugend* (Viking Youths) are under the leadership of Raoul Nahrath, former functionary in the Nazi party and considered to be one of the most dangerous brains behind the youth movement.

The seventh group at Idstein was the *Nationale Jugendgemein-schaft*, directed by Hans Schulz who had sent out the invitations to the merger meeting to the other six. Schulz is a man with a nebulous biography. Not long ago, it has been alleged, he was a member of the East Zone Socialist Unity Party (SED).[5]

In addition to the seven groups which met at Idstein, there are others, many of them small and insignificant, organized on a purely local basis. Several of importance, not represented at the merger meeting, are:

Jugendbund Adler (Eagle Youth League) which is associated with a right-wing political party called *Deutscher Block* (DB—German Bloc).

Junge deutsche Gemeinschaft (Young German Association) connected with the *Deutsche Gemeinschaft* (DG), another right-wing

[5] According to Thomas Gnielka, Schulz came to Western Germany for not fully clarified reasons. He took up with a small local party of right-wing tendencies in the Hessian university town of Marburg. Schulz soon became head of the party's youth organization and editor of the party publication's youth pages. He also established contact with numerous other right-wing organizations.

Shortly after the publication of Gnielka's article, Schulz and several of his friends were investigated for subversive activities.

When portions of Gnielka's report were reprinted in *The Overseas Weekly* an English language newspaper for Americans in Europe, Schulz demanded retractions. He denied the allegation that he had been an SED official, explaining that he had fled the East Zone when thirteen years old and had absolutely no Communist affiliations. He also said he was a foster son of well known Pastor Martin Niemoeller. Asked to prove his claims, Schulz backed down.

In an interview with a reporter from another American newspaper overseas, Schulz was asked how Pastor Niemoeller felt about the "youth activities." Schulz remarked, "He doesn't like them."

Whether Schulz is or was a Communist agitator or not is immaterial. However, there appears to be some substance to the theory that certain rightist groups and neo-Nazi incidents have occasionally been Communist-influenced.

political party, headed by former Adenauer supporter and co-worker August Haussleiter.

Junge Kameradschaft, the youth organization of the German Reich party.

Whereas the nationalistic youth groups have won their greatest support in large cities and industrial centers, a bouquet of militaristic organizations has cropped up, drawing most of its members from the smaller cities and the provinces. The majority of these organizations are sponsored by, or closely affiliated with, similarly named adult "veterans'" groups. The largest and most active are:

Deutsche Jugend im Verband deutscher Soldaten (VdS), (German Youth in the Association of German Soldiers). Its members are the sons of *Wehrmacht* men killed in action and the sons of members of the sponsoring organization, the *Verband deutscher Soldaten* (VdS), a rightist veterans' group.

Deutscher Jugenbund Kyffhäuser (German Kyffhäuser Youth League) trains its members in the handling of firearms, horseback riding, signaling, map making, and distance measuring. It sponsors camps and has a distinct conservative tradition.

Jugendkorps Scharnhorst (Scharnhorst Youth Corps) is closely associated with the adult *Stahlhelm* combat vet organization, providing its uniformed followers for *Stahlhelm* demonstrations and ceremonies.

Marinejugend (Navy Youths) is an organization which emphasizes nautical training. But it is closely associated with the adult *Marine Bund* (Navy League), a veterans' association which identifies itself with the principles and achievements of grand admirals Karl Doenitz (German *Führer* after Hitler's death), and Erich Raeder.

Although it is difficult to find a single common political purpose prevailing among these various organizations, there are some common ideological denominators and historical interpretations which can be detected. Prevalent is the glorification of the Germanic spirit, the belief in Germany's mission and destiny of power. Most of the groups aim toward the "preservation of Germany's cultural heritage." They teach that "traitorous elements" on the home front were at fault for Germany's defeats in two world wars. While only a few approve of Nazism per se, most of them take a conciliatory attitude in their approach to Germany's most recent history.

Paramilitarism and martial training, as well as the wearing of uniforms, is a common activity for both the militaristic as well as the nationalistic groups. In general, their attitude toward democratic efforts during the Weimar Republic and the anti-Nazi resistance movement during the war is a disparaging one. Their desire to avoid open conflict with the laws of the Federal Republic, however, has forced many of them to veil their real policies behind high-sounding, but foggy and mystical ideals and a veneer of democracy.

Although some of the militaristic organizations proclaim publicly that "today's democracy is not the way of life for Germany's future," it appears that they advocate change, particularly in the balance of political power and in the rights and position of the military within the framework of the present laws. They hope to strengthen the army's position, making the military more palatable.

The situation among the nationalistic groups is somewhat more crass. Here there are elements which already speak of a "new order." Thoughts about "X-day" have been smoldering in the minds of many of their leaders, and their present aims are to gain sufficient numerical support to force a change in German politics "when the time is ripe."

Although democratic youth organizations, educators, and youth leaders had been aware of the right-radical groups and had attempted to prevent their growth on a local basis, there was little that could be done without public awareness of the problem. Of course, these organizations did not establish themselves overnight. For years they were numerically too weak to earn any popular attention or arouse widespread public concern. Even in those areas where they had gained sufficient strength to create trouble, they were not taken seriously. Less than a year before Thomas Gnielka's eye-opening exposé, official government sources still reassured the public and themselves that reports of fascistic and militaristic youth activities were unfounded. In April, 1958, when Social Democratic *Bundestag* deputy Moritz Priebe mentioned in parliament that units of a neo-Fascist youth organization had been conducting military maneuvers in his constituency, the federal ministry of interior replied it had no knowledge of such "werewolf youth clubs."

After the publication of Gnielka's article, widely quoted throughout the rest of the country, Germans asked themselves how such organizations could have started and grown. What made young people join these groups? they asked. Gnielka himself provided part of the answer.

"For thirteen years we have refused to take them seriously," he wrote. "For thirteen years we have refused to accept the possibility of something like this happening."

He cited the example of a Bavarian political leader who had been too busy to realize that his own teenage son had become pith-helmet-wearing Alfred Zitzmann's adjutant. The position of "adjutant" meant that the boy had to hold Zitzmann's shaving mirror on camping trips.

Thus far, active agitation on the part of the right radical youth groups has been relatively limited. But one organization has been mentioned frequently in *Putsch*-style incidents. That is the *Bund Nationaler Studenten* (League of National Students), some of whose members were arrested following the midnight Nazi songfest in Berlin.

The *Bund* made international headlines in August, 1959, when members of its Heidelberg University chapter attacked and beat several students distributing copies of an anti-Nazi article on the campus. The author of the piece, Bernhard Schoenung, was hospitalized as a result of the attack.

Schoenung's article originally had been written for the campus newspaper, *Forum Academicum*, and scheduled for publication in May, 1959. Entitled, *Man Trägt Wieder Braunhemd* ("Brown Shirts Are Popular Again") it exposed neo-Fascist student groups at the university such as the *Bund*. The *Bund* won an injunction barring further distribution of the issue of the *Forum* which contained the article. By that time, however, only five hundred of the original six thousand copies remained to be distributed.

The author and some of his friends ran off several thousand additional copies of the article in handbill form and distributed them individually on the campus. They were attacked by members of the *Bund* and severely trounced. Schoenung, a partial cripple, was hospitalized.

Although the fact that forty thousand young Germans belong to rightist and militaristic youth organizations is alarming, in all fairness one must take into consideration that these forty thousand represent only a small fraction of Germany's entire "teen" and "twen" population. In comparison, the Federal Youth Ring, embracing fourteen organizations, and the various state youth rings, has a total membership of nearly 6 million. The ring encompasses the Catholic and Protestant youth activities with a membership of about 1 million each, the Boy Scouts, Junior Red Cross, and numerous other groups, including the Social Democratic Falcons with some hundred and fifty thousand members.

In fact, the nationalistic and militaristic groups represent less than 1 per cent of all Germany's organized young people. Instead, there are thousands of jazz clubs, movie fan clubs, athletic organizations, cowboy clubs, and hundreds of other activities, all of them democratically oriented. The federal government has given considerable financial aid to the youth program, allocating more than $6 million annually for the maintenance of youth hostels, welfare organizations, and support of youth activities.

Another development deserves mention, too. There has been an ascending "juvenile delinquency" curve which some observers greet as a welcome sign. The German interpretation of juvenile delinquency, however, is somewhat different from the American. No wide-spread juvenile crime wave has been recorded, and organized gangs are virtually unheard of. Instead, the Germans are concerned about what they term *halbstarke*, or "half-strong ones," by which they refer to unruly teen-agers who like to rock and roll and "soup up" motor bikes to where they will go faster than the permitted maximum speed. Strange as it may sound to Americans, this "juvenile delinquency" is, in a way, a blessing for postwar Germany because it signifies a breaking away from discipline and tradition.

In some societies, such as our own, this departure from discipline is very undesirable because there is already a noticeable lack of restraint in the behavior of the young people. But in other societies, such as the German, a breaking away from discipline represents a departure from tradition and a revolutionary development in the attitude of young people toward their elders, their teachers, the social establishment, the state, and authority.

History has demonstrated tragically that many of Germany's problems are rooted in a bedrock of discipline and obedience. This has always been considered one of the Germanic "virtues." Discipline and obedience are what the Kaiser demanded and what he got. Discipline was the spirit of the Kaiser's time just as it was of the Third Reich. Without these "qualities" millions of Germans would not have accepted unquestioningly the dictates of Adolf Hitler.

It is this same discipline for which the "warriors" of yesteryear yearn in the Germany of today and tomorrow. Blue-jean wearing, gum chewing, leather-jacketed motorbike riding, rocking and rolling teen-agers are anathema to old-line Germans. To many of the older generation, it all reflects a lack of self-restraint and inability to resist foreign, "un-Germanic" influences on the part of Germany's youth.

Just this lack of blind obedience, however, is what makes most young Germans less susceptible to the cancerous entanglements of dictatorship than their parents were. The forty thousand young people who belong to nationalistic and militaristic youth organizations undoubtedly are being traditionally "disciplined." That is why they follow unprotestingly a code of morally bankrupt ideals. Fortunately, they are not many. And thanks to Thomas Gnielka many unsuspecting Germans have been put on their guard.

Germany's hope for the future lies in the young people who meet in jazz cellars, in the *avant garde* bookshops and galleries, and the coffeehouses, who read postwar authors and participate in Anne Frank memorial celebrations. They belong to the forty thousand Berlin students who rallied and demonstrated *against* Nazism and anti-Semitism just a few days after that other handful sang Nazi songs and waved swastika flags in Glienecke Park.

What about the adults?

Since the end of the war, hundreds of neo-Nazi, neo-Fascist, right radical, and ultranationalist organizations have started up in Western Germany and disbanded again. A number of them had their origins in economic pressure groups which had been organized to lobby for pensions and public assistance for veterans, former civil servants, and one-time Nazi officials. Some such as the rabidly anti-Semitic "Movement of the House of Ludendorff" existed even before Hitler came to power. They were disbanded during the Hitler régime because they were competitive to the Nazi party, then resumed their "work" immediately after the war.

The majority, however, such as the Socialist Reich party (SRP) which was outlawed in 1952 [6] as unconstitutional, or the extreme right-wing German Reich party (DRP), can trace their development to the first military government sponsored local elections in 1946 or to 1950 when Allied political licensing requirements were lifted.[7]

Today the rightist political parties and political organizations number more than three dozen. The list ranges from the increasingly

[6] The SRP, generally considered a reincarnation of the Nazi party, was formed in the fall of 1949 by the ultraradical wing of the *Deutsche Rechtspartei* (German Rightist party) which had polled 8 per cent of the vote in Lower Saxony in August, 1949. Two deputies in the *Bundestag*, elected on the Rightist party ticket, transferred their allegiance to the SRP, but one of them was arrested in February, 1952, after it became known that he was a former Nazi party functionary who had assumed a false name after the war.

In the May, 1951, Lower Saxony state elections, the SRP polled 367,000 votes, that is, 11 per cent of the total. It won fourteen seats in the legislature out of a total of 158. The SRP led in four election districts, came in second in twelve others, its strength being concentrated among the Protestant peasants of the Lueneburg Heath and the Frisian territory, where Nazism had deep roots.

Only after this showing in Lower Saxony was the spotlight of publicity focused on the SRP, although it already competed in the 1950 elections in North Rhine Westphalia and Schleswig-Holstein. In October, 1951, after the Lower Saxony elections, the SRP won 7.7 per cent of the total vote in the cosmopolitan city state of Bremen. In March, 1952, elections to the constituent assembly of the Southwest State, the SRP polled 3.85 per cent.

The federal government announced that it would expect state authorities to initiate steps "necessary to counter excesses of the SRP." The paramilitary units of the party were outlawed, especially its strong arm, *Reichsfront*, and its youth organization, *Reichsjugend*. In November, 1951, the federal government filed a brief with the federal constitutional (supreme) court under provisions of Article 21 of the constitution which outlaws "parties that according to their aims and the behavior of their members seek to impair or abolish the free and democratic order," under which the Communist party was outlawed in 1956. The supreme court banned the SRP in 1952.

[7] In the course of 1947, requirements for obtaining prior approval for political meetings, of reporting on membership changes, and so on, were first modified, then abandoned in the United States zone of occupation. From early 1948 on, it was no longer necessary to notify the military government of public meetings. The responsibility for the licensing and regulation of political parties and associations was transferred to the German state governments in November, 1949. On January 12, 1950, the Allied High Commission decided on a similar transfer of powers to the German authorities in the British and French zones, and on March 17, 1950, a law was enacted to that effect. Although the federal government has passed no specific licensing law, Article 21 of the constitution also states that political parties "can be freely formed. Their internal organization must conform to democratic principles. They must publicly account for the sources of their funds."

powerful German Reich party to the insignificant but vociferous "Battle Group Germania," which celebrates January 30, the day of Hitler's ascension to power; April 20, Hitler's birthday; November 9, the day of the beerhall *Putsch*, as well as other important dates in Nazi history.

No right-wing political movement, however, is as well known abroad as the German Reich party. It can credit most of its notoriety to the desecration of the Cologne synagogue. The two swastika smearers, Strunk and Schoenen, were members of the Cologne county organization of the DRP.

The DRP evolved out of the dissolution of the German Rightist Party in the first *Bundestag*, and made its greatest initial organizational strides in 1952 and 1953 following the banning of the Socialist Reich party. For the federal elections of September, 1953, the DRP presented the following list of candidates:

Hans Grimm, right radical author of the book *Volk ohne Raum* (*People Without Room*).

Ex-Colonel Hans Ulrich Rudel, a famous Nazi *Luftwaffe* ace.

Hans Heinrich Scheffer, former *Wehrmacht* officer, and at that time national DRP chairman.

Ex-General Alexander Andrae, and former *Wehrmacht* tank officer Adolf von Thadden.

Star candidate was Wilhelm Meinberg, honorary SS major general, *Reichstag* deputy, Prussian state counselor, holder of the Golden Nazi party emblem, high-ranking Nazi agricultural official, and "proud of the fact that I was a Nazi."

Scratched from the list of candidates in the last minutes was Dr. Werner Naumann, state secretary in Josef Goebbels' propaganda ministry, who had been released from Allied confinement shortly before the 1953 election.

The party didn't win enough votes, however, to place a single deputy in the *Bundestag*. As a result, in November, 1953, there was a basic reorganization of the party leadership. Meinberg was elected national chairman, Andrae became second in command, and Thadden was named as executive secretary. Other members of the board of directors included Otto Hess, a relative of Hitler's right-hand man. The total membership at that time was estimated to be two thousand.

A half-hearted 1953 attempt to outlaw the DRP as unconstitutional failed when damaging evidence, collected by Lower Saxony state officials, was rejected by the federal ministry of interior as "too insignificant" to support a successful supreme court case.

By 1955, DRP strength had doubled to four thousand dues-paying members, of which half were registered in Lower Saxony, one fourth in neighboring North Rhine Westphalia, and another fourth in all the other German states. The circulation of the DRP's often belligerent publication *Der Reichsruf*, stood at five thousand.

Nevertheless, even in its strongest area—Lower Saxony—the DRP still had not attained the same popularity in state elections as the Socialist Reich party had registered four years previously. In only two election districts did the DRP win a substantial vote accounting for 12 to 14 per cent of the total. Even in those districts the results were below those of the SRP in 1951. In twenty-two other districts the party tabulated between 5 and 12 per cent of the total.

One year later, in city and county elections, the DRP won a total of 210,000 votes in Lower Saxony, the equivalent, however, of only 2.3 per cent of the total. Despite this poor percentage showing, some 258 DRP candidates were elected to municipal, county, and village offices. In some town councils the DRP won pluralities, majorities, and in the case of two small communities, unanimous control. The DRP has continued to grow, until in January, 1960, party officials estimated the membership at more than sixteen thousand. Outside sources judge it even higher. The circulation of *Der Reichsruf* is twenty thousand.[8]

The party demands that foreign troops be kicked out of Germany. It repudiates the "disgusting self-accusation that Germany alone was guilty for two world wars," and promises to create a "new epoch" in history without repeating Hitler's "mistakes."

Meinberg and Thadden are waiting for the death of Adenauer

---

[8] At the head of the party today are Meinberg, Thadden, Otto Hess, and Professor Dr. Heinrich Kunstmann, considered the DRP's chief ideologist. Meinberg, however, relinquished active party leadership at the national convention of the DRP in Hildesheim July 10, 1960, in favor of Kunstmann. Kunstmann joined the Nazi party in 1930 and the SA a short time later. He became an SA regimental doctor. He once was considered a leading candidate for the post of Hitler's personal physician, but eventually was not named for the job. After 1945, it was reported, he hired Grand Admiral Karl Doenitz's wife as a receptionist.

when, they prophesy, the German people will rally behind them. They believe the Germans "must be independent. Treaties with the West must disappear and Germany must be reunified."

"We are a nation of 80 million people in the heart of Europe," Meinberg and Thadden say. "We must fulfill our destiny." [9]

Official party pamphlets and propaganda material denounce the "historic lie" of German war guilt, brand President Franklin D. Roosevelt as a "war criminal," and refer to the "irresponsible game" about the number of Jews killed in concentration camps.

Publicly, the party has as its emblem the Germanic eagle and the black-white-red flag of Hitler and Imperial Germany. But one newsman, interviewing DRP members in a beer cellar, photographed a never-before-publicized emblem which, if turned and twisted in the proper manner, would be a perfect swastika.

The DRP believes also that the "poisoning of the minds of German youth is part of the reeducation which we have experienced since 1945." The party spokesman called Cromwell, Napoleon, Mussolini, Hitler, and Stalin "geniuses" who flare up in history as rarely as bright comets. According to DRP tenets, resistance fighters against Nazism were "traitors," and the figures about gas chambers and concentration camp victims have been cooked up to justify the actions of these "turncoats." Even Berlin Mayor Willy Brandt is termed a "traitor." The Nazi party, on the other hand, is described as an "essential and timely element in the battle for recognition of nation and Reich.

"We are the party of the future," says the DRP. "Bonn belongs to yesterday. . . . We are the National Opposition. . . . We don't believe that the Germans are better than anyone else, but neither do we believe they are worse than everyone else. . . . We believe in Europe, but feel we should not forget our own nation. . . . All great accomplishments of humanity have been of a nationalistic character."

Within two days after Paul Schoenen and Arnold Strunk were arrested for their swastika and slogan smearings in Cologne, public attention was focused on the role the DRP had played in the incident. North Rhine Westphalian Minister of Interior Josef-Hermann Dufhues ordered an immediate investigation of the party and

[9] Meinberg and Thadden in an interview with London *Daily Express* reporter Colin Lawson, January 10, 1960.

Strunk's and Schoenen's associates. Dufhues declared that he had determined the DRP was under the leadership of former Nazis.

How the German Reich party would react to these allegations became clear immediately after Dufhues' statement. Strunk and Schoenen were expelled from the party and the Cologne county organization was dissolved. The *Reichsruf* called the former party comrades "vandals, crackpots, East zone agents, and provocateurs." Meinberg challenged Dufhues to prove his "unqualified attack and slander" of the DRP, emphasizing that Strunk and Schoenen were known to have made "repeated trips" into East Germany.

Cologne police commissioner Theodor Hochstein, however, left little doubt as to where the two young smearers had assimilated their ideas. At a press conference in Cologne, Hochstein displayed photographs taken in Strunk's apartment. They showed his wardrobe painted with the DRP emblem and colors; his bookshelf filled with DRP literature glorifying the Nazi régime, and a portrait of air ace Rudel on one wall.

On December 28 the Federal Government announced that it would move to outlaw the DRP, allowing that sufficient grounds could be found under the provisions of Article 21 of the constitution. The statement by federal Interior Minister Gerhard Schroeder (himself once a Nazi) left open the question of whether enough documentation could be gathered to file a suit of unconstitutionality against the DRP. The major obstacle was that the party had successfully avoided a direct clash with the law, remaining always out of reach.

The actions of Strunk and Schoenen were unanticipated and caught the party, so to speak, with its pants down. Meinberg and Company took immediate steps in ousting the two smearers to make themselves decent again. The major problem was whether this temporary nudity would suffice for legal action.

As government officials mulled over the possibilities of a case against the DRP, the anti-Semitic and Nazistic incidents continued at the rate of some twenty per day. On January 8, attention suddenly shifted from the national scene to the state of Rhineland Palatinate where the DRP planned a state convention in the city of Kaiserslautern for the following weekend. The Rhineland ministry of interior banned all public meetings of the party on the ground that DRP members had been arrested in connection with anti-Semitic outbursts. The state government also cancelled its contract with the party for the use of a state-owned Agricultural Hall.

Meinberg went to court and got a temporary injunction permitting him to hold public rallies. A second court ruling on the hall took until convention day to obtain. In the meantime, the DRP delegates convened in a beerhall.

When the convention finally moved to the Agricultural Hall, DRP state chairman Hans Schikora took the platform and launched a hysterical tirade.

"Allies, get out," shrieked Schikora, the DRP's only deputy in the Rhineland-Palatinate state legislature. "The Allied troops on German soil are unbearable for us. They support those who are governing us and who prevent German unity. We can't bear any foreign troops on German soil. Get out, go away!"

The three hundred delegates applauded wildly.

Meinberg told them the party is going through a phase of "Slander, hatred, and terror" from outside. He exclaimed that he would look forward "with confidence" to any constitutionality trial.

Although state officials had lost the first round to the DRP, they continued to fight. In several turbulent sessions of the state legislature, state premier (governor) Peter Altmeier fired a series of charges against the DRP, in particular Schikora, who, it turned out, had been a member of the outlawed Socialist Reich party. Schikora—and this is typical of developments among rightist groups which have learned to use the law for their own interests—won an injunction against the governor ordering Altmeier to desist from making further remarks about Schikora's background and principles unless he could prove his statements.

That, apparently, was a declaration of war. On January 27, without any constitutionality trial, without any court orders, Rhineland Palatinate authorities outlawed the DRP. They had merely relied on an earlier decision in the case of the Socialist Reich party in which the German supreme court empowered local and state officials to dissolve all "substitute" organizations for the SRP. To document their order, Rhineland Palatinate officials simply proved that Schikora had been a member of the SRP and had moved into a high position in the DRP one day after he had joined it. In the years since, the state officials charged, Schikora had successfully maneuvered former Socialist Reich party members into key positions in the DRP's organization. At no time, the dissolution order explained, were there less than 30 per cent former SRP members in the state organization of the German Reich party.

While federal officials looked on, dumfounded by Altmeier's audacity, other state governments made plans to take similar steps against the DRP. No other bans have been imposed, however. The state supreme court ruled the ban unconstitutional on November 24, 1960, but Rhineland Palatinate officials said they would appeal the decision to the federal supreme court.

Arnold Strunk and Paul Schoenen were not influenced entirely by the German Reich party, though. Investigations revealed that their anti-Jewish sentiments had been formulated too by the "Movement of the House of Ludendorff."

Dr. Mathilde von Ludendorff, widow of the World War I general, has been spewing out her hate-filled theories about "noble races," which include the Germans, and "subraces," among them the Jews, for nearly forty years. Her theories were too radical for even the Nazis.

The Ludendorff movement, spread all over Western Germany, is subdivided into a "Federation for Recognition of God," a "Federation of Free Soldiers," and others. Most of the movement's activities are cloaked in foggy, imaginative, but incomprehensible pseudo-religious philosophies, liberally spiced with Germanic legend and ritual. Widow Ludendorff, a creaking octogenarian, has been transformed into a demigod and a myth for her followers.

In the four decades that she has developed her "movement," the widow has written volumes of essays, pseudoscientific and pseudophilosophical books, treatises, and articles. Racism and the fight against a phantom of "Judah's rule of the world," mark the basic principles.

She has tried, with varied success, vociferousness, and fanaticism, to prove to the Germans that all world history is the result of a synagogue plot. The Jews, she teaches, try to instigate all people in the world, particularly the Germans, to wage war on one another, robbing them, by means of intrigue and murder, of their cultural and political leaders toward the eventual aim of enslaving them all.

The "movement" combats all so-called "powers above the state." It fights Jewry as well as Christianity because it sees Christianity as

an offspring of Judaism. Other enemies of the movement are
Marxism and Free Masonry. A brief quote from *Der Volkswart*, one
of the movements publications, will give a clearer idea of Frau von
Ludendorff's aims.

"Political parties pollute a people and divide it. Neither the black
nor the red parties (in Germany that could only mean the Christian
Democrats and the opposition Socialists) have a Germanic origin.
Their origins, instead, are with Moses and Marx. Red and black
are un-Germanic, representing the coffin nails of the Germanic
spirit."

One of the leaders of the organization is Franz Karg von Bebenburg, Mrs. Ludendorff's son-in-law. As editor of the biweekly *Der
Quell* [10] one of the movement's periodicals, he was sentenced to a
two-month suspended jail term and fined 1,500 DM in February,
1960, on a criminal slander and libel charge.

The conviction, in itself a judicial afterthought, because Bebenburg had first been acquitted by a municipal court, then found guilty
on appeal by the prosecutor in a state court, stemmed from an
article in the January 5, 1959, edition of *Der Quell*. This article,
which purported to reflect the opinions of Arab students who had
visited Western Germany, slandered Berlin's senator of the interior
Joachim Lipschitz and German Jewish leader Heinz Galinski. It
"quoted" one "student's" impressions of West Germany and West
Berlin:

West Berlin is the most terrifying example of moral degeneration. A
hungry woman stands at every street corner and offers herself. All West
Berlin looks like an Israeli colony. Two Jews (Lipschitz and Galinski),
bursting with hatred for the Germans, tyrannize the disenfranchised German people in West Berlin. The Jews get the nicest homes and businesses
—and there's nothing left for the Germans. All of it is called a "Free
World."

The article was written by a man named Felix Wiethold, alleged
to be a pen name for former Nazi propagandist Dr. Johannes von
Leers, now a Nasser associate in Cairo, Egypt.

The "report" also quoted one "student's" feelings about Hitler:
"I am a young man and don't believe in glorifying the dead. But

[10] Circulation 7,500.

what I liked about Hitler was that he fought the Jews and killed so many of them."

The Ludendorff movement also sponsors several youth organizations and conducts summer camps. In 1959 there were more than a dozen camps and widow Ludendorff's concepts of the "recognition of God" undoubtedly played an important part in their spiritual program.

But these two organizations merely head off a seemingly endless list. One of them, second in importance only to the German Reich party, is the *Deutsche Gemeinschaft* (DG—German Association), an extreme right-wing movement under the leadership of August Haussleiter.

Once associated with the BHE—*Bund der Heimatvertriebenen und Entrechteten* (Bloc of Expellees and Victims of Injustice),[11] the

---

[11] The BHE is a conglomeration of refugee political interest groups which became a party in 1950 after the first *Bundestag* was already in session.

A total of forty-one refugees had been elected to the first parliament on the tickets of the established parties. They were politically impotent as a pressure group within their own parties.

Conditions for banding together of expellees and refugees were most favorable in Schleswig-Holstein, the state with the heaviest concentration of such newcomers. The BHE was founded there early in 1950. The "victims of injustice" had been added to the party title to attract not only refugees, but other malcontent groups such as air-raid victims, war veterans, the disabled, and those penalized in de-Nazification proceedings.

Although it started from scratch, the BHE scored a decisive victory in Schleswig-Holstein state elections in July, 1950, polling 307,000 votes, or 23.4 per cent of the total, winning fifteen seats in the state legislature. It won representation in the state cabinet, and the party chairman, Waldemar Kraft, a former SS captain and wartime manager of the Reich Corporation of Agriculture in occupied Poland, became Schleswig-Holstein's deputy minister president (that is, lieutenant governor).

The BHE spread its influence all over Germany very rapidly. Allied with the *Deutsche Gemeinschaft* it won 14.7 per cent of the total vote in Baden-Wuerttemberg and 12.3 per cent in Bavaria in November, 1950. In the Lower Saxony state elections of May, 1951, the BHE polled 14.9 per cent, obtaining twenty-one seats in the state legislature.

In the first *Bundestag*, the BHE, steered in some areas by former high-ranking Nazis, in others by political novices, was represented by three deputies. In the 1953 elections, the BHE snared twenty-seven seats in the *Bundestag*, becoming a member of the Adenauer coalition government. One of the leaders, Professor Theodor Oberlaender, became minister of refugee affairs. In the 1957 elections, the BHE didn't place a single candidate and has remained influential only on the state level, particularly in Bavaria, Schleswig-Holstein, Lower Saxony, and Hesse. Oberlaender switched to the CDU and remained in the cabinet.

Deutsche Gemeinschaft has been most influential in southern Germany. It at one time was represented by several deputies in the Bavarian state legislature. Its secretary-general is Dr. Renate Malluche, once a leader in the German Girl Movement (equivalent to the Hitler Youth). Haussleiter, one of the founders of the Christian Democratic Union (CDU/CSU) and once a member of the board of the CDU, together with Adenauer, is today an avowed opponent of what he terms the "clerical Adenauer course."

The *Deutsche Gemeinschaft* supports "world-wide nationalism." In a recent advertisement the organization searched for *Landsknecht* drums for the "education of German youth." [12] The organization plans on a great "breakthrough offensive when the downfall of Bonn's politics becomes apparent." In the meantime, one of its state officials has declared publicly that "Nazi concentration camps were not rough enough."

A Haussleiter resolution at his party's 1959 convention in Kaiserslautern said: "The justice ministers of the individual German states have established a central board for the investigation of crimes committed by Germans before 1945. But they rejected unanimously a proposal to establish a central board for the investigation of crimes committed *before and since 1945 by foreigners against Germans*. That is proof that German justice is under pressure of a systematically organized hate campaign. . . ."

The *Deutscher Block* (DB—German Bloc) is a militant Bavarian rightist group whose program includes a government without political parties, a strong military force, state security, and "a people's community." It has been relatively unsuccessful electorally and does not introduce candidates, waiting, instead, for a certain "X-day" when it hopes to gain control with an effective "battle group." The Bloc's leader, Karl Meissner, was sentenced to a suspended six-month jail term on March 17, 1960, when a Munich court convicted him and another member of his organization of criminal libel, slander, and violation of the public demonstration laws.

In the course of years, internal strife has resulted in the splintering of various elements off the DRP, SRP, DG, DB, and German Rightist party. Key manipulator to unify these splinter groups and individual malcontents was Erwin Schoenborn, former *Reichsar-*

---

[12] Type of drum used by mercenary soldiers in the sixteenth century.

beitsdienst (Reich Labor Service) official who has been jailed twice for his right-wing activities.

Schoenborn ran into trouble with Berlin authorities for organizing storm-troop units similar to the SA and was sentenced to a five-month jail term. After his release from prison, he moved to Mainz, capital of the Rhineland Palatinate, and founded the *Deutsche Freiheits Bewegung* (German Freedom Movement), followed shortly by a National Circle of Comrades. In early 1959, aided by former German Reich party members, he started the *Freie Soziale Volkspartei* (Free Social People's party) which he first wanted to name Free Social Reich party, modifying the name for "tactical reasons." Then he was convicted of slandering and libeling *Bundestag* president Eugen Gerstenmaier, and sentenced to eight months in jail. He was released from the Mainz prison in October, 1959.

The resort town of Wiesbaden hosts the headquarters of yet another rightist group called the *Deutsche Soziale Bewegung* (DSB— German Social Movement), led until his death on April 16, 1960 by Karl Heinz Priester, a Hitler Youth official and SS officer who allegedly escaped war crimes prosecution because of a head injury which renders him mentally incompetent to stand trial.

Priester joined the right-radical Hessian National Democratic party (NDP) in 1948, soon sliced a splinter of his own from it and called it the National Democratic Reich party. Later he converted this into the Bloc of Fatherland Associations. He has been identified with a conglomeration of nationalistic, right-radical, and fascistic organizations, including Per Engdahl's Swedish Fascist movement. His publication, *Europäische Nationale*, has attempted to blame the Russians for 3.4 million of the 6 million murders of Jews in concentration camps and ghettos.

Certainly not to be overlooked is the political activity of Dr. Otto Strasser, one-time Hitler sidekick, who returned to Germany in March, 1955, from a twenty-two-year exile that took him all over the world, finally to Canada. Strasser first made news in March, 1920, as a participant in abortive Kapp *Putsch* in Berlin.[13] That

---

[13] On March 13, 1920, Wolfgang Kapp, American-born German radical, dressed in morning coat, striped trousers, top hat, and spats, marched through the Brandenburg gate at the head of two brigades of German marines, turned into Wilhelmstrasse to the chancellory, and proclaimed himself chancellor of

same year his brother Gregor, one of the founders of the National Socialist party, introduced Otto to Hitler. Otto joined the NSDAP in 1925, and the following year the two Strassers formed a publishing house from which they issued the *Berliner Arbeiterzeitung* and *Der Nationale Sozialist*, as well as a flood of books and pamphlets.

But Strasser drifted further and further away from the Hitler group, finally making a clean break in 1930. He remained in Germany until the Nazis took power in 1933, then fled to Vienna, from there to Prague where he agitated against the *Führer*. Gregor was killed during the Roehm purge of 1934. When the war ended Strasser was in Canada. In 1946, a friend, banker Waldemar Wadsack, started the *Bund für Deutschlands Erneuerung* (League for Germany's Renovation) in Strasser's name. Strasser lost no time in trying to return to Germany but was turned down first by occupation authorities, later the Bonn government.

In November, 1954, a court decision paved the way for his return by restoring the German citizenship which had been revoked by Hitler. He arrived in March, 1955, and immediately started to work for a political comeback. His league proved ineffective, but he started the *Deutsche Soziale Union* (German Social Union) with such slogans as "Neither Wall Street nor Moscow" and "From Aachen to Beuthen, from the Memel to the Saar, Germany Forever!"

The organizing convention was held in Miltenberg, Bavaria, in June, 1956. The party emblem was a crossed hammer and sword over two ears of corn, against a stark black background. Some three hundred delegates were present as Strasser strode to the platform to speak. He didn't get very far. One of his followers tossed a tear gas bomb at some anti-Strasser demonstrators who had forced their way into the meeting hall. Chairs were thrown, fist fights ensued, and five persons were injured before police restored order. Finally, Strasser managed to outline the new party's program. He demanded Germany's reunification on the basis of armed neutrality, a strong army of volunteers, not draftees, a compulsory youth service for boys and girls, and the removal of "red tape" from government.

Germany. His aim, and that of his co-conspirator General Freiherr von Luettwitz, was the restoration of the monarchy. Kapp's reign lasted for one hundred hours. Later he and Von Luettwitz fled to Sweden. Kapp returned voluntarily and died in jail in 1922. Von Luettwitz returned after a general amnesty for the *Putchists* in 1925 and died in 1942.

Since then Strasser has made relatively insignificant progress. Although its membership at present is believed to be in excess of two thousand, the Strasser Black Front concept of "old-time" fascism apparently doesn't harmonize with the ideas of Germany's modern rightists.

The parties and movements which have made their debut since the lifting of the Allied political party licensing regulations in 1950 are many and varied. There are associations and committees and parties for "Peace and Freedom," "Tradition," "Freedom and Truth," and even for "Kaiser and Reich."

There are or have been a German National party, National Democratic party, German Workers' party, National German Workers' party, Radical Socialist Freedom party, Party of Good Germans, Bavarian Homeland and Royalist party, German Conservative party, and a European party.

The list has included such innocent sounding right-radical front organizations as the Reich Movement, League of Reich Royalists, The Never-Forgotten-Homeland Association, League of Prussians, The German Circle, Historical Association, and Union of Independent Democrats. Some have mysterious titles such as Circle of Friends for the Perservation of Nordic Culture, Federation for the Determination of Historic Truths, and Spearhead Squad Against Bolshevist Subversion. Others are more blunt, calling themselves, Reich Front, Black Legion, and Black Corps.

At present there is little danger they will unite and form a real neo-Fascist front. Repeated attempts to iron out differences of personality and philosophy between even the largest organizations, such as the German Reich party, the German Association, German Bloc, and Strasser movement, have consistently run aground, leaving an even deeper cleft between them. However, the rightists continue to try and, unless there is close supervision, some day they *may* join forces and be too strong to combat with purely legal and constitutional means.

One of the most dangerous sources of power and initiative toward a unified neo-Fascist, neo-Nazi movement is presented by the right-wing veterans' groups and so-called associations of "victims of de-

Nazification and injustice." Basically, these organizations have one outward goal: financial assistance, rehabilitation of their members in society, and "comradeship." However, they all try to minimize the crimes of Nazism and Germany's responsibility for World War II. They justify German actions before and during the Third Reich and try to shift the blame for Germany's actions on some other nations.

Six of these groups merged in 1955, forming the *Bundesverband ehemaliger Internierter und Entnazifizierungsgeschädigter* (Federal League of Interned and Victims of De-Nazification). Instead of the brusque, boot-wearing approach its members once favored, the league adopted smooth lobbying techniques. It aimed toward public sympathy for the "suffering" of its members at the hands of the Allies in internment camps, POW camps, and war-crimes prisons. "We don't condone the crimes committed under the Nazi régime," was the slogan. "But if we don't condone those, then Germans should not condone the crimes committed by the Allies against us."

In April, 1959, the German government outlawed the league as subversive and unconstitutional, but little time passed before a substitute "Fighting Federation for Freedom and Justice" took its place, sporting the same old faces and the same old demands in a different wrapping.

Extremist military and pseudo veterans' organizations such as the *HIAG der Waffen SS* (the previously mentioned self-help association of the Army SS) also pose a significant right-wing danger.

HIAG claims to represent members of the Army SS in Germany as well as Army SS volunteers in countries all over Europe. Its leadership has for years attempted to nurture the idea among the German public that the only similarity between the SS as such and the *Waffen SS* (Army SS) is that of title.[14] There is, however, only a very

---

[14] HIAG members insist there were two types of SS: the regular black-uniformed Elite Guard and the so-called Death's-Head organizations which ran the concentration camps, on the one side, and on the other, the *Waffen* or Army SS, which, HIAG claims, was not really an SS organization but merely designated so by Himmler and Hitler. In reality, the Army SS was started in 1935 when Himmler and Hitler ordered Lieutenant General Paul Hausser (now a leader of HIAG) to form a reservoir of fighting SS men which could, in case of emergency, be detailed to the *Wehrmacht* in a ratio of one SS division to thirty-five army divisions. By 1940 the term *Waffen SS* was already used to designate these units. By the end of the war, there were approximately six hundred thousand *Waffen SS* members, all of them volunteers. Contrary to the theory which

thin dividing line between the two and the so-called *SS Toten-kopfverbände* (SS Death's-Head Units).

Former SS members started to organize on a local basis after the war. Their goals were political and financial rehabilitation. The major obstacle in their way was the verdict of the International War Crimes Tribunal at Nuremberg, which had branded the SS collectively as a "criminal organization." Out of these local efforts grew the HIAG. Of late, Major General Kurt (Panzermeyer) Meyer, once sentenced to death for war crimes by a Canadian court, then interned for life, and eventually freed in 1953, has been functioning as HIAG's chief spokesman. Since his release from prison in 1959, Sepp Dietrich has also been active in the organization.

HIAG, which draws thousands of former SS men to its annual meetings, publishes a magazine called *Der Freiwillige (The Volunteer)*. Until a few years ago, when he was moved out of the organization by political differences within HIAG, Erich Kernmayer, former Nazi propaganda chief for the Saarland, served as its managing editor. Its annual "help find lost comrades conventions" are wild affairs. At the 1957 clambake in the small Bavarian town of Karlburg, not far from Wuerzburg, some eight thousand former SS men showed up. Principal speakers were Panzermeyer and "Papa" Hausser, the former general so named because he helped organize the *Waffen SS*.

A band blared out old, in some cases illegal, marches. More than once the veterans sang a favorite SS song, "We Are the Guard the *Führer* Loves." Before Hausser started to tell his comrades what he planned to do for them as official lobbyist in Bonn toward getting pensions and treatment equal to that of other soldiers, bouncers in the audience went to the press table and shut off a reporter's tape recorder. When a news photographer snapped his camera during the incident, an ex-SS man started taking pictures of every reporter and cameraman in the gigantic tent. "They're for our files," he explained. "We don't want to forget your faces. We might need the pictures someday."

HIAG is attempting to propagate, the great mass of *Waffen SS* officers, noncoms, and even enlisted men were SS men first, army men second. Certainly all senior officers in the *Waffen SS* had originally been members of the Elite Guard organization. Throughout the war, the *Waffen SS* remained under direct orders of Heinrich Himmler, *Reichsführer SS*. They were neither a police force nor an armed service, but a separate organization on loan to the *Wehrmacht*.

In a one-and-a-half hour speech Panzermeyer said, among other things, "SS troops committed no crimes except the massacre at Ouradour. And, that was the action of a single man. He was scheduled to go before a court-martial, but he died a hero's death before he could be tried."

The SS vets denied being in any way responsible for the massacre and destruction of the Czechoslovakian town of Lidice. "The *Waffen SS*," Meyer emphasized, "was as much a regular army outfit as any other in the *Wehrmacht*."

Meyer criticized all the political parties in Bonn except one—the right-wing *Deutsche Partei*. He called for an end to government policies which "treat former SS troopers as second-class citizens. They did nothing more than fight for their country." He attacked the theory of "collective guilt," and said there was no such thing in Germany as an "extralegal" or "illegal" state and "the SS wasn't part of such a state."

The ex-general also blasted away at German illustrated magazines which have printed a number of articles about the "old army." "These are a mixture of sex, sadism, and cruelty," Meyer said. "What they write is completely untrue. Watch out, comrades, that your children never get hold of these magazines." The SS veterans hailed Meyer's speech by singing the illegal first stanza of the German national anthem, *Deutschland, Deutschland über Alles*.

Participation at the 1958 convention was nearly double that of 1957: some fifteen thousand men. In addition to the basic claims and demands, Panzermeyer also took pot shots at the government policy of prosecuting "so-called war criminals."

One of HIAG's primary functions is political lobbying. Unfortunately, the former SS members are considered an important "vote potential" by even liberal politicians and members of the parliament. While the HIAG is a veterans' organization fighting for legitimacy of its members, other more conservative, often traditional organizations have become increasingly active and powerful. They all are closely associated with rightist and nationalist political movements and parties.

One that has grown in stature steadily is the *Gemeinschaft der Ritterkreuzträger* (Association of Wearers of the Knight's Cross).[15]

[15] The *Ritterbreuz* was the highest medal awarded in the *Wehrmacht*.

The organization gained its major impetus through the 1956 law which permitted the wearing of Hitler and Kaiser medals [16] again. Among the three hundred delegates to the society's 1959 convention in Regensburg, Bavaria, were Sepp Dietrich and Duke Joseph of Austria-Hungary, last commander-in-chief of the Imperial Austro-Hungarian army.

In 1959, unlike preceding years, the *Ritterkreuz* wearers held most of their convention behind closed doors. Music for the ceremonies was provided by a *Bundeswehr* band, and Defense Minister Josef Strauss had made a special dispensation for the convention allowing *Bundeswehr* holders of the *Ritterkreuz* to wear the cross strung around their necks—in traditional style—instead of as a ribbon on their chest—as per *Bundeswehr* regulation.

The 1959 meeting was nowhere near as informative as conventions in the past, when society members displayed their political colors more openly. Chief speaker at a memorial ceremony for the second annual convention in 1957 was an ex-colonel, now a Wiesbaden pastor, named Hans Dingeldey. Addressing a crowd of monocled, serious-faced heroes, the pastor said:

Dear generals, officers, and comrades. These are important days, because we again can salute you as the bravest of the brave. Thank God for that.

We must not forget the many years during which one could not utter the word "bravery" in our fatherland. Many of us have had to hide our medals and citations, if they hadn't been taken forcibly from us. For the past few weeks, however, we have been able to wear them openly and with pride again.

. . . I know what you have done to defend the fatherland, said Dingeldey. There were seven thousand of our comrades who were cited with the *Ritterkreuz* in World War II. Most of those comrades are close by in our memories but they are a long way from here—perhaps under a simple white cross in some far-off cemetery.

Today we want to think of all our fallen comrades, not just those cited with the *Ritterkreuz*. It is only fitting and proper that we greet all our fallen comrades who died in uniform defending their fatherland.

We can't rub out a war that changed the course of history. We can't rub out a war that spilled the blood of all peoples all over the world. But

[16] Without swastika emblem, however.

we must learn to serve our fatherland in peace. That does not mean, though, just sitting down and putting our hands in our laps.

If a new fire comes, we'll have to say again, we're afraid, but we won't fail you.

If the German people are attacked *once more*,[17] we'll have to go to the battlefield again.

Other veterans' organizations and leagues of old soldiers include the Navy League, Federation of German Paratroopers, *Luftwaffen-ring*, the all-powerful *Verband Deutscher Soldaten* (Association of German Soldiers), and the *Stahlhelm* organization of former front-line soldiers. There is even a *Legion Condor* Comradeship, made up of volunteers in the German legion which fought on Franco's side in the Spanish Civil War.

Two of these organizations still deserve special mention. The Federation of German Paratroopers has taken a very critical attitude toward the democratic development of the *Bundeswehr*. At its various conventions speakers expressed a definite longing for the return to "better days." In an atmosphere of march music and cheers a variety of provocative speakers have been featured. Among them have been ex-Field Marshal Albert Kesselring, ex-General Kurt Student, and ex-General Bernard Ramcke, all three convicted war criminals.

The main trend of attitudes has remained the same in the organization. General Student jarred observers at the 1955 convention by greeting them with an upraised arm salute and shouting, "We don't want politicians in our ranks and we don't want to serve foreign purposes," neglecting to say which foreign powers, however. He went on to warn the veterans that "our fight is against those who accuse us of being war criminals, robbers, pilferers, and collectively guilty. We object to accusations that we are Fascists."

Student and his comrade-in-arms Ramcke pleaded for a return to an army with tradition, because an "army without the living values of tradition has no force. . . ."

The federation came in the public limelight in 1959 when Ramcke filed suit against German author Erich Kuby and radio editor Ruediger Proske for a network dramatization of the defense of the city of Brest, France. Ramcke had commanded the 2nd Airborne Division

[17] Author's italics.

in the surrounded city. In the radio show Kuby severely criticized the "last-ditch stand" which caused needless death and imprisonment of 10,000 German soldiers. Ramcke lost the suit, but that didn't dampen his enthusiasm for a fight-to-the-last-man type of military campaign. At the Paratroop Federation's 1959 convention, the general took the stand, amid thunderous applause. Screaming, his fists clenched, he blasted away at "elements which could never slander or libel me." Student continued along the same lines in 1959 that he had used for all the years in between: "Put an end to the defamation of German soldiers."

The only change in attitude of these military groups, as reflected in the paratroop convention as well as in those of other veterans' organizations, is that as time has passed and the German *Bundeswehr* has become a fact, the federations, leagues, and associations are trying to become more respectable so they, too, can take part in Germany's "military reconstruction." At the 1959 convention in Freiburg, for example, the *Bundeswehr* was officially represented by a marching band. The commanding general of the 1st *Bundeswehr* Airborne Division and a United States Army general were among the "guests of honor." The *Bundeswehr* later issued a public "apology" disassociating itself from individual speakers at the clambake, though not the entire federation.

Decidedly more vociferous and regimental in its approach than the paratroopers is the *Stahlhelm*, which traces its history back to the First World War. Active in the formation of the private armies that rocked and terrorized the Weimar Republic, it marched together with the SA on January 30, 1933, the day of Hitler's appointment as chancellor, only to be outlawed later by the same *Führer* to whom it had given its support. But that was no bitter lesson for the *Stahlhelm*. In fact, one must ask oneself whether the *Stahlhelm* has learned anything in the meantime.

The organization attracted widespread public attention in June, 1955, when its steel-helmeted, boot-wearing, and uniformed members paraded in Goslar, Lower Saxony, for their annual convention. When Goslar citizens, labor union members, democratic youth clubs, and church organizations staged a protest demonstration against the uniformed convention, the police drove away the demonstrators and protected the *Stahlhelm*. This experience was so reminiscent of the

Stahlhelm's might and protected activities as a private army in the 1920's that a major debate ensued a few months later in the *Bundestag*. Both CDU and SPD deputies pronounced their distinct displeasure at the *Stahlhelm* activities. The uniformed convention cost the organization many followers and considerable support, and for several years following it was almost a meaningless, ineffectual society for the "preservation of traditions."

Over the years the *Stahlhelm* attitudes can best be illustrated by a few excerpts from its publication. The magazine said in August, 1958:

Our present Western Germany is only half a nation, without ideas, uprooted and hopeless. We all must fight for the maintenance of our nation. We have room only for those men in our ranks who will do battle for a clean fatherland in the size and scope of the old Reich.

In September, 1958:

The concept of honor was the center of all being in the Germanic Occident. . . . The only ballast which Germanic men carried with them was the concept of personal honor. All power, all property, all relations, every action was in the service of honor. This concept of honor is the nerve of fate which touches our entire history. This personal honor fosters courage and self-discipline. This concept of honor has remained a basic ingredient of our people. . . .

In November, 1958:

. . . If the Germans were really all Germans, then everyone would be quite satisfied with us [*Stahlhelm*]. But that isn't the case and people don't understand or don't want to understand us. "But we knew what we were doing, for we remained true to the Fatherland."

In March, 1959:

The First World War broke out in 1914. Despite heroic courage, it was lost after four and a half years. There were too many enemies. On November 9, 1918, the Empire capitulated. The German people were torn internally. In the same castle in which the Emperor had been crowned in 1871 the victors dictated a shameful treaty to the German people. Our people had to suffer want and misery. The enemy squeezed virtually everything out of our fatherland. The Weimar Republic was formed. Terrible unemployment settled over the country. The republic ended in 1933 and Hitler took over control of the state. For him, too, there was only a short period of rule. The Second World War, no doubt the most terrible of all wars, started in 1939. Despite heoric fighting and millions of sacrifices on the part of the entire people, we had to capitulate in 1945. The result was the collapse of a nation such as the world had never seen. And what were things like in our fatherland? Even worse than after 1918: moral and spiritual decay; wherever one looked a race for the material benefits. Our youth matured without proper education. Which of them knows the fear of God, the sense of sacrifice or fulfillment of duty today? Who still understands the concept of Fatherland? Nothing of the Prussian spirit is left, and today we know why the Allies destroyed the Prussian state.

In June, 1959:

In this politically active period in which one must face the existence or nonexistence of Germany, active *Stahlhelm* participation is essential . . . so that we can really develop into a battle group, not just a society for the preservation of traditions.

How many people belong to the *Stahlhelm?* In the 1920's there were 200,000 members. Today, the membership is more than 30,000. The *Bundesführer,* until his death on July 16, 1960, was ex-Field Marshal Albert Kesselring.

Generally all these organizations demand reconstruction of the fatherland and reunification. They pine for the old virtues and traditions of "Kaiser and Reich," "honor and sacrifice," "courage and love of the fatherland," and the "rejuvenation of Nordic culture."

How far these traditionalists have infiltrated military and public life is difficult to estimate. Their attempts, certainly, are "valiant." Many former generals, most of them members of such organizations, have found well paying positions in industry where they again exert considerable influence on German public officials as well as help formulate German attitudes.

And last, but not at all least, among the organizations bringing right-radical pressures to bear on Germany's postwar way of life are the expellees and refugees from the territories of Pomerania, Silesia, East Prussia, and the Sudetenland, and the so-called ethnic Germans.

The official expellee and refugee party, the BHE (Bloc of Expellees and Victims of Injustice) includes many former Nazis. Its founder was an SS man. Today many high-ranking SS, SA, and Nazi party functionaries are politically active in its ranks. The same goes for other organizations of refugees and expellees. Numerous leaders of the Sudeten German associations throughout Germany were functionaries of the Fascist Konrad Henlein movement in Czechoslovakia and later took over important positions in the German rule of the country.

While the Silesian and eastern expellee groups have not been as politically active, the Sudeten Germans have come closest to what might be called a revengist policy. They clamor that the federal government not give up its rights to former ethnic German territories in exchange for union with the East zone. While German unification is still an unrealistic dream, they already lay claims to the territories east of the Oder-Neisse line.

The Sudeten Germans, organized in a variety of uniformed and costumed organizations, are particularly active. They also represent the greatest reservoir of former Nazis. Sponsorship of youth organizations is one of their major objectives, and the younger generation, raised in Western Germany, is again being taught the principles of a greater German Reich.

The refugees and expellees form a potentially very dangerous force. They number approximately 9 million. The federal government and Allied occupation authorities attempted to fuse them into the West German society as effectively as possible, but unfortunately a great number has remained an undigested entity. Having lost most of their worldly possessions when they were driven from their homes, they form a nucleus of malcontents despite the general economic recovery of West Germany.

But just as they were the "German minorities" in their native countries whom Hitler sought to "liberate from foreign oppression," they are a minority within the Germany they now call their own. Once an economic burden for the states in which they settled, they are still disliked by the indigenous populations. They generally hold to strong nationalistic and Reich-inspired ideals which tend to fire the latent nationalistic imagination of the Germans living around them.

Since they represent 15 per cent of the entire West German population, they form an important pressure group. Their demands for return of their homelands, and their clamors of "unjust" treatment at the hands of the Russians, Poles, and Czechs, present some of the most sensitive problems. Touched off, they could become a rallying point for all other nationalistic, neo-Nazi and neo-Fascist interest groups.

Chapter VIII

Skeletons in the Public Closet

The Nazis are not "back in power." Nor are they "everywhere in government." However, it would be either pure whitewash or unrealistic optimism to deny that there are many ex-Nazis in all facets and at all levels of public life.

Even Chancellor Adenauer admits that much. He once acknowledged that two thirds of all senior officers in the foreign ministry had been Nazi party members. When criticized and asked why he had permitted this infiltration, the chancellor retorted: "You can't create a diplomatic corps with amateurs."

The chancellor may be right. But how does he explain the fact that several ministers in his cabinet were once storm troopers and that his closest advisor wrote the official commentary to Hitler's 1935 race laws? He does not. In fact, he attempts to refute the allegations or tries to minimize the importance of the role his associates played in the Third Reich. When cornered in a parliamentary debate on this subject once, Adenauer merely replied: "I think it is about time to end the witch hunt for Nazis."

The chancellor once said that the world should recognize that the majority of Germans had served Nazism "only under the hard pressure of dictatorship." That also may be true. However, the men in

121

Adenauer's cabinet, the hundreds of judges, district attorneys, senior civil servants, members of parliament, and state legislators for whom the chancellor is being reproached were not nominal Nazis. Many of them were enthusiastic supporters of Hitler.

One of the first German officials to hang these matters out for international airing was Dr. Otto John, former chief of West Germany's "Bureau for the Protection of the Constitution," a hybrid FBI, CIA, and OSS amalgamated into one agency. The occasion for Dr. John's blast—that the Nazis have "regained power in public and political life"—was a press conference held in East Berlin, three weeks after the West German security chief had defected to the Soviet zone.

Who was this Dr. John?

He was born in 1909, the son of a civil servant. He attended school in Wiesbaden, where he counted as one of his best friends a half-Jew named Wolfgang Hoefer. John was a brilliant student in high school and college and considered a fierce idealist. At the age of twenty-eight, he was named legal advisor to Lufthansa, Germany's state-run passenger airline.

During the war, as rumor has it, while working with the airline, John was also an informer for the British. It was not long before he identified himself with the group of officers and government officials who were plotting Hitler's assassination. When the July 20, 1944, bomb plan failed, Dr. John fled to England. His brother Hans, a *Luftwaffe* soldier on the Russian front, was imprisoned and executed.

In the United Kingdom, John met London *Daily Express* reporter Sefton Delmer, a British intelligence agent during the war. Delmer hired John as an agent, and when hostilities ceased, Dr. John returned to Germany in British uniform. He interrogated and helped prosecute numerous high-ranking Nazis, among them ex-Field Marshal Erich von Manstein, who was convicted as a war criminal, later pardoned, and now holds an important advisory post in the West German defense ministry. In 1950, when the Allied High Commission authorized the new Bonn government to establish a security agency, Dr. John was employed on its staff. Six candidates proposed by the federal government for the post of bureau chief were rejected by the Allies. John, the seventh, was approved.

From the outset he had many enemies, due in part to the fact that he was an avowed anti-Nazi and that there were many former National Socialists in the new government. But more than that, he was a controversial figure because his responsibilities included spying on everyone else in the government for the purpose of ferreting out subversive elements. Dr. John was relatively successful in detecting subversives on the right, but he discovered only few on the left.

On July 20, 1954, Dr. John went to West Berlin for the tenth anniversary of the abortive uprising against Hitler. In addition to finding former SS officers at the ceremonies, he also encountered several old friends. One of them was his Wiesbaden classmate Wolfgang Hoefer, who had immigrated to the United States to escape Nazi persecution and had returned to Germany in the uniform of a United States Army Counter Intelligence captain. Rumors at the time had it that Hoefer had tipped off Dr. John that he was suspected of spying for his old British friends. United States Army intelligence allegedly was keeping John under surveillance.

Another friend in West Berlin was Dr. Wolfgang Wohlgemuth, trumpet-playing, Don Juan-like society gynecologist who, as a *Wehrmacht* field surgeon, had once saved brother Hans John's life on the Russian front by extracting a number of Soviet bullets from his chest. Wohlgemuth was known as a salon Communist. Dr. John visited the gynecologist's office the evening of July 20. What happened then is still shrouded in mystery. John today insists his old friend drugged him and abducted him across the sector border into East Berlin. Wohlgemuth's ex post facto version is that John asked to be driven into the Soviet part of the city.

Three days after John's disappearance Hoefer committed suicide. Shortly after John had arrived in the Soviet zone he broadcast an explanation for his actions over the East German radio network, saying he had left West Germany because of all the ex-Nazis who had gained a foothold in the government. These former Nazis, John said, had slandered and libeled him and had made it impossible for him to continue his work for the democratic reconstruction of Germany.

Some three weeks after his defection (or abduction) Dr. John held a press conference, attended by three hundred Western newspapermen, Sefton Delmer among them. John charged that the Bonn government was harboring ex-Nazis and listed them by name. Among them was Theodor Blank, at that time head of the "defense office," whom John accused of employing former SS men. Others were Dr. Paul Leverkuehn, CDU *Bundestag* deputy, whom John accused of collaborating with Fascists; Hasso von Manteuffel, another *Bundestag* deputy and ex-general; Professor Theodor Oberlaender, minister of refugees, chairman of the BHE refugee party, charged by John with hiring Nazis in his ministry; Bernhard Ramcke, retired paratroop general; Dr. Werner Naumann, former Goebbels aide, active in the German Reich party; and many others.

All of them denied John's charges categorically.

"I see no reason why I should defend myself against this character John. I don't consider myself accused by his allegations," said Hasso von Manteuffel who, five years later, was convicted of war crimes by a German district court in Duesseldorf.

Oberlaender, who has been subjected to a barrage of attacks for his storm trooper activities and alleged participation in mass murders, also denied Dr. John's denunciations.

John's unofficial bill of indictment sounded so much like the familiar, hackneyed invectives of the Pankow propagandists that the Bonn government uninhibitedly shouted "turncoat" at John to depreciate the importance of his allegations domestically and minimize their impact abroad. There was no skirting the issue, however, as the Paris *Le Monde* pointed out. ". . . Whatever one may think of John's attitude, one must admit that it is presented openly and sincerely. The Bonn government does not improve its prestige by flatly denying the facts and attempting to categorize John as a 'traitor and agent of Soviet propaganda,' " wrote *Le Monde*.

Nearly a year and a half later, Otto John reappeared as mysteriously as he had disappeared. A Danish newspaperman helped spirit him back into West Berlin. He soon faced prosecution by West German authorities on charges no one had ever heard of before: damaging the reputation of the German Federal Republic and giving away "false state secrets." The latter count stemmed from the fact that, although he had given information to his Soviet zone hosts, the data had been incorrect. What most observers still haven't figured out is whether this was merely because John was poorly informed or whether he had deliberately given false information.

At his trial, as controversial as his disappearing act, Dr. John pleaded not guilty, basing his defense on the version that he had been drugged by Wohlgemuth and abducted across the border. Although he was convicted and sentenced to four years in prison, which he served only in part, the real motive for his trip to East Germany may remain a riddle. Some German newspapers, disgruntled about censorship attempts preceding the trial, suggested that the government was afraid to let the truth come out.

In retrospect, there seems little doubt that John's defection or abduction—whichever one chooses to believe—was related to his anti-Nazi sentiments. But there was more than just idealism involved. His appointment to the bureau presidency had been contested. It is known that Chancellor Adenauer never liked him. John, on the other hand, was incensed that he could never get past the desk of Adenauer's advisor, State Secretary Hans Globke, the man who had written the race law commentary. John was unpopular among his coworkers because of his pro-British sympathies and his defection to the United Kingdom during the war. Although he repeatedly told his friends that "political developments in Germany don't suit me any more," there is strong evidence that John didn't suit the politicians any more.

Dr. John has been described, even by his friends, as "a crackpot idealist who sees Nazis in every ministry just as an old maid sees men underneath her bed. The difference is that while the men under the bed may be imaginary, the Nazis are not." "Isn't it strange that on the very day when Otto John, one of our resistance leaders against Hitler, was sent to prison, former SS Colonel Joachim Peiper, convicted for his leading part in the Malmédy massacre of 1944, was paroled from Landsberg war crimes prison?" asked one observer at John's trial.

The Otto John affair had three concrete results. First, through his dramatic disappearance and his allegations, John became the first West German official of importance to draw attention to the problem of former Nazis in government. The unfortunate second effect was that, by making his allegations from the Russian zone, he detracted from their political impact, enabling the respondents of his accusations to rebut. They pointed to John's defection and his "treasonable relations" with the East, thus damaging the reputation of all resistance fighters. The third development was the most unusual. Until then the East Zone's most popular propaganda game had been to shout that West German officialdom is "riddled with old Nazis." When John heaped his indictment on top of the propaganda pile, the Adenauer government had to retaliate, and the propaganda war has become a two-sided one, dominated by a political parlor game called, "You expose my Nazi, I'll expose yours."

Indeed, there are plenty of Nazis in the East Zone to uncover.

Following the German Democratic Republic's (DDR) last general election in 1958, the number of former National Socialists in the *Volkskammer* (parliament) increased from twenty-nine to forty-nine. The chief justice of the East German supreme court is reported to be an old-time Nazi. The head of the East German academy of state and legal sciences is alleged to be a former SS officer. Ernst Grossmann, a member of the central committee of the Socialist Unity party (SED) and a close personal friend and advisor of Walter Ulbricht, the party's chief, has been tagged as a former SS guard at Sachsenhausen concentration camp. Arno von Lenski, former major general in the East Zone People's Army and deputy in the *Volkskammer*, is reputed to have been an honorary judge of the *Volksgerichtshof* (Nazi People's Court) in Berlin.

The London *Bulletin on German Questions*, October, 1957, reported the following ex-Nazis in political posts in the East Zone:

Theophil Beust, former official in the Nazi party, now secretary of the National Democratic party [1] in Langensalza, member of the

[1] Both in Eastern and Western Germany, the same four political parties were licensed in 1945. Counting from left to right they were the Communist party (KPD), the Social Democratic party (SPD), the Christian Democratic Union (CDU) and the Liberal Democratic party (LDP). The LDP changed its name to Free Democratic party (FDP) in Western Germany in 1948. After the enforced amalgamation early in 1946 of the Socialist and Communist parties in the East zone into what is now called the Socialist Unity party (SED), certain Social Democratic sympathizers, opposed to this amalgamation and unwilling to support religious criteria in political life as the CDU favored, threw their support to the LDP at the East German polls. In the October 20, 1946, state legislature elections of the Soviet zone, the LDP garnered 22 per cent of the vote. Thereafter, the Communists never again permitted non-Communist parties to compete with the SED in elections. When the *Volkskammer* was chosen in October, 1950, the only avenue open to the voter was that of approving a four-hundred delegate unity list which included sixty members of the LDP who had been found satis-

city council, and an instructor for the "National Front."

Siegfried Dallmann, Nazi student leader, member of the central executive committee of the National Democratic party (NDP), member of the *Volkskammer* (parliament).

Manfred Einenkel, once member of the Nazi party, now secretary of the Liberal German party in Leipzig, deputy in the *Volkskammer*.

Horst Gossinger, once a Hitler Youth leader, chairman of the NDP in Rudelstadt.

Franz Hahn, former member of the Nazi party, now chairman of the NDP in Cottbus and *Volkskammer* deputy.

Heinrich Homann, at one time in the SS, now vice chairman of the NDP in East Germany, and deputy in the *Volkskammer*.

Vilmos Korn, once a member of the Free Corps Rossbach and the Nazi party, now in the directorate of the NDP.

Eva Ludwig, former member of the Nazi party, active in the Nazi women's movement, now a member of the *Volkskammer* and active in the NDP.

Hans Luthardt, former Hitler Youth official, member of the directorate of the NDP in Thuringia, deputy in the *Volkskammer*.

Charlotte Sender, member of the Nazi women's movement, today a deputy in the *Volkskammer*, head of the women's committee of the NDP for Saxony.

There is no denying it. The DDR also has its political skeletons in its public closet, but far fewer than West Germany. The Soviet zone officials have exploited the propaganda value of this fully. Many of the ex-Nazis in the West German officialdom have been "exposed" or "uncovered" by hard-hitting, well aimed, and carefully timed press announcements and research reports. Nearly half of all the West German political "exposés" and "scandals" have had their origin in documentation supplied by the DDR or other satellite countries. Although the motives for publication of this documentation are

---

factory to the Communists. Noting that confidence in the CDU and LDP as independent entities was dwindling, the Communist régime, in mid-1948, launched two new political parties which, they hoped, would be less suspect in the eyes of the public. One, the Democratic Peasant party (DBP) was designed to enlist peasant support. The other, the National Democratic party (NDP), was designed to capture, for Communist ends, the political potential of the right-wing middle-class nationalists, ex-Nazis, and former officers. The NDP has never competed at the polls since no real elections have been held since 1946.

more than obvious, that has thus far failed to detract in any way from the accuracy of the charges and allegations.

Some of the Nazis in the West German government regained their posts through loose interpretation of the "131 Law." [2] Others successfully concealed their Nazi past until documentation, either of Eastern or Western origin, ripped off the disguise. Many were unmasked accidentally by some action, speech, or political activity which smacked of Fascist tendencies and resulted in closer probing into the individual's past. And, in the case of a few, their political biography has been a matter of public record since the end of the war. These have been protected by Chancellor Adenauer or other government officials.

There are two basic groups—elected officials and civil servants—which can be divided into several major categories. These are: (1) members of the Adenauer cabinet or senior civil servants in the Adenauer government; (2) *Bundestag* deputies; (3) judges, district attorneys, and other judicial officials who were members of the NSDAP or served on special Nazi courts; (4) *Bundeswehr* officials and advisors; (5) elected state and local officials; and (6) local and state civil servants.

Take the cabinet and senior civil servants first. Until March, 1960, three ministers in Chancellor Adenauer's cabinet were former storm troopers and Nazi party members. One of them was finally pressured out of office. The political pasts and attitudes toward Nazism on the part of the others is still debatable. One member of the cabinet rose to the position of a well paid industrialist under the Nazi régime and has drifted further and further to the radical right since being a member of the government.

Although Chancellor Adenauer himself was a victim of Nazi persecution, being under constant Gestapo surveillance and arrested twice, he was banned from political activities in October, 1945, by British occupation authorities on grounds of "obstructionism and noncooperation."

Interior minister Gerhard Schroeder became a Hitler storm trooper in 1933, a Nazi party member in 1937.

2 See p. 41.

Professor Ludwig Erhard, minister of economics, was the head of a Nuremberg institute for industrial and market research during the Nazi régime.

Fritz Schaeffer, minister of justice, finance minister from 1949 to 1957, practiced law during the Nazi régime but was imprisoned at Dachau concentration camp in 1944 for anti-Nazi remarks. The United States Military Government appointed him minister president (governor) of Bavaria in May, 1945, then dismissed him the following September, and in 1946 barred him from all political activity. The restriction was lifted in 1948 following his de-Nazification.

Dr. Hans-Christoph Seebohm, Adenauer's minister of transport, was a mining engineer, mine manager, executive and director of mining enterprises, corporations, and manufacturers' associations until 1945. Since 1946 he has been a member of the executive committee of the conservative, right-wing *Deutsche Partei* (DP—German Party), part of the Adenauer coalition government. Seebohm provoked an Allied High Commission protest to the federal government in December, 1951, when he stated in a public speech that he "bows in homage before *any* symbol under which Germans have given their lives."

In September, 1959, Seebohm was elected "federal speaker" of the Sudeten German Union, thus representing virtually all Sudeten German leagues, clubs, and associations. At the time, he became subject to considerable press criticism but rode over it almost unruffled when Chancellor Adenauer declared there was nothing wrong with Seebohm's "extracurricular" activities. On March 27, 1960, Seebohm rocked the federal boat when he addressed a group of Sudeten Germans and demanded that they be given the right to return to their old homeland in Czechoslovakia. Although he ruled out a military venture to win back the territory, he declared that the *Sudeten Germans must take the lead* in "wiping out Bolshevism not only in Czechoslovakia, but in all of Eastern Europe as well." [3] "We don't want to fight for freedom with force," Seebohm said. "What good would it do for us to have a devastated homeland."

Other speakers at the same meeting said the Czech-Germans would not find themselves in their present plight if Woodrow Wilson and

[3] Associated Press dispatch, March 27, 1960.

Franklin D. Roosevelt hadn't gone to the international conferences too ill to make their views prevail.

Unquestionably, the most controversial member of the Adenauer cabinet was Professor Theodor Oberlaender, minister of refugees and expellees, an old-time Nazi who served the Third Reich régime as an expert on Eastern Europe and had been captain in the SA (storm troopers) and lieutenant in a battalion of pro-German Ukrainian nationalists which marched into Poland in *Wehrmacht* uniform in the summer of 1941.

Oberlaender was national chairman of the BHE party (Bloc of Expellees and Victims of Injustice) and won a seat in the *Bundestag* in the 1953 elections. In 1954 he became a member of the Adenauer cabinet. He came under fire shortly after his appointment when he replaced CDU civil servants in the ministry with members of his own party, some of whom had never been in the civil service before but had been very active in the Nazi party instead.

Always the focal point of embarrassing attacks against the Adenauer government, Oberlaender quit the BHE before the 1957 general elections and transferred his allegiance to the Christian Democratic Union. He was reelected on the CDU ticket and resumed his post as a cabinet member. The subject of numerous political flurries from the time of his appointment, Oberlaender became the object of a hurricane of protests in 1959 when he was accused of participating in the massacre of 2,400 Ukrainians, Poles, and Jews at Lvov, Poland, between June 30 and July 6, 1941. The charges leveled by the left-wing *Vereinigung der Verfolgten des Naziregimes* (VVN—Association of Victims of the Nazi Régime) were based on incriminating documents which the association turned over to the center for the investigation of Nazi crimes in Ludwigsburg in September, 1959.

The center passed on the material to the Bonn district attorney for further study. The Bonn prosecutor was asked to determine whether a petition for the suspension of Oberlaender's parliamentary immunity from trial was warranted. The allegations were made public through an article in *Die Tat*, a publication closely linked with the VVN. Oberlaender, however, won an injunction against further distribution of the issue containing the charges on the grounds that they were unsubstantiated and libelous. He denied the accusations, saying that the massacre in Lvov had been committed by the retreating

Russians, not the Germans. And, he insisted, he had plenty of witnesses to substantiate his claim.

Oberlaender said his unit, nicknamed the "Nightingale Battalion," because its Ukrainian members were all good singers, had discovered the blood bath left by the Soviets in the city's jails and prisons. The twenty-four hundred victims, he insisted, had all been political prisoners who had opposed the Soviet régime. The refugee minister relied on his war diaries to prove his contention that the battalion, whose major mission was anti-Soviet propaganda among the Poles and Ukrainians, had been camped on the outskirts of the city on June 28, 1941, when news of the prison massacre leaked through. The unit, he stated, did not enter the city until June 30. There were no Russian soldiers left and the populace turned out en masse to greet the Germans and the *Wehrmacht*-uniformed Ukrainians with flowers. Although all vital spots in the city, including the jails and prisons, were occupied immediately, the refugee minister claimed, he and his singing propagandists had come too late to prevent the massacre. The majority of prison inmates, Oberlaender explained at a press conference where he strove to exonerate himself, had been shot two days previously. "In the six days our unit was in Lvov, not a single shot was fired and there wasn't a single atrocity reported," said Oberlaender who had been adjutant of the Nightingale Battalion.

Oberlaender emphasized that at no time had Polish war-crimes proceedings ever mentioned the Nightingale Battalion or any of the other units such as the Brandenburg Division or the 99th Mountain Division which had participated in the German siege of Lvov. As evidence, Oberlaender produced articles, written at the time, in newspapers of neutral countries, and unsolicited statements from witnesses. The material substantiated Oberlaender's claims that the Soviets had been responsible for the mass murders in the prisons.

As Oberlaender continued to deny the charges, however, folders full of damaging data accumulated—the greatest proportion of it from the East Zone or other Communist sources. Although Oberlaender insisted the documents had been forged, most German experts have reached the reticent conclusion that "it isn't all fraudulent." Information about Oberlaender's somewhat misty past is available in his personnel file from the former Reich ministry of interior, now in the possession of the East Zone, which DDR officials have offered to make available for West German judicial inspection. Some of the evidence against Oberlaender came from West German sources, too, such as the historical archives and institutes. Although none of these documents validates the VVN claim that Oberlaender and his musical Ukrainians participated in the prison massacre, there were other atrocities committed in Lvov, and it has not yet been determined conclusively whether or not the refugee minister shares any responsibility for them.

By his own admission, Oberlaender's was the only *Wehrmacht* unit composed of foreign nationals to be stationed in the city from June 30 to the early morning hours of July 7, 1941, at which time the Nightingale Battalion moved on to a new position. Oberlaender may insist that not a single shot was fired and not a single atrocity committed during this period, but official SD (security service) and eyewitness reports, made public since the VVN allegations, discredit at least this claim. On June 30, according to the Nazi security police and security service reports, Ukrainian citizens in Lvov gave vent to their pent-up anti-Communist feelings by mistreating about one thousand Jews and delivering them one by one and in groups to prison. One eyewitness maintains that he and some five hundred other Jewish citizens had been beaten with rifle butts and stabbed with bayonets by Ukrainians in German uniform. Most of the five hundred, he stated, had been mishandled and mistreated so horribly that they died from their injuries. According to SD (security service) reports, some seven thousand Jews were arrested and executed in Lvov between June 30 and July 6, 1941. Yet Oberlaender is adamant that "not a single shot was fired," and to make sure, the refugee minister said, he personally had controlled the guard posts and made numerous inspection tours through the city.

To further implicate Oberlaender in the crimes at Lvov, the East zone government published a "brown paper" containing allegations against the West German cabinet member. In an effort to clear his name, Oberlaender asked the German section of the "Union of Resistance Fighters for a Unified Europe" (URPE), an association of World War II partisans and victims of Nazi oppression, to form an independent committee to investigate the charges against him. For a while, this proved to be an excellent propaganda counterattack. Then, newspapers in Germany and other West European countries began to scrutinize the circumstances surrounding the formation of this committee and the background of its secretary.

The members were former Danish foreign minister Ole Björn Kraft; Karl Richard van Staal, the chairman of the "Association of Former Political Prisoners in Holland"; Dr. Floor Peters, a Belgian professor of international law; Henri Michel, general secretary of the French Committee for Research of World War II; Norwegian Hanns Cappelen; and Swiss parliamentary deputy Dr. Kurt Schoch. The controversial secretary of the committee was a Dutchman named Joop Zwaart, alleged to have been a one-time leftist who has moved far, far to the right.

Within two months after this investigative committee had been formed, the majority of Dutch, Scandinavian, and German resistance organizations had disassociated themselves from the project, claiming the group had already come to the foregone conclusion that Oberlaender was innocent. Germany's Social Democratic party was exceptionally critical of the committee, going so far as to allege that the group had received between 80,000 and 100,000 DM for its work from the secret government funds of Dr. Hans Globke, state secretary to Adenauer and the chancellor's closest advisor. Two important members of the German section of URPE, *Bundestag* deputies Boehm and Frenzel, resigned their membership in the association in protest against the way the committee was handling the investigation. Most other resistance fighters and their organizations charged that the investigative committee was deliberately protecting Oberlaender and that the probe as such was a farce because the committee members had already agreed to exonerate Oberlaender from any responsibility for the Lvov massacres.

Finally, toward the end of February, 1960, three of the committee members resigned their posts and a month later, on March 23, the committee dissolved itself without ever reaching a decision as to Oberlaender's guilt or innocence. In the meantime, the honor council of the Christian Democratic Union started an investigation of its own, but also called a halt to its work when, on April 5, the SPD demanded the formation of a *Bundestag* subcommittee to conduct a full parliamentary probe into Oberlaender's political past.

Throughout the often tempestuous controversy that surrounded Oberlaender from the end of September, 1959, until spring, 1960, the refugee minister clung to his cabinet post as tenaciously as an oyster to its shell. Repeated public demands that he resign were completely ignored. Oberlaender insisted he would take no steps toward resignation unless Chancellor Adenauer fired him or asked him to step down. Oberlaender refused to resign and Chancellor Adenauer apparently refused to dismiss him. The subcommittee investigation loomed as unavoidable because the Social Democrats had enough votes to force its formation. In addition, it appeared that many CDU deputies would support the SPD demand for an open hearing of the charges against Oberlaender.

The issue was threatening to split the CDU. The CDU decided to compromise. On April 7, 1960, an agreement between the CDU and SPD *Bundestag* factions was reached. Oberlaender would take his annual leave, extending over May 1, his fifty-fifth birthday, when by rights he could apply for retirement from his ministerial post and assure himself a healthy 3,000-DM-a-month pension. He agreed to resign after that date. In exchange the SPD agreed to withdraw its demands for an investigative subcommittee. Thus, an April 7, after six years in the Adenauer government, it appeared as if Oberlaender would make an ungracious withdrawal from politics. But matters did not develop quite that smoothly, for two weeks later the refugee minister announced that he would not resign or retire until a parliamentary committee had investigated his case and cleared him of what he insisted were unfounded allegations. Finally on May 3, 1960, he submitted his resignation.

Oberlaender's basic claim to innocence has been the decision of a 1947 de-Nazification board which categorized him as "exonerated because he became a bitter opponent of the Nazi régime after he had realized and understood its full meaning and learned of its ultimate goals." Oberlaender maintains that his opposition to the mass liquidation of Poles and other East Europeans resulted in his being sentenced to death. He escaped execution only through the intervention of friends, he contends, then was excommunicated from the Nazi party and discharged from the *Wehrmacht* in 1943.

What factual basis there is to the Communist- and non-Communist-oriented allegations against Oberlaender may remain for a court of law to determine once his ministerial and parliamentary immunity has been lifted.[4] What is clear, however, to most observers and the majority of Germans is that even if none of the charges can be substantiated Oberlaender's record as an enthusiastic Nazi and ardent supporter of Hitler's Eastern Europe expansion policies make him dangerous ballast for the Federal Republic's reputation. Why Chancellor Adenauer persisted in protecting him for so many years escapes the perception of some of the most loyal supporters for the Christian Democratic Union. Guilty or innocent, they assert, a man such as Oberlaender had no place in a democratic government's cabinet.

It is an almost irrefutable axiom that politics make strange bedfellows. One of the strangest in Adenauer's political bed is Dr. Hans Globke, state secretary in the federal chancellory and "The Old Man's" closest advisor.

"So long as Chancellor Adenauer remains in office, I'll remain in mine," Globke once boasted. Those are bold words for any political figure, but not for Dr. Globke, one of the most mysterious, most suspected, and most powerful forces in the senior civil service. The bond between Globke and Adenauer has grown steadily in the past ten years. The chancellor has had to defend his advisor before the *Bundestag* on four separate occasions, each time replying: "In the long period that I have been active in government and public life, I have never met a civil servant with such objectivity and dedication as Herr Globke."

Globke's power is greater than that of any cabinet minister, for it is the extended power of Adenauer himself. According to the German constitution, the chancellor determines the policies of his government. But they are implemented in cooperation with his state secretary. Globke carries them out. All cabinet decisions are sent through the state secretary's office. Globke prepares the agenda for cabinet meetings. The ministers send their bill proposals, their personnel appointments, and their policy recommendations to and through him. These suggestions, usually accompanied by Globke's comments and opinions, constitute the basic source from which Konrad Adenauer's "personal decisions" emerge.

Globke's unusual role as the chancellor's "administrative assistant"

[4] His *Bundestag* term expires in 1961.

is buttressed by his sole administrative control of a multi-million-mark slush fund, and supervisory authority over the German government's principal propaganda instrument—the Press and Information Office. In addition, he exercises extensive jurisdiction over the two largest secret service and intelligence organizations in Western Germany: "The Bureau for the Protection of the Constitution," [5] and the counterintelligence group headed by ex-General Reinhard Gehlen.

Globke can rarely be seen at public functions. He seems to shy away from public appearances, so essential to the popularity rating of vote-hungry politicians. Globke requires no popularity. He needs no votes. He is dependent on the support of only one man: the chancellor. His real power did not become evident until September, 1955, when Adenauer took his assistant, then fifty-seven years old, to Moscow. Shortly after their return, the chancellor became ill. Globke literally assumed management of all German governmental affairs. He was responsible for all but the most vital policy-making decisions.

The extent of his influence over Adenauer, even in the determination of party and government policies, became apparent during the 1955 coalition crisis between the CDU and the Free Democratic Party (FDP). Thomas Dehler, one of the FDP chiefs, complained that Globke sat next to Adenauer during the coalition conferences and continually handed him slips of paper which formulated the German chancellor's opinions and decisions. The real attacks against this persuasive administrator, aimed at exposing his unsavory past, were launched when the FDP left the ranks of the Adenauer government.

Who is this right-hand man of Chancellor Adenauer and why is he so vulnerable to attack?

In 1936, as a senior civil servant in the Reich ministry of interior, Globke co-authored a legal interpretation and commentary on the notorious Nazi race laws. His associate on the project was SS Lieutenant General Wilhelm Stuckart. Despite this contribution to the Hitler régime's racial policy, Adenauer has consistently defended Globke against parliamentary criticism. The occupation forces, Adenauer maintains, gave Globke a clean bill of health and many Jews have thanked Globke personally for saving their lives. The parliamentary opposition countered bluntly that Himmler too had saved the lives

[5] The organization of which Dr. Otto John was director.

of many Jews. Then, during a 1953 *Bundestag* debate on Globke, Adenauer baffled the deputies by saying he thought it was time to end the witch hunt for Nazis in Germany.

Globke's personal history is relatively simple to trace. He studied law and in 1929 entered government work and became a well paid civil servant in the Prussian ministry of interior. After the Nazis took power, the Prussian government offices were amalgamated into the Reich administration, and Globke found himself working for the Reich ministry of interior.

Although he had no part in the drafting of the racial laws, at the 1935 Nazi party convention in Nuremberg, Globke voluntarily wrote the commentary and interpretation which, with five thousand copies on the first edition, netted him royalties of 3,000 Reichsmarks. He declined to revise the text for a second edition on grounds that he was too busy. This legal commentary is what has made Globke so controversial.

Globke has made many friends and acquired many defenders in addition to Adenauer. Five Jewish jurists declared that Globke's commentary and interpretation of the race laws were the most liberal of four such books published. Other Jews in Germany defended Globke for his support of restitution payments. Even some Social Democrats (Walter Menzel, for instance) said that Globke's book was a "virtual treasure chest of defense arguments against the race laws in the Nazi days."

But others, such as Dr. Adolf Arndt, also of the SPD, have been more critical. "It is as impossible to make the racial laws the subject of a legal treatise as it would be to write a treatise about the by-laws of an association of criminals or about the house rules of a bordello," Arndt contends.

Some of Globke's interpretations indeed were very strict. In respect to Paragraph 3 of the Law for the Protection of Blood,[6] Globke ruled that the paragraph is necessary to protect German housemaids from "racially impure sexual dangers." A Jewish household, according to Globke, is constituted when a Jewish man is head of the household or when a Jewish man is part of the household. According to

---

[6] Decreed that Jews are not permitted to employ female domestic servants of German citizenship under the age of forty-five.

Globke's interpretation, an Aryan family which permitted its Jewish subtenant to partake not only of room but board as well was not permitted to employ a maid younger than forty-five unless she, too, was of the Jewish faith.

Another of Globke's interpretations: "A full German-blooded grandparent who converted to the Jewish faith when he or she married a Jew counts, as far as the grandchildren are concerned, as a full Jewish grandparent. . . . The length of time that the German grandparent belonged to the Jewish faith is immaterial. Even a temporary membership suffices."

Globke was eulogized for his legal work by no less a figure than "Bloody" Roland Freisler, chief judge of the dreaded *Volksgerichtshof* (People's Court) in Berlin. Freisler termed Globke's book "exceptionally valuable . . . a must in every law library."

The laws on which Globke wrote commentaries were the "Reich Citizenship Law of September 15, 1935; the Law for the Protection of German Blood and German Honor, also of September 15, 1935; and the Law for Protection of the Hereditary Hygiene of the German People of October 18, 1935." Despite these "contributions," Globke has a book full of testimonials which clear him of Nazi taints. In 1951 Adenauer permitted a host of German newspaper editors to study them carefully. They indicate that Globke helped many Jews escape the interpretations he himself had made of the racial laws. He has been praised by many anti-Nazis for courageously and cleverly aiding many Jews and half-Jews. And although Globke's co-author SS General Stuckart,[7] recommended him, Globke's application for membership in the Nazi party was never accepted. When he claims today that he never swore allegiance to Hitler, he is technically correct.

Globke's role in the Nazi hierarchy will always remain a controversial one. Praised by some Germans, damned by others, he remains one of the great enigmas in German public life today.

After Germany's capitulation in 1945, Globke was interned by the Allies. As luck would have it, an old friend, Robert Kempner found him there. Kempner, once an official in the Prussian ministry of interior who had had his office near Globke's, had immigrated to the United States after Hitler came to power. He returned to Germany

---

[7] State secretary in the Reich interior ministry.

as a United States army officer and became one of the chief prosecutors at the Nuremberg War-Crimes tribunals. Kempner picked out Globke from the internment camp and used him as one of the star prosecution witnesses against the top Nazis.[8]

Later, Globke even helped to prosecute his own co-author, General Stuckart, who was sentenced to three years' imprisonment.

"Globke aided us immensely," says Kempner. "He was very valuable to us."

After the excitement of the war-crimes trials was over, Globke gained a foothold in postwar governmental life with a minor position in the Aachen municipal administration. From there he moved to a senior civil service job in the North Rhine-Westphalian state government, and finally entered the federal chancellory in 1950.

Now let us discuss the status of *Bundestag* deputies. Reports in American publications in the spring of 1960 stated that one out of every ten legislators in the East zone of Germany and that one out of every three in the Federal Republic had been members of the Nazi party. While the East zone figures come closer to reality, those for Western Germany seem wildly exaggerated. Were the figures accurate, one would have to conclude that more than half the members of Chancellor Adenauer's Christian Democratic Union had been Nazis, for it would seem inconceivable that any Social Democrats had been in the NSDAP.

Actually, only three present *Bundestag* deputies can be associated closely with the Hitler régime. One of them is Professor Pascual Jordan. In his book *Die Physik und die Geheimnisse des organischen Lebens (Physics and the Secrets of Organic Life)*, written during the Hitler régime, Jordan said that World War II, no matter how it ended, would have one clear-cut result: the demise of the parliamentary-democratic way of thought. "There are no serious differences of opinion about that," wrote Jordan. "The only decision that remains to be made in the face of this fact is whether one accepts it reluctantly or joyously. . . ."

As the methods of government become unified all over the world, Jordan explained, only one basic difference remains: "Not every na-

[8] On the witness stand Globke admitted that he had been aware that Jews were being exterminated systematically.

tion is endowed with a man [Hitler] who has the energy of a volcano."
Professor Jordan is a *Bundestag* deputy from Lower Saxony.

A fellow legislator, representing the Christian Social Union (CSU)
from Bavaria, is Dr. Fritz Kempfler, alleged to have been an active
member of the NSDAP from 1932. In 1938 he was recommended for
the post of lord mayor of Bayreuth. He rose to the rank of SS colonel
and was interned for three years following Germany's surrender.

Dr. Helmut Schranz, former Nazi mayor of Offenbach, Hesse, is
also a deputy in the *Bundestag.*

The number of former Nazis in the federal parliament has dwindled
steadily. Many of them were members of the smaller splinter parties
which have been eased out of *Bundestag* seats during the two elections
since 1949 because of Germany's electoral laws, under which a party
must score at least 5 per cent of the total vote before it can be represented. Thus, where once there were ten political parties in the lower
house, today there are only four. And of these, only the Social Democrats and the Christian Democrats are influential, while the Free
Democratic party (FDP) is too insignificant to alter the governmental
course and the *Deutsche Partei* (DP), originally a Lower-Saxony
conservative party, has joined the CDU in the governmental coalition.
Out of a total of 497 seats, the DP is represented with 17, the FDP
with 41, the SPD with 169, and the CDU/CSU with 270.[9]

Although there are relatively few former Nazis remaining in the
German parliament, there was a time when this problem appeared
much more acute. One of the most controversial and bitterly attacked
by Dr. Otto John during his East Berlin press conference in 1954 was
Hasso von Manteuffel, an ex-general and one-time commander of
Hitler's 7th Armored Division on the Russian front. Manteuffel served
as an FDP deputy in the *Bundestag,* later quitting the party to join
the conservative DP. He was DP chairman for North Rhine-West-
phalia.

Although he had frequently been criticized for his role in the
Third Reich, accusations against Manteuffel were not investigated
extensively until 1959. In August of that year he was charged with
manslaughter for ordering the execution of one of his subordinates.
The specifications, drafted by the Duesseldorf district attorney, cen-

---

[9] The CSU is the Bavarian wing of the CDU.

tered around the trial of two unidentified German soldiers who had failed to fire at a Russian reconnaissance patrol which had penetrated their lines and captured a German corporal. The soldiers were court-martialed. One was acquitted, the other convicted for failure to carry out orders and sentenced to two years' hard labor. Manteuffel, as convening authority of the court, reviewed the trial and upheld the one acquittal. However, he changed the two-year term for the other soldier to the death penalty. The man was executed on the spot, without further trial or a rehearing. Although there were numerous witnesses who could reconstruct the case, no one could remember the name of the executed trooper.

Manteuffel defended the arbitrary execution, asserting he had been authorized to take such drastic steps by "Fuehrer Order No. 7" which prescribed the maximum penalty, without trial, for any man or officer guilty of cowardly retreat before the enemy. Discipline in his division, he explained, had deteriorated to the point where "I was compelled to set an example." The Duesseldorf court sentenced Manteuffel to eighteen months in prison. Although he filed an immediate appeal, it was rejected and the ex-general, once a star performer for the *Bunestag*'s conservative factions, has gone to prison. Manteuffel himself lambasted the court's verdict as an act of "vindictive justice in the Fourth Reich." Most liberal Germans disagreed with him, feeling, instead, that the sentence had been unusually mild.

The German Metal Workers' Union criticized some of the trial procedures in an article in its weekly publication *Metall*, objecting primarily to the fact that a man such as Manteuffel could have been permitted to take on an active and important role in postwar German political life. The union objected strenuously to the fact that the public prosecutor had greeted Manteuffel at the start of the trial with a hard handshake and that a former *Wehrmacht* judge advocate, himself suspected of war crimes, now a public official in Berlin, had been called to the proceedings as an expert witness.

Accounting for leeway in the actual figures and in the roles they played, some two hundred judges and prosecutors in postwar German courts are also former Nazis. The majority of them were associated with either the notorious *Volksgerichtshof* (People's Court) in Berlin or the so-called "special courts" which served the cause of

Hitler justice in Germany proper and in the occupied countries. The burning question which has plagued German officialdom since December, 1959, is how many of these jurists participated in passing out unwarranted death sentences.

The *Volksgerichtshof* and the "special courts" meted out forty-five thousand death penalties between 1933 and 1945. Most of them were for transgressions of the demented conceptions of law and order which characterized the Hitler régime. Capital punishment was prescribed for "resisting the war effort by criticizing the régime," "failure to report escaped war prisoners," "refusing to show Nazi officials legal identification cards," "assaulting a customs police dog," and "delivering laundry to a relative wanted by the Gestapo."

These courts were not legal bodies in the ordinary sense of the word. Dr. Max Guede, attorney general for the Federal Republic, has said that the *Volksgerichtshof* was "a political instrument from its inception." [10] "It was created as a political tool and that is the function it fulfilled," said Guede. "Basically, only the judges sympathetic to the régime sat on its benches, together with high-ranking party, SA, and SS functionaries (as lay jurors). Who could expect justice from such a court?"

Guede explained that an official of the People's Court once had confided to him that the court's purpose was not to dispense justice but to destroy the opponents of the Nazi régime. But, the chief West German prosecutor said, it would be unfair not to differentiate between the *Volksgerichtshof* and the special courts, which were initiated as purely auxiliary bodies to normal courts and did not assume their political character until some time had passed and the war approached its climax.

More than a thousand German prosecutors and justices were assigned to these courts and, according to Guede, the majority, all of them civil servants just as German judicial officials today are civil servants, were ordered to sit in on the special court benches or prosecute defendants before them. Although it would have been impossible for a judge or district attorney to decline an appointment to a special court, Guede explained, there would have been ways and means of curtailing the period of appointment. Guede, for example, told the

[10] Guede made this and most of the following comments during a TV interview over the South German radio network in January, 1960.

TV audience that he had given considerable thought to the problem during the Third Reich and had decided that if he were assigned to a special Nazi court he would pass judgments that would assure his immediate removal.

The Nazi judges had far more leeway and autonomy on these extraordinary courts than is generally believed today, Guede said. "Although more and more laws were being phrased so as to give the judge no leeway and calling for only one penalty, execution, many of the statutes still provided escape clauses which would have permitted a milder sentence. Many of the death sentences were unwarranted even in the terms of the law in those times," Guede commented. The attorney general pointed out that he knew of no cases where jurists or prosecutors had suffered death or injury in any form for passing mild sentences in these courts. One judge was retired prematurely, but there was no gamble with life, limb, or property involved.

These judges and prosecutors, active in German courts today, have been the subject of ceaseless debate within the Federal Republic and objects of an avalanche of criticism from abroad. In Guede's opinion, the decisive question is whether the judges had a part in unjustifiable death sentences, for many death sentences passed by the special courts were for crimes of violence which, until 1949, had always been subject to capital punishment in Germany.

Neither is it a logical consequence that a special court or *Volksgerichtshof* official, on the bench in postwar Germany, is of necessity unfit for the legal machinery of a democratic state. Some have been reassigned to civil courts, others have become prominent for their outspoken anti-Nazi beliefs and policies since the war. A classic example is that of Bavarian district judge Adolf Paulus who presided over the concentration camp trial of Martin Sommer. Paulus has been accused of unusual harshness during the Third Reich for rejecting the clemency appeal of a Ukrainian slave laborer, on trial for murder because he had accidentally killed his German master. The Ukrainian was executed. Yet Paulus' rulings and verdict in the Sommer case, contrary to what some observers had feared beforehand, were above reproach.

A substantial majority of the judges and prosecutors in the West German judiciary were reinstated in their posts by the Allied occupation authorities following de-Nazification. Others have returned to the bench through provisions of the "131 Law." Despite generally careful scrutiny of their backgrounds, however, an appalling number of Nazi judges are in office again. Although there had been sporadic attempts to retire or impeach them in various isolated areas, no concerted moves in that direction were undertaken until December, 1959, when the East Zone government launched a sensational propaganda campaign against the Federal Republic's judiciary. Under the slogan, "Yesterday Hitler's Blood Judges—Today Bonn's Judicial Elite," East Zone agencies released voluminous documentation which implicated dozens of West German legal officials in Nazi crimes and verdicts.

The spontaneous reaction was to label this Soviet zone material as a "pack of lies" or "blatant propaganda designed to smear the Federal Republic's reputation in the Western world." Not until shortly before Christmas, 1959, did officials make a complete about-face in their attitude toward this East zone documentation. Chiefly responsible for the sudden reversal was a young Berlin student, Reinhard Strecker, who apparently had gone to East Berlin where authorities supplied him with photostats and documentation to support their allegations. Strecker, a member of the West German Socialist Students' League (SDS),[11] took the documents to Karlsruhe, seat of the German supreme court, rented an exhibit room in a city-owned hall, and put the material on public display, embellished with the title: "Unatoned Nazi Justice."

Despite the general apathy which the Karlsruhe citizens displayed toward Strecker's exhibit, word of this extraordinary collection of court documents spread through town and it was not long before young Strecker was invited over to Attorney General Guede's office. Max Guede took a close look at the collection of death sentences and concluded that there was little reason to doubt the authenticity of the photostats.

The federal attorney general's stamp of approval had an immediate effect on the attitude of Baden-Wuerttemberg's Justice Minister Wolfgang Haussmann. He conceded that, on the basis of the documents

[11] Affiliated with the Social Democratic party (SPD) until July 20, 1960.

which Strecker exhibited in Karlsruhe, the circle of judicial officials involved in improper Nazi verdicts and judgments "appears to have expanded." The result was that an independent commission of experts was appointed by the judiciary committee of the Baden-Wuerttemberg state legislature. This commission will study the allegations and take action against judges and district attorneys "where it is warranted." Two judges and a professor of jurisprudence were appointed to the commission and Stuttgart district attorney Erich Nellmann is helping them in their probe.

On the basis of the East German material, some sixty-six jurists out of Baden-Wuerttemberg's total judicial staff of nearly fifteen hundred may be involved. Of the sixty-six, four practiced as prosecutors before the *Volksgerichtshof*, sixty-two were assigned to special courts; an additional twenty-three reportedly had been military judge advocates. However, only the Baden-Wuerttemberg minister and Stuttgart district attorney Nellmann appeared interested in pursuing the allegations and investigating them more closely.

Strecker, facing reticence on the part of other officials to take him seriously, boldly dropped the responsibility for action right in the laps of responsible judicial authorities: he filed manslaughter charges against forty-three of the judges and prosecutors, located all over West Germany. Soviet zone officials took advantage of Strecker's unilateral action and announced that East German archives would make additional material available on request to any law enforcement agency in the Federal Republic. Then other satellite countries which had been under Nazi occupation joined the propaganda chorus. The Polish and Czechoslovakian ministries of justice suggested that West German district attorneys contact their counterparts in Poland and Czechoslovakia for further documentation.

For the most part, German agencies remained aloof from the Communist offers, and eventually Strecker himself was accused of being an "Eastern provocateur." Several leading newspapers and magazines came to Strecker's aid, vouching for his integrity while pleading for a more realistic approach to the problem of the Communist documents. "The question is when and if law enforcement agencies in the Federal Republic will find it appropriate to look at Eastern, but nevertheless authentic, material," jibed the news magazine *Der Spie-*

gel.[12] "Federal Attorney Guede answered the question in a telephone interview, saying: 'All in all, I would say that it is certainly more desirable to have the material checked, regardless of where it may be located, by really competent people, not just students.' "

"Granted, it is a somewhat unusual situation for a democracy to obtain help from representatives of a totalitarian state in ridding itself of the handymen of yesterday's dictatorship," editorialized the liberal *Frankfurter Rundschau.*[13] But if documents proving possible guilt are available, one has to investigate them and come to a decision, regardless of where the accusations originated.

"Without a doubt, it is not concern about the judicial purity of our West German state which has provoked [Roland] Freisler's imitator [Dr. Ernst] Melsheimer [14] to throw open his archives for inspection by our ministers of justice. Certainly every jurist we will impeach will be earmarked for the East German propaganda mill. What of it? The ulterior motives behind the Soviet zone's offer of help should not become a hindrance to action. When confidence in our judicial system is at stake one should not become finicky about the gory titles on the [Soviet zone's] brochures."

And *Revue,*[15] one of Germany's mass circulation weekly illustrated magazines, even sent a reporter-photographer along with Strecker to inspect judicial documentation in Prague. The magazine reported after the trip that most of the material in the Czechoslovakian archives appeared to be quite genuine. In a sensational story, *Revue* named some of the judges and prosecutors involved in the accusations and challenged them to prove their innocence.

Federal Justice Minister Fritz Schaeffer, speaking at a press conference following the April 8, 1960, conference of state ministers of justice, declared that the initiative on the part of the Eastern bloc countries in compiling such lists was designed to defame Germany's reputation at the then forthcoming summit conference.

The case of Judge Paulus in the Sommer concentration camp trial indicated clearly that association with Nazi courts does not necessarily

[12] *Der Spiegel,* February 17, 1960.
[13] *Frankfurter Rundschau,* February 16, 1960.
[14] Attorney general for the German Democratic Republic.
[15] *Revue* of March 12, 1960 (circulation 1,000,000).

imply prejudicial judgment on the part of a jurist. On the other hand, there are many judges and prosecutors on the bench who were Nazis in spirit while never having been in any way implicated with the *Volksgerichtshof* or the special courts. How in postwar Germany such judicial officials are still able to twist paragraphs of the criminal code to suit their own ends was demonstrated in Hamburg, West Germany's largest city, and one of the electoral strongholds of the Socialists.

In the center of the controversy was a Hamburg state judge, Dr. Enno Budde, who had refused to initiate a trial against two men accused of slander and subversion in connection with an anti-Semitic tract they had published and mailed to all federal and state parliamentary deputies in Germany. The pamphlet, entitled, *Wieviel Welt (Geld) Kriege Müssen die Völker noch Verlieren?* ("How Many World [Money] Wars Must the People of the Earth Still Lose?"), had been written by Friedrich Nieland, a sixty-two-year-old lumber dealer, and published by Adolf Heimberg, a seventy-seven-year-old printer.

The tract contained such fantastic nonsense as the "fact" that "international Jewry" itself had been responsible for the extermination of 6 million Jews during the Nazi régime. Only the Jews could have been so ruthless, Nieland said. In reality, he contended, the Jews rule the entire world and even Hitler had been controlled and guided by world Jewry. He analyzed the words *Nationalsozialist* (National Socialist) and *Nationalsozialismus* (National Socialism) and maintained that in the secret code of international Jewry, they actually meant "O Zion a la Stalin" and "Zion ist a la Mussolini." Therefore, he asserted, racial laws such as those enacted at the 1935 Nazi party convention in Nuremberg should be implemented to prevent Jews from acquiring positions of importance or responsibility in business or government.

Most of these ideas had originally been incorporated in a twenty-six-page letter which Nieland sent to Federal Interior Minister Gerhard Schroeder on September 16, 1956. When Schroeder ignored the treatise, Nieland printed the tract. It was mailed to every *Bundestag* deputy, to each federal and all the state ministers, and to each representative in all the state legislatures. The majority of parliamentarians threw the tract into the wastebaskets. Only two of the recipients initiated any action against the Hamburg lumber dealer. Maxim Kurauer, SPD deputy in the Rhineland-Palatinate state assembly, filed a criminal complaint against Nieland. On April 4, 1957, Karl Wittrock, SPD *Bundestag* member, made an official inquiry in which he asked what the ministry was doing about the pamphlet. Schroeder replied that extra copies of the tract had been confiscated and an investigation started.

In December, 1957, the Hamburg district attorney filed charges. As is customary under German law, the prosecutor turned over all his evidence to the district court, requesting that Nieland and Heimberg be brought to trial. Because it was considered a political offense, Judge Dr. Enno Budde, who specialized in such matters, was assigned to the case. Budde studied the evidence [16] and decided to have Nieland tested for his sanity and mental competence.

In January, 1958, a psychiatrist, after extensive interviews and studies, pronounced Nieland completely sane. In the following months Judge Budde questioned Nieland in preparation for the trial. When the lumber dealer realized that his booklet might get him into real trouble, he told the judge that he hadn't meant Jews in general, not the Jewish people, but just an indefinable "international Jewry." Budde ruled that such "international Jewry" does not exist and therefore dismissed the charges against Nieland. The case never went to trial. It was settled in the judge's chambers.

Budde's dismissal opinion reads like the brief of a well paid defense attorney. ". . . The writing involved indicates on pages two, six, ten, eighteen, twenty-nine, thirty-four, and thirty-five, that there is a difference between Jews in general and the group mentioned," Judge Budde explained. "Although the comments on page thirty-two could be interpreted to mean all Jews, taken in context, however, they indicate that there is a difference between the Jewish people as such and 'international Jewry.' . . ."

On November 27, 1958, a day after the dismissal ruling, Ernst Buchholz, the Hamburg attorney general, filed an appeal with the

[16] Customary in German jurisprudence, where judges are not required to be ignorant of the facts in a case beforehand. On the contrary, they conduct the trial, much as the prosecutor in Anglo-Saxon law, have all testimony before them, and vote on verdict and sentence.

state supreme court.[17] Buchholz also added a new charge against Nieland and Heimberg in his appeal brief.

"Yes, it is unusual for an attorney general to file an additional complaint," Buchholz told newsmen, "but the matter was so important to me and I was distressed by Budde's dismissal of the charges. I consider it untenable that the publishers of such a violent hate sheet should go unprosecuted."

Buchholz' intervention, however, achieved nothing. The high state court upheld Budde. Not only that, the supreme court's decision, announced on January 6, 1959, made it legally impossible to take any further action against Nieland or Heimberg. Until then the Nieland case had passed almost unnoticed. But Hamburg mayor Max Brauer (SPD) traveled to Bonn to speak with Chancellor Adenauer, in the hope that some means of prosecution might remain in federal courts. The story broke. After the initial headlines had been digested, most newspapers started delving into Judge Enno Budde's background. The first fact onto which most researchers stumbled was that Judge Budde had been involved in another major legal controversy only a few years previously when he sentenced seven young men, accused of beating up a *Bundeswehr* soldier,[18] to terms ranging up to three years in prison.

Just why Dr. Budde had taken such a protective attitude toward an anti-Semitic pamphleteer but had ruled so harshly against that group of anti-rearmament demonstrators is explained more clearly perhaps by his political past. The judge's first contact with the law was recorded in 1925, when Herr Budde was only twenty-four years old. On that occasion, he sat on the other side of the judicial bench, defending himself against a charge that he had violated a political law which protected the Weimar Republic from slander and revolution. A junior judge during the Third Reich, Enno Budde gave moral support to the Nazi régime by writing spare-time essays which eulogized the brownshirts. Although his anti-Semitism, on the face of

[17] Hamburg (like Bremen) is not only a municipality, but one of the ten states in the German Federal Republic. The other eight are Bavaria, Baden-Wuerttemberg, Rhineland Palatinate, the Saar, Hesse, Lower Saxony, North Rhine Westphalia, and Schleswig-Holstein. West Berlin is not a legal member of the federation. Bremen and Hamburg trace their status as states to the Hanseatic period when they were free cities.

[18] See page 65.

his essays, is not as rabid as lumber dealer Nieland's, it no doubt was effective.

His first essay, entitled, "Maintenance of Race and Property in Lower Saxony," was published in 1935. It read in part:

Racial purity and property faced a new danger in Germany toward the beginning of the nineteenth century because of the emancipation of the Jews and the peasants. The [Hanoverian] Guelphs met these two perils with unusual legislation, based on the eternal ideal of racial purity. The Hanoverian Jewish Law restricted the Jews even more than our present Aryan laws. . . .

His essay explained how Lower Saxony had struggled alone through the years to maintain the purity of blood and landed property until, in 1933, the Nazi régime had come to the state's aid.

From the days of Arminius the Cheruscian,[19] through the Guelphs right up to National Socialism, Lower Saxony has been the keeper of the great seal and defender of German ways, German blood, German land, German justice, and German customs against the attacks of foreign races, Budde wrote. Who knows how Germanicism would have fared had it not been for these [Lower Saxon] leaders? Lower Saxony—Germany—*Heil!*

In 1936 he published another essay:

Race and blood . . . have been entrusted to us . . . by God. They are our gift of greatness from God. We can thank Adolf Hitler for making us aware of this.

Budde's postwar history as a district court judge,[20] presiding over most of the political cases in Hamburg, reflects accurately the ideas he expressed in his Third Reich essays. In 1950 he presided over the trial of two former *Wehrmacht* officers who, during the war, had denounced another officer for making anti-Nazi remarks. The denunciation resulted in the officer's internment at a concentration

[19] Arminius was chief of the Cherusci tribe that inhabited what is now part of Hanover and Brunswick (Lower Saxony). He became a hero for his defeat of Augustus Caesar's legions in the Teutoburg Forest A.D. 9.

[20] He was reinstated by the British.

camp. To everyone's astonishment, Budde acquitted the two informers but chastised their victim, asking him: "Why did you even file a complaint against your two comrades? That wasn't very charitable or Christian."

In October, 1951, Budde convicted a former Gestapo agent charged with eight counts of mistreating prisoners during his Nazi career. He sentenced the man to two years in jail, but deducted fifteen months pretrial confinement from the term and ordered the Gestapo man released on parole for the remaining nine months.

In 1956 and 1957, when seven young men, aged twenty to twenty-two, stood before him accused of assaulting a soldier of the *Bundeswehr*, Budde convicted the seven of assault and battery. Most of them had never been in trouble before, but the prison terms ranged up to three years. However, a concentration camp guard, accused of knocking a former prisoner's teeth out, was freed by Budde.

In another concentration camp case, when Budde had no choice but to find the defendant guilty, he commented to the complainant: "Listen, you were a reserve officer. The defendant was a reserve officer, and I was a reserve officer. Certainly there must have been a way of settling this matter other than with a criminal complaint."

On September 16, 1952, Budde presided over the trial of a Hamburg policeman accused of disrespect toward the West German national colors. The policeman had pointed to the flag, flying at half-mast for the death of then Federal President Theodor Heuss's wife, and called it "black-red-mustard" and a "dirty rag." [21] Budde acquitted the policeman, and in his written explanation for the verdict said, among other things: " 'Black-red-mustard.' If the defendant had uttered only these words, then perhaps there would be a violation of the criminal code. But the defendant's statements have to be taken in context. By adding the words, 'Dirty and torn, the . . . rag ought to be washed,' it appears the defendant was referring to that particular flag which was very dirty and badly torn."

The judge's record, from 1950 until 1959, was one of consistent pro-Nazi rulings. Yet even in predominantly Social Democratic Ham-

[21] The black-red-gold colors of postwar Germany are as unpopular with rightists as they were during the Weimar Republic. The policeman's comments, it was believed, had been made out of affinity for the black-red-white flag of Imperial and Hitler Germany.

burg no one had taken action against Budde until the legal calamity of the dismissal ruling. Generally, newspapers were responsible for digging into the judge's past. When the publicity barrage became too apparent, Budde requested a transfer from the criminal to the civil chamber.

Although most high-ranking officers, many junior officers, and enlisted men in the *Bundeswehr* had been carefully screened for their Third Reich activities before being permitted to reenlist, the federal government has admitted the fact that some ex-Nazis have gained a foothold in the new army. The government concedes that four hundred to five hundred former SS men are in uniform, though insisting adamantly that none of them were concentration camp guards.

Most of the senior officers, especially those in the grade of colonel or above, have no Nazi past to hide. There are, however, civilian advisors to the *Bundeswehr* and it has been charged frequently that among them there are numerous ex-Nazis who exert as much influence on the *Bundeswehr's* policies and attitudes as do the uniformed soldiers.

One such advisor who has been under fire steadily is ex-Field Marshal Erich von Manstein. Manstein was convicted of war crimes and sentenced to eighteen years in prison for having directed the mass extermination of Jews, ordering the destruction of Polish villages, and participating in several massacres. Chief prosecution witness against him was Dr. Otto John. Documentation at the British war-crimes tribunal implicated Manstein in the hanging, gassing, and drowning of large numbers of Jews and Russians, the deportation of Russian slave laborers, and the dynamiting of Polish villages and synagogues.

Although German officers have come to his defense, saying he was a member of the anti-Hitler resistance movement, there is no record of his participation in any opposition activities. Certainly, if Manstein had taken even a secret part in the plot against Hitler, Dr. John would have had some knowledge of his role and then would have abstained from the British prosecution effort. None of the detailed reference works concerning the resistance movement mentions him as one of the rebels.

Documents from his headquarters which appeared as evidence

against him at the war-crimes trial indicate, however, that Manstein was an ardent supporter of Hitler's racial theories. One order to his subordinates spoke of the "Jewish-Bolshevist system which must be destroyed, once and for all. It must never again infiltrate our European sphere. Therefore, the German soldier is not only charged with destroying the military might of this system, but must also act as an agent of the idea of racial supremacy. He must avenge all atrocities perpetrated upon him and the German people. The soldier must understand and appreciate the necessity for strong action against Judaism which is, in fact, the spiritual support for the Bolshevist terror. It is important for the soldier to realize this so he can 'nip in the bud' all uprisings which, generally, are instigated by the Jews."

Former National Socialists have scored their greatest political triumphs in local and state elections. It is in this area that the extreme right-wing postwar parties have demonstrated their greatest strength, and it is here that "unrehabilitated" Nazis have successfully infiltrated the democratic parties and won seats in state legislatures and on municipal councils.

While a former Nazi in the *Bundestag* is likely to draw fast fire from the opposition parties, he could pass reasonably unnoticed for many years in the state assemblies and city legislatures. Thus, ex- and neo-Nazis have come to power through such political parties as the Bloc of Expellees and Victims of Injustice (BHE), the German Reich party, the Socialist Reich party, and other extremist organizations.

For example, Gustav Hacker, Hesse's minister of agriculture, a member of the BHE fraction in the Hessian *Landtag*, has been accused of close association with the Konrad Henlein Fascists in the Sudetenland and membership in the NSDAP. Hacker was a member of the Sudeten German party and deputy in the Czechoslovakian national parliament. He was a captain in the *Wehrmacht* and after Germany's capitulation, was sentenced to four years in prison by a Czechoslovakian people's court.

Dr. Walter Stain, Bavarian minister of labor, has also been accused of Henlein and Nazi activities in the Sudetenland.

There is Hans Schikora, former Socialist Reich party functionary, now German Reich party deputy in the Rhineland Palatinate.

A former German Reich party member, later allied with the FDP (Free Democratic party), Leonhard Schlueter, who reportedly once said, "National socialism is the healthiest movement there has been in Germany since 1900," served for a time as minister of culture and education in Lower Saxony.

Waldemar Kraft, former SS captain, founding father of the BHE, served as deputy minister president (lieutenant governor) in Schleswig-Holstein.

But the most incredible political victory was scored on September 28, 1958, by Heinz Reinefarth, a former SS lieutenant general, mayor of Westerland, and defendant against serious war-crimes charges. Reinefarth became a candidate for the Schleswig-Holstein legislature on the BHE ticket. When his candidacy was announced in the summer of 1958, political opponents accused him of atrocities committed during the 1944 Warsaw rebellion. An investigation into his past was launched, and state officials were faced with the ironic paradox that Reinefarth would probably escape prosecution if he were elected to the state legislature. He would then be protected by the immunity law for representatives. Some unusual political situations have arisen in Germany, but this was the first time that a man under investigation for war crimes was at the same time a candidate. As soon as he was elected and took office Reinefarth succumbed to public pressure, asked the legislature to lift his immunity, and requested a leave of absence from his post as mayor of Westerland.

Most of the allegations against Reinefarth, tagged as the "Henchman of Warsaw," by Polish officials, stemmed from Dr. Hans Thieme, professor of law at Freiburg University. During the war, Thieme had been the adjutant of a *Wehrmacht* artillery unit stationed in Warsaw. In letters to the editors of several German papers, Thieme related that he, his commanding officer, and SS General Reinefarth had been watching a column of Poles being driven out of Warsaw by the Germans. "It was a tragic picture which made tears come to our eyes. But Reinefarth turned to my commanding officer and said, 'See, that is our greatest problem. We don't have enough ammunition to take care of them all.'"

Reinefarth, in his election campaign, ridiculed Thieme, saying: "This professor seems to have a compulsion to write letters to newspapers. The professors whose lectures I attended when I was in college didn't have compulsions like that. They were steeped in scientific work. Even if I did say that we couldn't take care of all of those people because we didn't have enough ammunition, what about it?" Reinefarth asked his constituents. "That wasn't violating any law, was it? It may have been nasty and shameful, but we didn't take care of them, after all. That's what counts. Not even this professor can prove that I killed anyone unlawfully."

Photostats of documents which implicated Reinefarth in mass murders were sent to the district attorneys in Hamburg, Hanover, and Karlsruhe by an East Zone documentary film producer. Reinefarth called them forgeries. Nevertheless, it has been documented that forty thousand armed Polish rebels and two hundred thousand Warsaw civilians were killed between August 1 and October 2, 1944. After this bloody suppression of the Warsaw rebellion, Reinefarth was awarded an oakleaf cluster to add to his *Ritterkreuz*.

The Flensburg district attorney closed the investigation for lack of evidence, because Reinefarth allegedly had entered the beleaguered city too late to participate in any crimes against humanity. By the time his battle group had reached Warsaw with orders from Heinrich Himmler to "drown the rebellion in a sea of blood," the prosecutor ruled the worst of the massacres had already ended. Despite violent protests from opposition parties, Reinefarth remained in office.

The problem of former Nazis in government becomes most apparent on the state and local civil service level, where thousands of former Nazi party members have been reinstated in their pre-1945 positions. Many of them, as Chancellor Adenauer has emphasized, were only nominal Nazis, those who served Hitler under pressure. Others, however, were enthusiastic volunteers in support of the régime and have regained their positions through false pretenses or by means of illegal or irresponsible interpretations of the "131 Law."

The most incredible case involves two civil servants in the Hessian restitution and reparations bureau, the office responsible for compensation payments to Jews and other victims of the Nazi régime. The two were accused of making anti-Semitic remarks and singing anti-Jewish songs in their office during a birthday party. Investigations by Hessian officials turned up that one of the civil servants had a background of "right-radical associations" and had displayed rightist sentiments numerous times. A probe of some of the restitution decisions they had made revealed that the two employees had done more to sabotage the program than to help it. In one case, for example, a former Frankfurt textile dealer had returned to Germany after a twenty-five-years' exile in Israel. He resettled in his native city and applied for the 6,000 DM "immediate aid" to which returnees and victims of Nazi persecution are entitled. The application was rejected in the Hessian restitution office on grounds that the returnee's German "was too broken and in the twenty-five years of his exile he had failed to take pride in his Germanic origin."

Another man, imprisoned because he had helped a Jewish woman in 1941, was denied a restitution payment for the time he spent in prison because "his own actions had resulted in his internment."

When the two officials were unable to reject claims outright, they tied them up in so much red tape that applicants were forced to wait for years for the first payments. Although Hessian authorities did not prosecute the two, they were transferred from the restitution and reparations office to a "less sensitive post."

Chapter IX

Business as Usual

In his final report to the State Department, Mr. John McCloy, the United States High Commissioner for Germany, wrote that ". . . one of the major Allied objectives for the decartelization and deconcentration program is . . . based upon the conviction that the legitimate demands of the German people for a wider diffusion of economic opportunity and for an expanding standard of living can be peacefully satisfied only in an economy in which competition rather than restraint of trade is the rule." [1]

"The establishment of a genuinely competitive economy," the report went on to say, "has also been regarded as essential to prevent the re-creation of the economic tensions which in the past influenced significantly the acceptance of a program for economic and military aggression."

The Allied decartelization program is based on military government laws which took effect in 1947. These prohibited price-fixing and other restraint of trade agreements and outlawed many domestic and international cartels in existence at the time. A variety of high commission laws provided the basis for deconcentration of various

[1] Report on Germany, September 21, 1949–July 31, 1952, Office of the High Commissioner for Germany.

157

industries, in particular steel and coal, film, banking, and chemicals. Thus, for example, Allied High Commission Law No. 27, enacted in May, 1950, prescribed the deconcentration of steel production of twelve closely integrated companies into twenty-four new, and four of the smallest of the old ones for a total of twenty-eight steel firms.

The sprawling I. G. Farben chemical complex, which accounted for 40 per cent of the world's chemical products before the war, has been decentralized into several smaller firms, sufficient, according to the high commissioner's report, to be "consistent with our program for the development of a competitive private economy in Germany. . . ." But despite these Allied efforts, most of the big industrialists have made a grand-scale recovery. Name them. They are virtually all back at the throttle today. Every industrialist who went before a war-crimes court, every firm that contributed measurably to the Hitler war effort, and nearly every concern ordered decentralized has returned or is on the threshold of economy power.

Krupp, Flick, Thyssen, Heinckel, Messerschmitt, I. G. Farben, Mannesmann, Kloeckner-Humboldt-Deutz, Stinnes, Robert Bosch, Siemens, Dresdner Bank, and even the former Reich-owned Ufa motion picture combine are names which today are closely linked with the German economic miracle. While some of them, such as Krupp, are flamboyant about their comeback—in November, 1958, for example, the Krupp concern erected a ten-foot-high neon sign on the banks of the Nile—others, such as the conservative, quiet trader Friedrich Flick, are reticent about any publicity. There are a few, such as Willy Messerschmidt, who have failed at a convincing resurrection.

Even the ominous I. G. Farben trust, while still legally limited to the decentralization agreements, is beginning to sing in cartel key once more. In June, 1958, for example, The New York Times reported that "the four companies carved out of the old I. G. Farben chemical empire (Farbwerke Hoechst AG, Badische Anilin und Sodafabrik AG, Farbenfabriken Bayer AG, and Casella Farbwerke Mainkur AG) have completed their first joint financing venture—the construction of a . . . synthetic rubber plant in the Ruhr. There has been no official disapproval of the financing venture nor is any West German official ready to say that it indicates the beginning of the reconstruction of the old empire. The cartel office, formed to enforce West Germany's new anticartel laws, refused to comment. . . ." [2]

Mannesmann AG, one of the four major coal-steel combines of prewar days, announced a reorganization which, according to the London *Financial Times*,[3] will undo the deconcentration decreed by the Allies. "Its six main subsidiaries, four of them wholly owned, are to be merged in the present holding company, thus reestablishing the prewar concern," the *Financial Times* said. The subsidiaries involved were Mannesmann Huettenwerke (steel); Mannesmann Roehrenwerke, a tube manufacturing plant; an iron ore company; Mannesmann Rohstoffwerke; Essener Steinkohlenbergwerke, and another steel plant, the Hanschewerke.

Similar reconcentrations have appeared in other fields, and although anticartel laws exist, many large cartels are re-forming or at least the feelers toward mergers are being stretched out. On the other hand, many of the divestment, deconcentration, and decartelization programs, ordered by the Allied High Commission and agreed upon by German representatives during the drafting of the Bonn Conventions, have not been carried out.

Friedrich Flick, one of the industrial war criminals, followed to the letter the United States Nuremberg tribunal's divestment order. But today he is again one of the most influential financial barons in Germany. A shy, reticent seventy-seven-year-old, he pulls the strings of his gigantic empire without any public show.

He started building his enormous fortune in the First World War, and by the end of World War II, when the Allies branded him a war criminal, Flick owned vast coal mine and steel properties. In addition to imprisonment for crimes against humanity and the peace, Flick, as well as other German industrialists, was ordered to sell and decentralize his holdings. Herr Flick sold out. In turn, he received 250 million DM in cash. He started to buy stocks and has been buying so steadily ever since that today he exercises dominant control over many industries. A tally of his holdings reads like a listing of German industry. According to the "Bulletin on German Questions,"

[2] *The New York Times*, October 6, 1958.
[3] London *Financial Times*, October 29, 1958.

in 1958 [4] he owned 88 per cent of the stock in the Auto Union plants at Ingolstadt and Duesseldorf, makers of DKW passenger cars and light trucks and motorcycles as well as manufacturers of the German-type jeep with which the *Bundeswehr* is equipped. Flick also owns more than 40 per cent of the stock in Daimler-Benz plants; 54 per cent of the Buderuswerke in Wetzlar; 51 per cent of the Kraus Maffei works in Munich; 30 per cent of Deutscher Eisenhandel, Berlin; 74 per cent of Ravene Stahl, Berlin; 93 per cent of the Metallhuette in Luebeck; 50 per cent of the Kieler Maschinenbau plant; 51 per cent of the Monopol coal mine in Kamen; all of Bayrische Schrott AG in Munich; 26 per cent of the Hessian Mine and Smelter Works, Wetzlar; all of the Maximilian Smelter in Sulzbach-Rosenberg; 34 per cent of Feldmuehle paper mill, Duesseldorf; 50 per cent of the Lauchhammer Machine and Steel Works, Duesseldorf.

Flick, it is common knowledge in Germany, has set his sights on the automobile business in the postwar economy instead of the mining and steel industry with which he was so closely associated before and during the Hitler régime. His interest in Auto Union is dominant. His share in Daimler-Benz is the biggest individual share, and he is assistant chairman of the board of directors. His Daimler stocks have a face value of 29 million DM but a sales value of 750 million, three times the amount he was paid for the sale of his entire holdings in the late 1940's and early 1950's. The name of Flick was pushed into the public spotlight again in the fall of 1959 when Daimler-Benz and the Deutsche Bank offered to lend 70 million DM to the deeply indebted Bavarian Motor Works (BMW). The proposal eventually was rejected at a BMW stockholders' meeting, but the loan would have given Flick a dominant position in Germany's automobile industry.

Far less successful is Willy Messerschmitt of fighter-plane fame. After floundering for more than a decade, the Messerschmitt concern is back in the airplane business although, for the time being, producing only the fuselage of a French-designed jet trainer on a franchise basis. The wings and the tails of the Fouga Magister are being built by Heinkel, another famous German aircraft plant.

[4] "London Bulletin on German Questions," October 29, 1958.

Messerschmitt's new start in the aircraft industry, belated as it comes, reflects a great deal of Messerschmitt trouble before, during, and after World War II. A brilliant engineer, Messerschmitt at many times has been too unrealistic for the demands of his surroundings and his associates. His genius at the drawing board far overshadowed his abilities to bargain with the board of directors. Although Messerschmitt has designed a jet trainer of his own since the end of the war, it was turned down by the German defense ministry in favor of the French ship which could be built on franchise. In 1938 Messerschmitt designed the first operational jet plane. The jet's plans were rejected by *Luftwaffe* General Erhard Milch in 1941 as "jokes and nonsense." Messerschmitt still claims that—had he been given approval—the jet could have been mass-produced as early as 1942 and might have changed the course of the war. Former *Luftwaffe* officials relate that Messerschmitt had test-flown a twin-jet fighter in the spring of 1943 with the then unheard-of level flight speed of 520 mph. This aircraft, the M262, did see battle, but by the time it got to the front too few qualified pilots remained to operate it and Hitler attempted to use it as a medium bomber instead of a fighter, the mission for which it had been designed.

After Germany surrendered, the United States Air Force reaped the benefits of Messerschmitt genius by confiscating research data at a laboratory in Oberammergau, putting United States jet efforts from five to ten years ahead. Messerschmitt boasts that he has had offers from the Russians "and almost every other country in the world" to work on jet and missile development. He spurned the offers, he maintains, to stay in Germany and "work for peace."

Unfortunately for him, his peacetime efforts ended in financial calamity. In 1949 he turned his hand to prefabricated housing, utilizing outsized bricks, manufactured in the shell of his Augsburg fighter plant. The State of Bavaria invested heavily in his scheme and he solicited orders from many war-ravished countries, but the venture failed. Next he converted the plant to the manufacture of sewing machines, auto parts and the *Rollermobil*, the bug-shaped, three-wheeled vehicles that look like plane cockpits on gocart frames. He sold thousands of them in Germany and abroad, but the venture was taken from his hands because of poor production planning. The sewing machine and auto parts business also failed, leaving Messerschmitt nearly 5 million DM in debt, mostly to the State of Bavaria. That is one unofficial reason why the German defense ministry didn't place orders for his two-seater ME200 jet trainer and turned instead to the French Magister.

The production of the Fouga Magister as a trainer for the *Bundeswehr*'s air force proved sufficiently lucrative to enable Messerschmitt to put in a successful bid for franchise construction of the United States F-104 Starfighter with which the *Bundeswehr* will be equipped. The first planes have been shipped complete from the United States. The remainder of the four-hundred-aircraft German fleet will be built to American specifications in Germany. (Messerschmitt's co-worker on the Fouga Magister and the F-104, incidentally, is the Heinkel Company, wartime manufacturers of bombers. Since 1945, Heinkel, too, has been active in the cabin scooter business.)

But while Flick shuns publicity, while I. G. Farben is deconcentrated but again working jointly, and while Willy Messerschmitt seeks to recuperate from the losses on his scooters and sewing machines by building French and American jets, Alfried Krupp von Bohlen und Halbach is slugging it out in public with Allied control and deconcentration authorities. Herr Krupp is the sole owner and heir of a 147-year-old industrial dynasty which, for more than ninety of those years, has been munitions makers by appointment to the world's powerful, among them two German emperors and one German *Führer*. During World War II the Krupp firm manufactured the huge 80-centimeter railway gun called "Fat Gustav" which was used in the campaign against Sevastopol. It was reminiscent of the 42-centimeter Big Bertha of World War I. In addition Krupp built 8.8-centimeter antiaircraft guns, 15-centimeter field howitzers, antitank guns, naval guns, submarines, and the widely feared Tiger tank.

Although Alfried did not get a job in the huge Krupp industries until 1936, did not become a member of the board until 1941, and did not take over the sprawling, privately owned concern until his father Gustav suffered an incapacitating near-fatal stroke toward the end of 1943, it was Alfried, then thirty-seven, who was arrested by American occupation forces and placed in pretrial confinement as a war criminal in 1945. Three years later Alfried and eleven members of his directorate went before a tribunal at Nuremberg. Only one of the board members was acquitted. The others, including Alfried, were sentenced to a total of ninety-six years in prison on charges of plundering and employing slave labor. They were acquitted of another allegation that they had helped prepare Hitler's war of aggression.

Alfried Krupp was sentenced to twelve years in jail and confiscation of all his properties. He was confined at Landsberg, where he worked in the prison machine shop making tools and wrought-iron lighting fixtures for the prison chapel. As Krupp started his term, the balance of his properties in Essen was ravaged and disassembled. Huge plants were sent piecemeal to the Soviet Union and other victorious Allies. German statistics indicate that 72 per cent of Krupp's industrial installations were destroyed during and after the war by bombs and dismantling.

For three years Krupp sat out strange developments in postwar Germany. He can thank the cold war and United States High Commissioner McCloy for the turn in events. On January 31, 1951, McCloy, following a sweeping review of sentences against the leading war criminals, scrapped the confiscation decree on grounds that it was "discriminatory to Anglo-Saxon procedures." Three days later guards brought Krupp and his ten directors their civilian clothes. For Alfried Krupp this parole had a hook, however, which to date still poses numerous difficult problems. He was not allowed to visit physically any of his properties and was not permitted to take any active part in the administration of his business. McCloy assured the public that Krupp properties still would remain subject to Allied High Commission Law No. 27 on the Reorganization of the German Coal, Iron, and Steel Industries. Krupp attorneys and Allied officials settled down to working out the details.

On March 4, 1953, Krupp signed an agreement with the Allies under which he would have to dispose of all his coal and iron mines and his steel mills, of which one in particular, Rheinhausen, was almost untouched by wartime or postwar damage. Other properties to be sold included the Essen-Rossenray mine, the Rheinberg and Rossenray coal fields, the Hanover-Hannibal coal mine in Bochum, the Constantine the Great mine in Bochum, and all iron ore mines in the Siegerland, Harz Mountains, and the Lahn area, and the Emscher Lippe mine in Datteln. In addition, the Allies decreed that

Krupp's sister Irmgard would get 8 million DM worth of shares in the subsidiary former Krupp firms of Capito and Klein and Westphalian Wire Industries. The same amount of stock in these two firms was to go to his nephew Arnold von Bohlen und Halbach, son of Krupp's brother Claus who was killed during the war. Krupp was also ordered to pay his brothers Berthold and Harald and his sister Waltraud 11 million DM each in cash. The principal sum is due in 1963 and in the meantime each brother and sister receive an annual interest payment of 100,000 DM.[5]

Krupp was permitted to retain all the manufacturing aspects of his empire. These included: the Essen Locomotive Factory, Krupp Technik, a consulting engineering firm; Rheinhausen Machine and Steel Works (which is adjacent to the Rheinhausen mill but separated by a fence erected by the Allies); the WIDIA Factory; Essen Machine Works; WIPLA Dental Works; Krupp Trading Organizations; the Essen Foundry and Forge; construction companies; the Weser AG shipyards where U-boats once were built but oil tankers are launched today; the Krupp Motor and Automobile Works in Essen; the Iron and Bronze Works in Hamburg; the Brune and Kapesser GmbH and Coal-Chemical Plants in Wanne-Eickel.

His gigantic enterprise runs the gamut from manufacturing special steels for dental plates, base chemicals for the production of shoe polish, metal drills, Diesel engines, locomotives, trucks, cranes, giant shafts for ship engines, freighters, and tankers, bridge and building girders, boilers, and steel containers. The Krupp industries today plan and build to order steel mills, steelworks, cement and chemical plants. One of the fastest growing developments is Krupp Technik which provides engineering consultant services all over the world. The total manpower of the companies which Krupp has been allowed to keep is approximately forty-five thousand. That of the mines and mills which he has sold or agreed to sell is another forty-three thousand.

[5] According to the testament set down by Great-grandfather Alfred Krupp, only one son or daughter in each generation falls heir to the giant Krupp fortune. The others are excluded from any role in management or ownership but the heir is obligated to make certain payments to his brothers and sisters. The Allies assumed this part of the Krupp family responsibility because Alfried had hardly had time to do so since taking over the business in late 1943 and going to jail in 1945.

Even with the mines and mills deducted,[6] Alfried Krupp is still one of the richest men in the world. He is now doing an $800-million-a-year business. Of the properties he was ordered to sell, he has sold all but two. One of those which he sold, has returned to Krupp control: the Constantine the Great mine which was purchased by the Bochumer Verein, a major steel enterprise. At the time of the sale, in 1957, Bochumer Verein was passing into the hands of Swedish industrialist Axel Wenner-Gren. In mid-1959 Krupp bought the Bochumer Verein. This has made him the leading steel producer in West Germany and his the largest heavy-industry concentration in Western Europe. He has failed to divest himself of two major holdings: the Rheinhausen smelter and the Hanover-Hannibal Mine in Bochum. Publicly, Krupp still proclaims that he has every intention of selling the properties and that he will make every effort to keep his agreement. The only problem, Krupp asserts, is that there are no buyers.

The original agreement was that Krupp would liquidate the holdings no later than January 31, 1959. A year's extension was granted at that time and in December, 1959, Krupp representatives appealed for another one-year extension to the "mixed committee," constituted under the Paris Treaties and Bonn Conventions for the purpose of regulating the deconcentration of the coal mining, iron, and steel industries.[7] The divestment order against Krupp as well as other German coal, iron, and steel magnates has been made part of the Paris Treaty of 1955 and the Bonn Conventions of 1952. The elements pertaining to deconcentration of coal, iron, and steel properties are included in the convention on the settlement of matters arising out of the war and the occupation. Under Article 4, Chapter Two (Decartelization and Deconcentration) the treaty prescribes:

Allied High Commission Law No. 27 on the Reorganization of the German Coal, Iron and Steel Industries, as amended by Law No. 76, together with all legislation issued thereunder, shall be maintained in force until such time as the deconcentration of the German coal mining

---

[6] Krupp is not allowed to set foot in them or in any way personally take part in their administration.

[7] This committee, consisting of three representatives of the Federal Republic and one each from France, the United Kingdom, and the United States and a Swiss chairman, has the power to grant extensions for deconcentration.

and iron steel industries in accordance with Law No. 27 has been carried out.

The powers of the Allied High Commission of the Combined Coal Control Group and of the Combined Steel Group under Law No. 27 shall be vested in an agency which is hereby established [the Mixed Committee].

Article 5 of the chapter, which deals with the establishment of the Mixed Committee, states, among other things:

The Mixed Committee shall extend the time fixed for the disposition of the securities provided that the applicant establishes that all of such securities could not, with the exercise of reasonable efforts, be disposed of on reasonable terms and on a basis which is compatible with the German public interest and that such disposition will not be possible within the remaining time without a disruptive effect on the German capital market.

Thus, the committee may grant an extension if it feels that no potential German buyer could be found and that a sale would upset the German economy. The Mixed Committee does not have the power to cancel the divestment order, nor can it even recommend cancellation. It can merely state its opinions. Only the governments of the United States, Britain, and France may repeal the order.

Krupp, publicly, has been very conservative about his hopes that the divestment order might be canceled. Most German sources report that he wants to keep his word. However, shortly after his release from Landsberg war-crimes prison, he appointed a young new general director, Berthold Beitz, with complete power of attorney to act for the entire firm. It is Beitz, unencumbered by any promises to the Allies or written agreements, who publicly has been vociferous about the deconcentration requirements. He has been more than blunt in his objections to the divestment order. According to Beitz, the divided Krupp empire can show a profit only in a time of economic boom. If Germany is hit by a recession, Beitz has said, Krupp interests would be in serious trouble, trouble they would not experience in times of recession or depression if they were reunited.

The Krupp companies have prided themselves for years on the

quality of their products. The decentralization policy, which cuts Krupp off from his own raw materials and steel, officials of the company say, has seriously impaired the quality of Krupp products. As an example, they cite the case of a huge turbine ordered by shipping magnate Aristotle Onassis. It developed a structural failure which, say Krupp experts, would never have occurred if the steel and iron for the turbine had come from Krupp's own smelters.

My great-grandfather's basic tenet, to deliver only the best quality merchandise, has been seriously infringed upon by the divestment order [Krupp explains]. Our specialty has always been high-quality steel products, such as drive shafts for ship Diesel engines. The steel for the shafts always came from our own mills. The responsible man in the foundry always worked closely with the responsible man in the mill on any given job. Today we have to buy the steel somewhere else and our foundry men aren't as familiar with the varying grades of materials as they were with that from our own mills. Thus it can happen that problems arise on a job and then you have delivery troubles.

What is also a simple economic fact for the Krupp concern as well as outsiders is that some elements of the sprawling operation may be making a profit while others are operating in the red. With the empire split down the middle, Krupp officials contend, there are money-losing subsidiaries under Krupp control while the majority of money-making operations are scheduled for sale.

Nevertheless, Krupp profits today are higher than ever before.

When he was released from Landsberg, Krupp pledged that he would never again build cannons. The company still stands behind that principle. However, it has been reported widely that Krupp has been asked to participate in arms manufacture for NATO and is currently engaged in some electronics work for NATO countries. Some Krupp officials have attempted to explain that the munitions business is really unprofitable and that conversion of a plant for munitions manufacture is, in the long run, impractical. "If you turn out cannons," one Krupp spokesman said, "you need special equipment. There is, after all, no other object in the world in which you would bore a long tubular hole in the middle. After the war is all over you have nothing but a big supply of useless machines."

It would be unfair to say that the Germans or the Allies have tried to forget the plans to decentralize large industries which played a major role in supporting the National Socialist régime.

But there is also no question, understandably, that the Germans affected by the orders and laws have dragged their feet. Most of the firms involved are vital to Germany's economic recovery and, considering the change in attitudes and the turn of events for Germany, many officials and many Germans in private life cannot understand why there is still the demand to decentralize and deconcentrate the industries which will strengthen the country economically.

Meanwhile, Krupp, in an apparent effort to win public sympathy in his passive opposition to divestment, has allocated 6 million DM ($1,428,000) for compensation to slave laborers employed in his plants during World War II. The firm announced on December 23, 1959, that it will pay approximately 5,000 DM (nearly $1,200) to each Jewish concentration camp inmate forced to work as a slave laborer for Krupp. Payment, according to the company spokesman, will be made regardless of the length of time the prisoner worked for Krupp. The claims of heirs will also be honored. Estimates are that approximately a thousand camp inmates were forced to work at Krupp, but if the present allocation does not suffice, it could be raised to 10 million DM (about $2,380,000). The payments, described as completely voluntary by company officials, are being offered by Krupp because he wants to "help heal wartime scars." Appropriately, the offer was announced at the time the Mixed Committee was deliberating on its recommendations for another extension on the divestment order.

Chapter X

Anti-Semitism: Real or Imagined

Between Christmas Eve, 1959, and January 28, 1960, complaints on 685 anti-Semitic incidents were registered with the police in West Germany. Touched off by the smearing of swastikas and anti-Jewish slogans on the Cologne synagogue, they ranged in gravity from sidewalk scribblings by children to an earnest arson attempt on a synagogue, Jewish school, and the home of a Jewish citizen. Some of the cases appear ludicrous in retrospect. And even those observers most shocked and most distressed by this sudden wave of anti-Jewish feeling couldn't help but laugh when a man arrested for shouting "Heil Hitler!" in a Berlin beerhall turned out to be a Jew. The Germans, smarting under foreign attacks, had their chance to point an accusing finger when one swastika smearer in the little Hessian town of Friedberg turned out to be an American soldier.

Although the avalanche of post-Christmas anti-Semitism soon rolled all over the world, it was Germany which had to shoulder the responsibility. This sudden outburst of racial and religious hatred, though not the first since the war, was the most serious. While Chancellor Adenauer attempted to blame Communist agitators, the Communists and other leftists pointed to the resurgence of right-wing movements and neo-Nazis in Germany as the basic cause. An analysis of the 685 incidents revealed that there was no organized movement behind them.

According to the federal government's white book report, some 215 incidents involved only scribbling by children. In 332 of the cases, according to the federal ministry of interior, only "a certain degree of political motivation" was involved. The remaining 138 incidents were instigated by individuals who manifested an anticonstitutional attitude or singled out churches, cemeteries, monuments, or public buildings for daubing.

It seems illogical that an anti-Semitic movement could grow anew in a country where the Jews represent only .05 per cent of the total population. Some thirty thousand Jews in a country of 60 million simply don't have enough impact on the society to incite anti-Semitic activity. At least it would appear so, unless one stops to recall the unbelievable hatred which served as the basis for the mass extermination and expulsion of all Germany's Jews. The thirty thousand who remain, or have returned, are merely the remnants, the flotsam and jetsam of modern history's most extensive and most brutal inquisition.

Although the exterminators, the sadists, the anti-Semites of yesteryear are still alive, although the hatreds which they unleashed between 1933 and 1945 are still there, enormous differences separate the Federal Republic from the Nazi régime. Today, any anti-Semitic act or statement is illegal and subject to stiff punishments.

Yet anti-Semitism does exist.

It is certainly not an inherent German trait. Although Chancellor Adenauer is grasping at historical fiction when he tries to convince the world that anti-Semitism was nonexistent in Germany prior to Hitler, it was, on the other hand, no more prevalent and no more of a problem in Germany than in any other Western European country. The emancipation of the Jews in nineteenth-century Germany was more extensive and effected sooner than in any of the Central or Eastern European countries. Neither can one forget or overlook the Inquisition in Spain four hundred and fifty years before Hitler came to power. Anti-Jewish feeling is strong in Great Britain and in France. And anti-Semitism is a strong factor in the United States.

What then is at the root of this hatred, of the anti-Jewish out-bursts in a nation with so few Jews?

The answer rests in recognition of the fact that anti-Semitism, as exploited by Hitler and his henchmen, took on forms more bloody, more violent than at any previous time in history. Although it may appear easy for many Germans to say they knew nothing of the con-centration camps and the Nazi terror, there is a great deal of truth to the fact that the *majority* were ignorant or only sparsely informed of the mass slaughter being committed by the Nazis. When the war ended and the sum of Nazi atrocities was bared to the Germans by Allied information programs, they were traumatically shocked. They were blamed, at least morally, and the result was both indignation and disbelief. The knowledge that these horrible crimes had been committed by Germans, by German officials, perhaps by the man next door or by someone in the family, that everyone shared in the moral guilt, was simply too staggering to comprehend.

It was, instead, more convenient to "forget," to stop thinking about the nation's moral bankruptcy. At first there was the ponder-ous task of postwar reconstruction, a much more apparent, much more personal problem than salving the national conscience. Then came the cold war and the accelerated pace of German recovery. As the occupation forces modified their attitudes toward Germany, the Germans regained their national pride. The Germans were welcomed back into the community of free and democratic nations. Instead of humility, the average German rather felt that the Hitlerite concepts of superiority had been sustained.

Certainly the majority of Germans recognize their guilt. But they had not yet expurgated themselves of their responsibility and it be-came infinitely more pleasant to point to the atrocities of others in an attempt to justify the Nazi crimes. To this was added the knowl-edge that many of the archcriminals had been pardoned and some of them had even regained positions of prominence. Those few in turn sought to minimize the debt of Hitler crimes.

Germany was too busy working toward the future to realize that the social pestilence of yesteryear was still alive, that the political termites, washed ashore by the tide of recovery, were again gnawing at the beams and foundation of the new democratic order. These "unrehabilitated" elements of bygone years sought out the weakest spots: restitution and the period of plundering and lawlessness set off by displaced persons and some freed concentration camp inmates immediately after the war.

In 1945, the few Jews who remained in Germany, most of them displaced persons who had been liberated from concentration camps, were afforded special privileges which set them apart from the defeated Germans. Whether justified or not, many of them poached on the German economy and profited from Germany's defeat. They were still hated because the Allied propaganda experts could not undo overnight the Nazi teachings which had been drummed into an entire people for more than a decade. They were still Jews, and the fact that they had suddenly been transformed from a "subrace" into the privileged dependents of the victors, enjoying Allied protection and profiting from the spoils, made matters even worse.

They were the only ones trusted by the wary, all-suspecting occupation forces. A number were licensed to open bars and night clubs which Allied soldiers were allowed to patronize. As the economy became more stable, it was a well established practice that soldier bars, the hang-outs for American GI's, were in Jewish hands. Today, the majority of these establishments are controlled by a syndicate. Invariably the criminal and rowdy acts, committed by American troops, are associated with these noisy, dimly lit bars and their Jewish owners. The bars in every garrison city are a public eyesore and it takes little imagination to see how and why the owners are despised.

Take into consideration, too, the extreme rightist groups which propagandize against restitution programs and attempt to convince the Germans that their high taxes are due to the government's compensation and reparations policy. The origins of postwar anti-Semitism begin to emerge more clearly.

The majority of German leaders are well aware of the problem, its sources, and the fact that these factors are no excuse. This became apparent in the January 20, 1960, declaration of the *Bundestag*, subscribed to by the four political parties in parliament.

There is no doubt that the shameful incidents can be traced to a wide variety of causes and offenders. Not one of these explanations can, however, satisfy us. The fact that the majority of rowdies had not reached their teens in 1945 and have never seen a Jew in their life, yet vent their peevish temper in anti-Semitic actions instead of overturning cars or perpetrating other wanton acts—that fact demonstrates that in many a subconscious mind there still remain dark corners full of decaying notions.

Perhaps parents are directly responsible for that state of affairs; or teachers; or inferiority complexes. Or perhaps there has remained in isolated spots a mental state in which such specters flourish.

As long as it is still possible to argue, without meeting with the sharpest condemnation, that the National Socialist attitude toward the Jews was gross stupidity because it antagonized the rest of the world . . . as long as it is still possible to argue, with the aim of self-justification, whether six million Jews were murdered or "only" three million . . . as long as there remains a single child that has not grasped the fundamental fact that not the question of the number of Jews murdered is relevant but the question whether one or none was murdered . . . as long as all that goes on, all of us have failed, not excepting those who managed to keep their hands clean during the terrible years. Moreover, we are destined to fail if we judge the malignant acts against synagogues, not by moral standards, but view them merely in the light of whatever damage the Federal Republic might thereby have suffered.

. . . Those sinister ideas that still have currency amongst us here and there can be destroyed only by facing them and grappling with them.

The tidal wave of anti-Semitic incidents which rocked Germany and shocked its allies during the winter of 1959 to 1960 is certainly not the first time that anti-Jewish, neo-Nazi sentiments appeared as an ugly apparition on the postwar horizon. The most recent events have become important in their own right only through extensive publicity and through their sheer number in such a short period of time. Postwar anti-Semitism has been a German problem all along. The basic question is whether these displays of anti-Semitism, particularly in recent years, are the result of an organized effort or merely reflect the scattered, reflexive convulsion of an ogre already dead.

Cemetery desecrations have been reported for years in Germany. Hardly a month passes without several such acts. They occurred long before the Cologne synagogue was reconsecrated and are included in the series of 685 incidents following Cologne. In October, 1958, the *Bundeskriminalamt* (Federal Criminal Bureau), Germany's equivalent to the F.B.I., released revealing statistics covering cemetery incidents in the ten-year period from 1948 through 1957. Of 378 desecrations, 203 were recorded at Christian cemeteries, four at cemeteries having both Christian and Jewish graves, and 171 at Jewish graveyards. Although the extent of vandalism at the Christian cemeteries exceeded that at Jewish ones, percentagewise the figures appear more alarming. According to the *Bundeskriminalamt* statistics there are seventeen hundred Jewish cemeteries in the country and the figure of desecrations would indicate that 10 per cent of the total had been damaged.

Bundeskriminalamt records on guilty parties indicated that at the Christian burial places 30 per cent of the vandals had been children, 70 per cent adults, while in the Jewish graveyards, 69 per cent had been children, 13 per cent teenagers, and 18 per cent adults.

The motives have been analyzed as follows by the *Bundeskriminalamt*: Approximately 54 per cent of the Christian cemetery incidents were traced to intentions of larceny, 46 per cent were motivated by juvenile vandalism. At the Jewish cemeteries, larceny was a motive in 7 per cent of the cases, juvenile vandalism served as the backdrop for the remaining 93 per cent.

Although the *Bundeskriminalamt* saw a political association in approximately half of the incidents at Jewish cemeteries, it must be mentioned that numerous Jewish graveyards are abandoned and located in isolated areas where they are used by children as playgrounds. The German federal government currently is renovating most of these burial places and will fence them off and provide guard service at government expense.

In addition to cemetery desecrations, there have been numerous other manifestations of anti-Semitism in the years since World War II. Some, like the case of café owner Kurt Sumpf or high-school mathematics teacher Ludwig Zind have made their way in headlines around the world. While some were brought to public attention by alert newspaper reporters and liberal publications, others have gotten only the barest notice in the press.

The attention of almost all Europe focused on the little Black Forest town of Offenburg in April, 1958, when Ludwig Zind, then fifty-one, a mathematics teacher at the local secondary school, was tried in court for insulting Kurt Lieser, a half-Jewish Offenburg textile dealer; defaming the dead (Jews in concentration camps) and approving of a crime (the mass execution of Jews).

The charges stemmed from a heated argument in an Offenburg

inn the night of April 23, 1957. Lieser and Zind had met each other there and had downed several drinks together. Everything had appeared amiable until the discussion turned to politics. The two—they had not known each other before—accompanied by two of Zind's students, started discussing the desecration of graves at a Jewish cemetery in Salzgitter during January, 1957. Zind let it be known that he approved of the Nazi régime and its methods. He told Lieser that he could see nothing wrong with painting swastikas and overturning gravestones. At this point Lieser expained that he was half-Jewish himself. Zind retorted by calling Lieser a "dirty Jew."

"Far too few Jews were gassed to death," said Zind in the course of the argument. "They forgot to execute you in the gas chamber. I'll take care of you, too, the same way I smashed the skulls of hundreds of Jews during the war."

Zind also threatened, "I'll do you and your wife in, but I'll let your children live. . . . Israel should be eliminated, and one of these days it will be."

The *Gasthaus* "discussion" continued for six hours until dawn. A few days later, when Lieser saw Zind walking down the street with a hunting rifle, he asked for police protection. Yet some time passed before criminal charges were filed against the teacher. Lieser filed a complaint against Zind with school officials who initiated an investigation and temporarily suspended the teacher. When this became public, the Offenburg district attorney preferred criminal charges against Zind.

The results of his sensational trial have been well publicized. Zind was sentenced to twelve months in jail. He appealed the conviction, and when Germany's highest court upheld the sentence and police came to arrest him, the teacher had disappeared. Some time later he turned up in Egypt.[1]

Who is this dapper schoolteacher with the Hitler mustache, the straight-edge part in his hair and a face criss-crossed with dueling scars?

A well known figure not only at the high school but as a director of the *Turnverein* (athletic club), Zind was born in Offenburg, the youngest son of a Reichsbank official. He studied natural sciences at

[1] See page 56.

Tuebingen and Heidelberg universities, passed his state teacher's exams in 1931, then taught in schools at Pforzheim and in Thuringia until 1939 when he returned to Offenburg and a position at the high school there. During his youth he was a member of the Andreas Hofer and the Viking leagues, joined the *Stahlhelm* and in 1933 became an officer in the SA. He shed his brown shirt two years later because of a general order to cut the *Stahlhelm* insignia off the SA uniform. In 1937 he became a member of the Nazi party, and during the war he served as a captain in the engineer corps.

His personnel records listed him as a member of the dreaded SD (security service), but Zind maintains that he was not associated with the SD. Instead, he claims, the entry was made on his records by a friend who sought to help him in his teaching profession. The SD was widely feared and any teacher who belonged to it was assured of rapid promotion in the civil service.[2]

After the war Zind was arraigned before a de-Nazification board which classified him as a "minor offender." He was prohibited from teaching for two years. Judging from Zind's behavior in court, however, he was anything but a passive supporter of the Nazi régime. In July, 1957, about two and a half months after the beerhall incident, the court was told, there had been an attempt to settle the dispute between Zind and Lieser. Lieser had agreed to drop his official complaint if Zind would apologize. "I wouldn't crawl in front of a Jew. I'd rather sweep the streets than take back my words," Zind retorted.

In court, Zind at first denied having made the remarks he was charged with during the beerhall argument. Under the pressure of prosecutor Dr. Paul Naegele's extensive cross-examination, however, he became enraged and made additional anti-Semitic comments. During the turbulent three-day trial Zind insisted that Hitler's Third Reich could never have been built had not the Jews been interned in concentration camps or expelled from the country. He denied, however, approving of their execution. During his testimony he frequently shouted and reeled off Hitlerite racial theories that repeatedly forced presiding judge Dr. Hans Eckert to threaten him with a contempt citation.

"Whenever I touch upon this subject [the Jews], I become en-

2 Teachers are civil servants in Germany and follow a set promotion pattern.

raged," Zind replied. When he told the court that the state of Israel was a pest boil in the Near East and that "I'm fully in accord with the Arabs" for wanting to stamp it out, spectators in the courtroom demonstrated their approval with applause.

Although it was apparent to all observers at the trial that both the prosecution and the judges were striving for a stiff penalty and that with it they had hoped to polish Offenburg's and Germany's somewhat tarnished reputation, it became equally obvious that the townsfolk had rallied to Zind's cause. As the teacher, his wife, and children left the courthouse, two hundred spectators milled around him. Some fifty persons, many of them weeping old women, shook hands with Zind, patted him on the back, and expressed their sympathies.

While Offenburg citizens mourned the one-year prison sentence, the presiding judge and German newspapers took the other side. Judge Eckert, in passing sentence, emphasized that the efforts of thousands of Germans to undo and make good the crimes and atrocities of the Nazi régime would fall by the wayside because of individuals like Zind.

Months before the Zind case had gone to trial, the German Teachers' Association published a stinging protest against him and Offenburg officials for being so slow to bring the teacher to court. In a press release entitled "Beware of the Beginnings" the German Teachers' Association expressed its indignation and shock about Zind's remarks and, in the name of its one hundred thousand members, lamented the fact that a man like Zind could have been reemployed as a teacher after the war. The federation expressed its anger and regret that school authorities in Offenburg at first had tried to protect Zind and hide the scandal. "Morally and spiritually defective individuals— those who will never learn from the past, those, in fact, who have already destroyed Germany once—still threaten the Federal Republic," the Teachers' Association charged.

The group also lambasted the fact that no legal action had been taken against Zind until a large national weekly magazine had publicized the incident. The federation demanded that the Offenburg school administration and Baden-Wuerttemberg ministry of culture and education explain to the public just what steps they had taken prior to the magazine story. German newspapers, which sent out reporters en masse to cover the trial, summed it up with stinging editorials in which they demanded that German school boards check more closely into their faculty records for other "hidden Zinds."

The warning was not unfounded. On the day Zind was convicted, Edgar Fernau, a grade-school teacher in Hanover, was charged with a similar offense. "It's too bad about the Jews, that they weren't all gassed to death, I mean," Fernau was accused of having said. A half year later another high-school teacher, Lother Stielau, was suspended temporarily because he had criticized a Luebeck school production of *Tom Sawyer* as "racial schmaltz." Stielau also asserted that the diaries of Eva Braun, the Queen of England, and Anne Frank were forgeries. (He stated this in an article in the school paper.) Anne Frank's father filed charges against Stielau, accusing him of slander, defamation of character, slander of the dead, and anti-Semitic remarks. Stielau was county chairman of the German Reich party at the time of the incident.

While the various teachers still made headlines, Germans started hearing about the troubles of Kurt Sumpf, a thirty-seven-year-old café owner who had become the victim of a torrent of anti-Semitic attacks in Koeppern, a village nestled in the Taunus Mountains some twenty miles from Frankfurt. In his futile desire to build a home and business in the Germany he had fled once before, in his frantic search for protection from brutality and anti-Semitic rowdyism Sumpf finally was forced to turn to the press for help. Not even the police had come to his aid. On the contrary, one of the men who finally went to trial for mistreating Sumpf was none other than a Köppern policeman.

Sumpf, the son of a Frankfurt Jew who was a highly decorated staff officer in the German army during World War I and owner of three food shops, had left Germany in 1936 with his parents after his father had been beaten up by SA men in one of his shops. They migrated to Israel. During the war, Kurt, only thirteen when his family left Germany, served as a seaman in the British Navy. Later he fought the British in the Israeli war for independence. He married a girl named Margot in Tel Aviv and worked as a baker. But his father was homesick for the old country and wanted to return to Germany. The entire family—Kurt, Margot, their son Peter, and Mama and Papa Sumpf—went back in 1956.

At first Sumpf went to work for the Americans, managing a beverage shop at the main post exchange in Frankfurt. The elder Sumpf filed his claim for restitution and settled down to a quiet life. In 1958, after he had saved and scraped together some $6,000, Kurt decided to buy the Café Winter in Koeppern. The café, on the main street, with a bakery attached to it, was one of the busiest in town. The bakery was lucrative and it included a concession for a local hospital. During the afternoons the café thrived on ice cream, cake, coffee, and confectionery. At night the villagers would come in to nurse their beer or wine while the younger set danced in a back room which had a jukebox.

Sumpf faced troubles from the start. The establishment was off limits to American soldiers because of a violent brawl between townsfolk and a group of off-duty United States MP's the preceding year. Although there was a liquor license, it was in the name of the previous owner and could not be transferred. Sumpf had to apply for a new one.

In court, almost a year later, Sumpf explained that he and his wife were the victims of threats almost from the first day. Sumpf's wife said she was warned several days after their arrival in Koeppern that there would be trouble and that young Peter, twelve, would have a rough time in school. When the boy started school, he came home one day and said other children had jeered him with anti-Jewish taunts.

At first, the Sumpfs shrugged it all off. Their one and a half years in Frankfurt, a big city where the few remaining and returned Jews are not noticed, had been very peaceful. But it became apparent that trouble was afoot. Sumpf was accused of selling liquor illegally and brought to trial. He was acquitted after he had proved that his application for a license had been filed with responsible authorities. The official answer was that the application must have been lost, very unusual in Germany's highly efficient civil service system.

Sumpf was also plagued by the county health board which ruled his establishment unsanitary and ordered a fresh paint job and new kitchen equipment. It took several months to get the off-limits order repealed. In October, 1958, trouble for Sumpf started full scale as a group of Koeppern citizens set out to make life unbearable. As Margot testified, one day that month Otto Roth, a twenty-four-year-old house painter, was asked to leave the café because of his disorderly behavior. Roth's father-in-law, Heinrich Weidmann, Sr., owner of a small trucking company, threatened Mrs. Sumpf. "We'll ruin you and break every bone in your body if you don't do as we want," he allegedly said.

One night in mid-November, Reinhold Katzorke, son of a former SA man, led a gang of five rowdies into the café. They had been drinking at a rival bar. Katzorke heckled Mrs. Sumpf and molested the waitress. Sumpf tried to restrain them. "Let's shoot the Jew," one of the group said. "A bullet is too good for him," replied another. A mortuary proprietor, one of the five, offered to bury Sumpf "free of charge."

Finally Sumpf ushered the gang out of the café. When, fifteen minutes later, he heard a noise on the courtyard gate and went out to investigate, a shot whizzed through the air, right past his head. Sumpf tried in vain to persuade the local gendarmerie to investigate. They considered the incident too inconsequential.

On November 30, Katzorke brought his five rowdies into the fray again. While two stood guard outside, three went into the café and one asked to use the phone. When Sumpf appeared to hesitate, one of the group launched a vicious anti-Semitic tirade. That was the signal. The gang jumped on Sumpf and assaulted him brutally. Mrs. Sumpf called the police. A radio car arrived and two state gendarmes, Focke Rademacher, forty-two, and another identified only as officer Otto, entered the café, followed by the two gang members who had waited outside. As the policemen checked for identity cards, Heinrich Weidmann, Sr., kicked Sumpf in the shins and two other members of the gang dragged Eduard Spohrer, a young guest who had come to Sumpf's aid, into another room and beat him up. When Sumpf protested and demanded protection, Patrolman Rademacher told him to "get behind the bar." Outside, a mob of townsfolk had gathered and shouted, "Drive out the Jew!" Sumpf angrily turned to Rademacher and again asked him to do his duty as an officer. Rademacher turned halfway to the crowd and allegedly said to Sumpf, "If you can't keep order yourself, why don't you close the filthy joint?"

Matters became worse. Mrs. Sumpf had been assaulted several times, Peter refused to go to school, and although one parent had come to Sumpf and apologized for the actions of his own child and a teacher had threatened to make any classmate write a composition for punishment if they taunted Peter, the kids came around every day and jeered beneath his window. Desperate now, Sumpf took his troubles to the press. He went to see reporter Botho Kirsch of the *Frankfurter Rundschau*. Kirsch investigated the situation and found Sumpf's charges substantiated.

At first the *Rundschau* reporter tried to mediate between Sumpf and the town. Koeppern officials agreed to cooperate. But the truce didn't last. Within a week the troublemakers were back and stirred up another incident which resulted in Mrs. Sumpf's being kicked in the stomach. Stumpf was attacked when he tried to protect her. This convinced Kirsch that there was nothing left to do but run the story. On December 20 it appeared on the *Rundschau*'s editorial page. From then on things got even worse. On New Year's Eve, Johann Gallus, a policeman assigned to the café to keep order because of all the previous trouble, remarked to a German newspaperman (the policeman didn't know the man was a reporter) that, if he had a chance, he'd hit Sumpf "not once, but ten times."

A *Bundeswehr* soldier, Helmut Hartmann, twenty-one, at home on leave in his native Koeppern, once said of Sumpf, "That's a Jew they forgot to gas."

The Frankfurt district attorney, Heinz Wolf, started an investigation into the complaints and eventually charges were filed against eleven men, including policeman Rademacher. After that violence ceased but in its place came a complete boycott of the café. His only customers were a handful of American soldiers and a tiny, insignificant group of Koeppern youths.

On January 10, 1959, the Koeppern community council released a statement to the press designed to whitewash the town. The council said the impression had been given in newspaper stories that all Koeppern citizens were at the most apathetic about Sumpf's troubles. This, the statement said, was not true. "The community administration extended the same rights to Kurt Sumpf as it did to every other citizen and will do so in the future. . . . Unfortunately a small minority disregarded principles of justice and tolerance."

But newsmen who investigated the incidents discovered that the majority of Koepperners were either completely indifferent or gave only passive support to right and justice in the matter. For example,

Sumpf told *Look* magazine's European editor Edward M. Korry: "You know who the real cowards are? The so-called good people; the ones who turn their backs and pretend it's none of their business. They have cowardice in their hearts. That night with the police you should have seen the crowd outside. It was a regular riot, almost a pogrom. When they heard that cop insult me, when they saw that the uniform was against me, they were all against me, too."

On January 22, he received a threatening anonymous letter: "How can you, you dirty Jewish pig, dare to bring charges against a decent German policeman?" it read. "Why didn't they gas you to death? Unfortunately, millions were forgotten. Otherwise the world would have its peace and quiet. But we won't forget you. This matter no longer concerns just Koeppern, but the Rumpelstiltskin SS squad of Frankfurt. In one of the coming nights you'll meet Jehovah. There you can continue to celebrate your Sabbath." The letter, closing on the words, "Down with Judea," was signed by "Rumpelstiltskin." But while the boycott continued, Sumpf also received other letters which promised hope for a new and better Germany.

In April, after eight months of ownership, Sumpf was finally forced to sell the Café Winter at a tremendous loss. He went to work in Frankfurt as a taxi driver, applied for a visa to the United States and waited out the trial, scheduled for October, 1959.

The defendants ranged in age from twenty-one to fifty-three. Nine of them had been from seven to sixteen years old when the war ended. They were raised in a time when the SS and SA and the *Wehrmacht* goose-stepped across the Continent. More than anything, their actions in Koeppern raised the question of how thorough the Allied reorientation and reeducation program had been and how effective it had proved. All described as upstanding citizens of the little town of 3,400, they represented nearly every walk of life. There was hatmaker Friedl Usinger; trucking company owner Weidmann; his son; house painter Roth; a county civil servant; a couple of truck drivers; a mechanic; Helmut Hartmann, the *Bundeswehr* soldier; and, of course, Rademacher, the policeman.

The trial, extending over several days, attracted a standing-room-only crowd. What became apparent even in the first session was that witnesses and defendants had suddenly suffered a tremendous lapse of memory concerning the events for which they were brought before the court. The prosecution fought an uphill battle all the way.

As the trial progressed, villagers were categorized by their own neighbors as "anti-Koeppern" or "anti-Sumpf," depending on the testimony they gave. German newspapers reported that some of the "anti-Koeppern" witnesses had suffered commercial disadvantages soon after their testimony became public. Considerable anger had been generated in the town, not over the attacks on Sumpf, but over the "bad publicity" the village received.

The results of the trial were disappointing to most observers who had expected the judge to set an example. Weidmann was sentenced to four months; Hartmann, the German soldier, was restricted for two weekends; Otto Roth, Paul Gentner, and Reinhold Katzorke were fined from 30 to 150 DM each. The six other defendants were acquitted.

One loyal native son of Koeppern had ten bottles of champagne on ice for the occasion of the verdict. He wanted to fete his fellow citizens on their acquittals and light terms. But while it was obvious that the majority of Koeppern citizens did not stand by and aid Sumpf, as the judge said they should have done, while it was apparent that the trouble stemmed only from a small group of men, it was equally clear that the great mass of Koeppern citizens were completely apathetic to Sumpf and his troubles. And when Sumpf turned to the press for aid, thus turning the world spotlight of publicity on a provincial village, he had even fewer friends. On the contrary, those villagers who might have been sympathetic turned against him because they felt he had dragged the town's good name through the mud.

One positive result remains, however: Sumpf made as many potential friends in other German communities as he ever lost in Koeppern. While the entire town boycotted his café and tried to write off the affair by saying, "It always did have a bad reputation," Sumpf received nearly twenty letters a day, written by well meaning people from all over Western Germany. They wrote of their sympathies for Sumpf and offered their help. In almost each letter shock and disbelief were expressed that such incidents as this in Koeppern could occur in postwar Germany.

"We just can't imagine and don't want to believe that all this really happened," many letters said.

"As a German, I'm ashamed that I have to read something like that," said one woman subscriber to the *Rundschau*.

"At first I thought it was a story about something that happened twenty years ago," wrote another woman from Cologne, who invited Peter to visit her during carnival time.

A nineteen-year-old German girl from Hamburg read the reports during her vacation in Switzerland and wrote: "I am amazed and shocked about all this."

A woman from Ansbach sent a box of local candy specialties for young Peter. A crippled woman wrote a fairy tale for the boy. From the Rhineland, an elderly couple asked whether the Sumpfs would send Peter to them during the Christmas vacation. The director of a children's home in Hamburg offered to board Peter so he could go to school there.

A student from Munich came to see Sumpf to hear in detail what had happened. He left behind a letter saying, "When you return to your own country, I beg you to take along, in some corner of your heart, the Germany in which we, your friends, live."

Only one letter out of every hundred reflected anti-Semitic feelings. And, strangely, even ex-Nazis, once important Nazis such as the one-time assistant managing editor of the Vienna edition of the *Völkischer Beobachter*, wrote Sumpf expressing his sympathies and his shock and disbelief at what had happened in Koeppern.

Even while Kurt Sumpf was fending off nocturnal attackers and trying to combat the town's unofficial boycott, another serious anti-Semitic incident rocked Germany's complacency. On January 17, 1959, the portals of the recently reopened Duesseldorf synagogue and a downtown Duesseldorf memorial to victims of Nazi persecution were smeared with swastikas. Although the incident differed little from the desecration of the Cologne synagogue nearly a year later, it received far less publicity. The circumstances, however, were suspiciously similar.

The Duesseldorf city administration posted a 1,000-DM reward, the state of North Rhine Westphalia 10,000 DM for information leading to the smearers' arrest. A few days later, Helmut Klier, a young carpenter, once a member of the German Communist party, was arrested as principal suspect because police had found smudges of the same white paint on one of Klier's sweaters as had been used on the synagogue. Organizations of which Klier was a member, among them a Catholic youth group in Duesseldorf, expressed angry disbelief that he could be in any way implicated. The trade union to which he belonged asserted that the type of paint found on the synagogue and on Klier's sweater is used widely in house construction and that it was insufficient evidence to connect Klier with the swastika smearing. The young carpenter's parents vouched that he had been home during the night the desecration took place.

Two weeks later a second suspect, this time a member of a right-radical organization, was arrested. During an argument in the Duesseldorf main railway station he had shouted with considerable bravado that he had painted the Nazi symbols. But even this public admission turned out to be merely an empty boast. No charges were ever preferred against anyone in the incident and it had been almost forgotten when, on Christmas Eve, 1959, the swastikas appeared on the Cologne synagogue and on a Cologne memorial to victims of Nazi persecution.

The portals to the Cologne temple had been smeared with swastikas. On the walls surrounding the building had been painted the slogan: "Germans demand: Jews get out!" News of the desecration jolted Christmas-minded Germany. Cologne police and district attorney officials initiated a city-wide hunt. Rewards totaling 15,000 DM were offered. Meanwhile, letters and cables of sympathy, sorrow, and apology came from officials and private citizens all over Germany to the twelve hundred members of the Jewish congregation of Cologne.

Within twenty-four hours police had arrested Paul Schoenen and Arnold Strunk, both twenty-five, who were trapped in the police dragnet on the basis of the fingerprints they had made on a paint pot left standing near the synagogue. Since both men had previous records of arrest and imprisonment, their identification required very little time.

What appeared at first as another case of vandalism soon mushroomed into a deluge of anti-Semitic incidents all over Germany and most of the civilized world. In the two months following the arrest of Strunk and Schoenen, both of whom had been members of the German Reich party, thousands of anti-Jewish, neo-Nazi, and neo-Fascist manifestations were recorded. The trail of hastily smeared swastikas and anti-Semitic slogans stretched all around the globe.

Despite the general panic in Bonn that the incidents would harm West Germany's reputation and weaken the West's bargaining position at the summit conference, the final tabulation of the effects of Strunk's and Schoenen's Christmas Eve painting spree may lean toward the positive. Although Chancellor Adenauer drew ridicule with his suggestion that private citizens should whip on the streets any swastika or slogan smearer they might apprehend, the hundreds of incidents following the Christmas Eve desecration have jarred many Germans out of their self-satisfaction and contentment with postwar developments. Although the government's white book discounted theories that the wave of anti-Semitic and neo-Nazi incidents had been organized or steered by a central agency or a number of left-wing or right-wing elements, German authorities were prodded into closer examination of right-radical organizations. True, they did not succeed in outlawing the German Reich party, but the cascade of bad publicity, according to unofficial sources, has resulted in a decrease in DRP membership.

Although hundreds of youth groups demonstrated against anti-Semitism and neo-Nazism during the succeeding weeks, the seemingly endless series of incidents have sparked vehement criticism of West Germany's postwar history education program. Schoolbooks and history courses are being scrutinized for possible sources of pro-Nazi influence. For the first time since the war, it appears, educators are seriously analyzing the educational program and its relationship to the development and training of a democratic-minded generation to which Germany can safely trust its future.

Although some Jews have stated publicly that their only protection in Germany is the presence of Allied troops, German courts, in prosecuting the post-Christmas incidents, have generally been severe, indicating that there are responsible authorities in the government and the judiciary who will fight neo-Nazism. German government leaders, not Jewish spokesmen, have spearheaded the drive to enact more effective legislation against racial, religious, and ethnic defamation and discrimination.

Disheartening and frightening as the many, frequently violent incidents may have been to those who have believed in or hoped for a solid democratization of Germany, one must acknowledge that thousands of Germans demonstrated their unequivocal antipathy toward the neo-Nazis and residual Nazis during the dark winter months of 1960. Hundreds of newspapers and magazines editorialized sternly against the social cancer which had made itself apparent. In protest meetings, in letters to editors, in seminars and adult-education discussions, tens of thousands of Germans took a clear, unrelenting stand against any rekindling of anti-Jewish and pro-Fascist flames.

The government's white book is perhaps somewhat overly optimistic in asserting that there is no indication whatsoever of any organized anti-Semitism in the Federal Republic or that anti-Semitic feelings play a role with only a negligible part of the population. An analysis of the government's own figures would lead one to conclude that more than two thirds of all the incidents occurred in two German states which have had a consistent record of neo-Nazi and neo-Fascist activity. Of the 685 incidents analyzed in the white book, 105 occurred in Lower Saxony, stronghold of the Socialist Reich and the German Reich parties. Another 167 took place in North Rhine Westphalia.

Of the 234 suspects who had been apprehended or convicted by January 28, some thirty-five turned out to be children under fourteen; ninety-five were teenagers between fourteen and twenty; forty-nine were between twenty and thirty years old; twenty-two between thirty and forty, sixteen between forty and fifty; eleven between fifty and sixty years of age, and six were sixty years or older.

The government report indicated that 48 per cent of the suspects had acted without traceable political motives, more in the spirit of pure rowdyism or vandalism; 15 per cent represented the children under fourteen; 5 per cent reportedly acted out of pathological motives; 8 per cent out of political conviction; and 24 per cent out of semiconscious or unconscious political and religious motives which made themselves felt following consumption of alcohol or as the result of a heated political or semipolitical discussion.

From the outset government spokesmen at all levels demanded that smearers and perpetrators of anti-Semitic incidents be punished swiftly and severely so as to curb the wave of incidents. Officials in

Berlin, where one sixth of all the incidents occurred, took decisive action. Trials were held within a few days after charges were preferred and the sentences were usually stiff. In a spectacular gesture, Berlin authorities even petitioned the Allied control council for permission to use occupation laws in prosecuting the neo-Nazi demonstrators. Under occupation law, painting or displaying swastikas is a capital crime.

Penalties throughout the country varied widely, of course, depending to a great extent on the tempers of the individual judges and communities. Aside from acquittals, the mildest punishment on record is a three-day juvenile jail sentence for a twenty-year-old Paderborn man who drew swastikas on a wall. The most severe sentence, one year and ten months in jail, went to an unemployed Wilhelmshaven seaman who was convicted of desecrating a cemetery.

Both the light and the severe sentences have been criticized widely in and outside Germany. When a Berlin civil servant was sentenced to seventeen months in jail for making anti-Semitic remarks in a beerhall, city authorities faced a wave of objections that the term was far too long for the offense involved. But when Paul Schoenen and Arnold Strunk were sentenced to ten-month and fourteen-month jail terms, leaders of the German Jewish community, labor union officials, and Social Democratic party representatives criticized the court for its leniency. There was bitter opposition to what was generally termed a "slap-on-the-wrist penalty," which the presiding judge had justified by saying that the "democratic order of our state has not been materially damaged or hindered by Strunk's and Schoenen's actions."

"Not yet," several newspaper editorials charged. And following pressure by parliamentary and Jewish leaders, the Cologne district attorney filed an appeal against the sentences and a new trial was scheduled in which, he hopes, Strunk and Schoenen will be dealt with more severely.

As public attention shifted from the incidents themselves to the question of how they should be punished, considerable thought again was devoted to the proposal of a special law for the protection of the Jews. Most Jewish leaders opposed it categorically on the grounds that such legislation was not in keeping with the democratic concepts upon which the Federal Republic had been founded. For all practical purposes, they explained, it would serve only to set the Jews even more apart from the German society.

The events in January and February, 1960, helped focus attention on a bill which had been under consideration by the *Bundestag* for some twelve months. This proposed law, which fixed stiff penalties for inciting racial hatred, might have passed in parliament inconspicuously had it not been for the resurgence of anti-Semitism. It is a bill which merely amplifies a section of the penal code dealing with breach of peace. The section itself dates from the nineteenth century, and prosecution under the law was made contingent upon the injured party lodging a complaint. The revised program, as drafted by Justice Minister Dr. Fritz Schaeffer, detailed and defined offenses and offenders and made the filing of charges obligatory for law enforcement agencies. In the final form, and the version in which it had been passed on two readings by the *Bundestag*, the bill called for not less than three-month jail terms for persons convicted of: inciting hatred of groups distinguished by nationality, race, or religious beliefs; defaming or libeling such groups, and making or disseminating defamatory allegations with malice aforethought about such groups.

The good intentions of numerous parliamentarians and the guilty conscience of many others had inspired the drafting of this bill shortly after the legal debacle of Hamburg lumber dealer Friedrich Nieland.[3] However, it met with opposition from Jewish leaders, in particular Hendrik Van Dam, general secretary of the Central Council of Jews in Germany, who expressed the belief that the proposed legislation singled out the Jews for special protection. Jewish organizations in West Germany had not asked for special protection. On the contrary, they were definitely opposed to such a special law. All they had demanded was a revision of existing laws so that the filing of a criminal complaint would be automatic instead of dependent on the action of the slandered or defamed party.

After almost an entire year in conference, the legal committee of

[3] See page 147.

the *Bundestag* produced three bills on March 17 which should serve to combat more effectively anti-Semitic and neo-Nazi incidents. One of these bills, a new paragraph of the penal code, calls for imprisonment of up to three years for anyone displaying in public Nazi signs or the symbols of outlawed political parties. Another bill alters slightly the provisions of an existing paragraph making it illegal and punishable to defame the dead. The third proposal is a revision of the bill which was introduced in January, 1959. The new version now reads:

Whoever attacks human dignity in a way calculated to disturb the public peace so as to: arouse hate against a section of the population; incite use of force or hostile deeds against them, or, malevolently subjects them to contempt or slander, will be punished with imprisonment of not less than three months.

This version has been criticized as too elastic for it could be used as a political tool to imprison outspoken candidates during elections because political parties, after all, are also "sections of the populations."

Despite the fact that nearly 75 per cent of the suspects arrested in anti-Semitic and neo-Nazi incidents during December, 1959, and January, 1960, were under thirty years of age, one of the most encouraging signs was the energetic reaction of Germany's youth toward the wave of anti-Semitism. On January 8, the German Federal Youth Ring, encompassing 6 million members, issued a declaration in which it not only disassociated itself from the synagogue smearings and neo-Nazi manifestations, but called on youths all over the country to demonstrate against anti-Semites and the neo-Nazis.

Make use of every opportunity to prevent incidents of this kind [the declaration suggested to all subsidiary youth groups]. Prove by word and deed that German youth refuses to have anything to do with this racial hatred of political instigation. . . .

In recent years German youth has often given proof of the fact that, to them, mutual esteem is the natural prerequisite for living together in a democratic form of society. These young people have shown that they are seriously endeavoring to overcome the Nazi past. This attitude has manifested itself many times when thousands of young Germans have paid homage at the memorials of the victims of Nazi persecution, in particular at former concentration camps.

During the first week in January, forty thousand Berlin students and adults demonstrated against the anti-Semitic incidents. They staged a torchlight parade during which they carried placards and signs reading "No Racial Hatred," "No Anti-Semitism," "Out with the Besmirchers," and "Nazis in the Lecture Halls, Get Out!" Similar demonstrations, though most of them less dramatic and with fewer participants, were staged in other German cities such as Frankfurt, Hamburg, Munich, and Bremen.

It speaks conclusively for the incongruity of Germany's postwar development that, despite these mass demonstrations by young people, the press and large segments of the population placed the major blame for the wave of anti-Semitic incidents on Germany's educational system. The absence of intensive modern history courses, the widespread evasion of any subject matter that touched upon the Nazi régime, and the general lack of knowledge of Hitler and the events of the Third Reich which young Germans have displayed has been criticized relentlessly since Christmas Eve, 1959.

The critical situation in the German educational system became alarmingly apparent in several of the trials for anti-Semitic comments and swastika smearings, in particular during the trial of Strunk and Schoenen. Pictures of Horst Wessel and Adolf Hitler had been discovered in one of the defendants' apartments, and when questioned about them he replied, "Horst Wessel is my idol and I bought the pictures of Hitler as a rare antique."

"Do you have any recollection at all of the Third Reich?" the presiding judge asked twenty-five-year-old Strunk.

"Barely . . ." Strunk replied.

The judge pointed out to him that the following books had been found on his shelf: *Ritterkreuz Holders of the Army SS, The Army SS in Pictures, The Army SS in Battle, Hitler as a Military Strategist, Hitler's Table Talk, From the Court of the Kaiser to the Reich Chancellory, The New Book of Soldiers' Songs,* and Hitler's *Mein Kampf.*

The judges wanted to know why Strunk and Schoenen had smeared black paint over Cologne's downtown monument which is dedicated to "Germany's Most Shameful Period of History: 1933 to 1945." The quiz session in court revealed that neither Strunk nor Schoenen had formed any political opinion until they had joined the Cologne section of the German Reich party.

"I joined the DRP to educate myself politically," Schoenen told the judges.

The results of this political education, in Schoenen's own words, are: "A limited dictatorship appears more advantageous to me than a democracy because that way one can bring the entire nation in line behind the government."

Strunk said he joined the DRP because he was concerned with the "welfare of Germany's youth." "I don't think the training of youth should be quite as strict as it was under the National Socialists," he explained to the baffled court members, "but certainly stricter than it is today. In other words, a labor service term for all men and a year in uniform for the girls. More than 60 per cent of the girls today don't know how to handle a stove. Moreover, the Jews should be expelled from all leading positions in politics, business, industry, and culture."

"Do you know any Jews personally?" asked the judge.

"No," Strunk replied, "but I have no sympathies for the Jews and I consider it a great danger if the Germanic race mingles and mixes with them."

When they read these and other excerpts of testimony, democratically orientated Germans were appalled. They asked themselves two basic questions: "Where were these two in school? What were they taught?"

Chapter XI

The Fault of the Schools

A democratically oriented educational system is the basic prerequisite for Germany's spiritual rehabilitation and reconstruction. Without it there is virtually no hope of an intellectual and moral German rebirth in the family of democratic nations.

How successful have the Germans been in achieving this? When one reads of Zind, Stielau, Fernau, and others of their ilk who have been entrusted with the responsibility of charting a democratic course for young minds, the hope for Germany's future dims considerably. But their presence in the German teaching profession is a natural outgrowth of the chaotic situation after the war. The pedagogues had to be recruited from somewhere, and because of the dire need for teachers, occupation and German educational officials were compelled to compromise between reality and their aspirations. The circumstances in the immediate postwar period are described pointedly in a report issued in 1948 by the Office of Military Government for Hesse.[1] The problem in Hesse was also that of almost every other area of Germany.

[1] *Hesse: A New German State*, Arranged by Dexter L. Freeman. Druck und Verlagshaus, Frankfurt am Main, 1948.

. . . The boys and girls who entered school in the last few years of the Third Reich had been appallingly duped by the sugar-coated poison dispensed through educational channels. One has only to glance through a few of the official readers used in Hessian grade schools to realize how total a job was done in the inoculation of German children with Nazism. . . .

. . . Primary readers . . . contained such chapter headings as this: "Heroic German Men and Women"; "Stories of the World War"; "Struggle and Victory of the Nazi Movement"; and "German Gods and Heroes."

With the glorification of anything German and, in particular, of the *Führer* principle of the prominent members of the Nazi movements, went a ruthless attack against anything that might endanger the success of Nazi plans. Ostensibly innocent paragraphs in grade-school readers, devised to improve pupils' *reading* skill, were spiced with statements such as, "The Americans use corn and coffee to feed their locomotives," and "Who is the farmer's greatest enemy? The Jew."

Finding books that were not tainted by militaristic and "master race" ideas was a problem . . . in the first year of occupation. Under pressure to get the elementary, middle, and secondary schools back in operation on a de-Nazified basis, Military Government education personnel undertook an intensive program of screening textbooks and planning new teacher outlines. Quickly discovering that practically all the texts dating from the Hitler régime (even arithmetics) were full of Nazi propaganda, the educators turned their attention to books of pre-Hitler days and arranged for a few elementary readers and arithmetics to be reprinted intact for temporary emergency use in schools.

The plan for picking up educational strings that had been left dangling in 1933 was by no means satisfactory in all cases. Military Government screeners found that even under the Weimar Republic many trends had developed openly in German schoolbooks which helped pave the way for World War II.

Responsible educators were agreed that any policy of importing U.S. manufactured texts and imposing them on the German schools would be unwise and even dangerous. The Chief of Education and Religious Affairs clearly expressed the official attitude: "We reject the idea of active reeducation. Our interpretation of active education would mean bringing in 50 million textbooks, fifty thousand teachers, and doing the job of educating ourselves. Such spoonfeeding of a nation by another nation we consider educationally unsound."

The alternative was clear: enough German manufactured books had to be dug up to get the schools started. In Hesse, German and Military Government educational authorities launched a book hunt that extended from musty school stockrooms to closed-down publishing houses and private libraries, while higher authorities in OMGUS [2] set about rounding up all available copies of acceptable German textbooks which had found their way abroad. Meanwhile, in the fall of 1945, emergency paper allocations covered the printing of a quantity of new textbooks for distribution to grades one through eight.

. . . Hesse's shortage of textbooks was no more serious than the shortage of teachers who could pass de-Nazification screening tests. Military Government found that the instructors had become imbued with NSDAP dogmas even more than their impressionable pupils. Before education officers could give Hesse's school system a passably clean bill of health, 52 per cent of the elementary and secondary school teachers had been banned from their classrooms, and of the remaining 48 per cent, there were many borderline cases. The situation was not surprising when one took a glance at the notorious Nazi educational policy files. . . .

The specific controls that Military Government had to exercise in redirecting education in Hesse were not aimed at dictating the reorganization of the German school system or its curriculum, but were designed to produce a far-reaching purge of the Nazi and militaristic elements. In October, 1945, an American observer visited a fourth grade class in Wiesbaden and gleaned some startling information. From several children he learned, for instance, that World War II was started by Jewish money-grabbers. And the only reason the United States had joined in the conflict, declared others in the class, was that Americans had become envious of the Germans' industriousness.

When the American visitor brought up the subject of concentration camps with the pupils, the teacher flushed with embarrassment. "You oughtn't discuss such matters," he said. "That's all past history."

In October, 1945, the schoolbells rang . . . for the first time since the war ended and nearly 229,000 elementary pupils (in Hesse) trooped into the classrooms, representing approximately two thirds of all children between the ages of six and fourteen years. The sad part of it was that there was only 2,707 teachers for the 1,345 schoolhouses. In 1939, 5,748 teachers had been employed to teach approximately the same number of children. The postwar lack of non-Nazi teachers produced an average pupil-teacher ratio of 85 to 1, while in some localities, the ratio soared as high as 120 to 1. In rural schools one teacher generally taught all eight grades of the elementary schools eight hours a day, five days a week. . . .

[2] Office of Military Government, United States zone.

. . . The secondary schools were a little slower in getting started, chiefly because of de-Nazification troubles and building shortages. . . . In May [1946] the teaching staff totaled 1,129, more than 700 short of the number needed to permit normal operations. And, at the end of the year, the figure was still more than 450 below par.

That was the situation in 1945 and 1946. What has happened since then? What has been done to solve the teacher and textbook problem? What is the attitude of German youths toward the facts of the Hitler régime, World War II, and the mass extermination of the Jews?

For some ten years after 1947, no one gave the problem much thought. Throughout Germany it was merely assumed that everything was in order, that the teachers were democratically oriented, that the textbooks were properly written. The new generation, the generation which had not been poisoned by Nazi propaganda, which had seen only the destruction and wreckage wreaked by the Nazi régime, was expected to emerge as the hope for the future.

It is difficult to determine just when this optimistic axiom was first questioned. The motivation may have been the Ludwig Zind affair, perhaps the Lothar Stielau and Edgar Fernau incidents, or the case of the Berlin high-school teacher charged in 1958 with having participated actively in the Crystal Night during 1938. Or it may have been the episode of Hans Venatier, Rhineland Palatinate high-school instructor who wrote neo-Fascist articles in *Nation Europa*, an extreme right-wing periodical. When a school disciplinary probe was initiated against him, Venatier committed suicide.

Then, too, many Germans had expressed their apprehensions at the state of education when a former German Reich party member became Lower Saxony's minister of culture and education. Whatever it was that suddenly touched off a close examination of the postwar school system, the discoveries, to say the least, were shocking.

Although the number of Nazi-oriented and Nazi-sympathetic teachers is widely exaggerated by extremist anti-Germans, what soon became embarrassingly obvious was that most teachers have shied away from any controversial discussion or detailed study of recent history. Textbooks devote only cursory attention to the Nazi régime. Since 1958, the German and foreign press has devoted many columns to reports about the inadequacy of the educational system's approach to the Third Reich and the moral lesson it should teach. One of the earliest and among the most alarming reports appeared in the *Süddeutsche Zeitung* which published a full-page survey on the status of history education in Bavarian schools.[3] One pupil, asked by a Munich newsman to explain who Hitler had been, said, "about what the Kaiser was. Hitler was the leader of all the Germans. He established the Greater German Reich and drove out the Poles and the Jews because they had become too powerful."

Another student, in the first grade of vocational school,[4] was asked the same question. "A shoemaker," he replied.

A classmate laughed, and said, "No, that was the captain from Koepenick."

"Oh, yes," the first teenager retorted. "Now I remember. Hitler built the *Autobahnen*, gave work to the unemployed, and started the war."

His answer, though unnusually primitive and simple, was typical for those given by many pupils in the lower schools. In the secondary schools, attended by only a minority of German youth, the training ground for Germany's intelligentsia, there was an equally amazing lack of knowledge about the Third Reich, its leaders, and the brutal system of terror they had spread all over Europe.

Educators, journalists, religious leaders, and government officials expressed their concern. Then a well prepared journalistic fuse was set off in the midst of Germany's miraculously recovered economy. It was delivered in the form of a forty-five-minute documentary television show entitled *Blick auf Unsere Jugend* ("Focus on Our Youth"). Produced and planned by Juergen Neven-DuMont of the Hessian Radio and TV network, the program was broadcast all over Germany the evening of April 29, 1959. The documentary, based on interviews with students in twelve secondary, middle, elementary, and vocational schools, as well as teachers and parents in Bavaria,

---

[3] *Süddeutsche Zeitung*, Munich, July 26, 1958. Circulation 225,000 daily.

[4] Eighty per cent of German school children complete their education with the *Volksschule* (elementary school) at the age of fourteen. They then take up an apprenticeship. However, they must attend a *Berufsschule* (vocational school) on a one-day-per-week, in some states on a several-hours-a-day basis for three or more days, until they are eighteen. In addition to vocational training, this school expands the regular elementary program.

Hesse, Lower Saxony, and North Rhine Westphalia, exposed a tragic gap in the teaching of modern history and current events.

Only one out of ten *Gymnasium* [5] students, for example, had been able to give accurate answers when asked to name and describe the political parts into which Germany was divided after the war. To the question: "What do you know about Hitler and national socialism?" only two upper school students out of ninety-five had been able to explain satisfactorily the Nazi system, the principles for which it stood, and how it had been possible for such a régime to come to power in Germany. Both of these students had read Hitler's *Mein Kampf* from cover to cover and had drawn from it a clear, objective appraisal of dictatorship.

"In my opinion," said one of the two, "Adolf Hitler knew full well that the science which he called national socialism was a pseudo science. It only served as a means to his ends, to gain control in Germany, in Europe, and eventually in the entire world."

These two, of the ninety-five he questioned, according to Neven-DuMont, had acquired their knowledge, not so much from what they had been taught in school, but on their own initiative. The others displayed an appalling lack of information and disconcertingly muddled thinking and ideas. Asked how many knew the number of Jews who had been killed during the Third Reich, only thirteen out of a class of thirty-three raised their hands. Nine of them gave reasonably accurate replies, their estimates varying between 4 and 6 million.

When Neven-DuMont queried them about the German resistance movement, its leaders, their names, their accomplishments, and the goals, the replies were alarmingly inaccurate. One high-school student said a man named Wahrendorff (not Count Klaus von Stauffenberg) had been the resistance leader. Another student, a girl who avoided mentioning names, believed the leaders of the opposition had been scientists. When pressed to name some of them, she replied: "Einstein." She named Ludendorff as another. Asked to mention that name again, she repeated it.

Finally, after an awkward pause, a timid voice from the back of the classroom said, "Stauffenberg."

[5] This is one term for the German secondary school, attended by approximately the upper 10 per cent of the population.

"The resistance leaders planned the assassination of Hitler at a time when the war was almost decided," explained one student inaccurately. "They made contact with the Allies who, in turn, did not guarantee a peace treaty. The opposition fighters acted completely vaguely. They didn't know what would happen, and, of course, today, we can see that the Allies proved [in their attack on] Dresden that it wasn't just Hitler they were fighting but the entire German people.[6] The Allies had fired themselves up to such hatred they would not have accepted any German compromise, not even a democratic one."

Not one of the students was able to name the date of July 20, 1944, which, after all, is the key date in the resistance movement. They cited a one-time sidekick of Hitler like Ludendorff as a resistance fighter, and the name of Stauffenberg was known to only a few.

Neven-DuMont's questions regarding the leaders of the East Zone German Democratic Republic (DDR) and its political structure were met with even more hesitant replies. About 10 per cent of the students knew something, the rest stumbled in the dark over terms and names which appear in the newspapers each day. He emphasized to his video audience that the students he had just interviewed were regarded as the intellectual élite of Germany's future generation, for only 10 per cent attend the secondary, and another 10 per cent the middle schools.

Understandably, the responses of *Volksschule* pupils were even hazier. Quizzed on their knowledge of Hitler, some offered puzzling replies.

"When Hitler drove through the streets, the people had to raise their hands and shout 'Heil Hitler.' If they didn't do it, they were punished somehow," said one youngster.

A few of the other answers: ". . . [Hitler] sold badges in order to take power for himself."

"Hitler always had a dog with him and had a little black mustache."

"He was the leader of the National Socialist party and Stresemann was against him."

"He gave work to the unemployed and built *Autobahnen.*"

[6] The February 13, 1945, air raid on Dresden in which thousands of refugees were killed is an often used argument for Allied brutality.

"It was pretty good under Hitler in a way. There were no murderers, such as taxi murderers, which there are today, or others . . . women murderers. They were done away with right away and the young people went into parties such as the Hitler Youth."

"Hitler also did a great deal for the workers. He sent them out on ships for low prices." [7]

"He also provided for mothers and the little children. Whether he had ulterior motives when he did that, one can't say. He wanted to make himself popular with his people."

"Hitler did a great deal for the German people. It only got bad when he went insane."

"I think that what Hitler did was quite good. With one swoop he gave work to 7 million people and he saw to it that kids didn't loaf around like they do now."

Shocking as the responses were, Neven-DuMont did not stop there. He also asked pupils whether they knew the names of other Nazi leaders.

"Hindenburg, Marshal Tito, Khrushchev," were several immediate retorts from various corners of the classroom.

"Goebbels and Goering also belonged to Hitler. They were National Socialists too," said one student. The same pupil, asked what Goebbels' function had been, named him head of the air force.

Some students mentioned concentration camps, in which "people were treated like beasts but nobody knew about it."

"Well," quipped one girl, "Hitler wasn't supposed to start the war, but he did and that's why the Jews were killed in the concentration camps."

"Poles, Jews, and enemies of the state were killed by the thousands, the tens of thousands, in the concentration camps," another girl rejoined.

"How many were killed?" Neven-DuMont inquired.

"I think about fifty thousand," said a boy. "Forty to fifty thousand," ventured another. "Thirty-five thousand." "Thirty to forty thousand." "About eighty thousand?" asked one girl uncertainly. "Maybe twenty thousand." "I think it was more who were gassed by Hitler," one pupil replied. "It was about 11 million." "I think it's

[7] Meant apparently were the "Strength Through Joy" excursion steamers.

about 2 million." "Well, there were many millions, but they weren't counted," one girl explained. "We know from the concentration camp trial which took place here in Bonn [8] what cruelties were committed in the camps," one pupil pointed out, refusing, however, to be pinned down to specifics.

Neven-DuMont emphasized that while the boys and girls had been disconcertingly vague on the number of Jews killed, the figures of pre-Hitler unemployed were amazingly accurate. Their replies, he indicated, reflected the contents of their history books.

Only one elementary student could make any comment on the resistance movement and named Stauffenberg as a leader. One girl said, "I think Anne Frank was among them."

The reporter asked them to explain how Germany is divided today and what the different parts are called.

"I'm not quite sure," admitted one. "I don't know," answered another. "In four parts, but I don't know the names," replied one girl.

"I don't know it, either." "I don't, either."

And one girl, in a class in Goettingen, twelve miles from the Hessian state border, said: "Hesse is under Polish administration."

The TV man asked them to name the capital of Germany and the answers were equally vague. Some listed Berlin, others Bonn.

"In Berlin," explained one girl. "That's the capital of the Reich, but the government is in Bonn."

"Which government?" asked the narrator. There was a pause, and he asked again.

"I don't know that," she flashed back. "I don't really know what the capital is. I've asked about it and no one seems to be quite clear about it."

Only a refugee from the East zone gave a realistic and accurate response.

When he tested one class on their knowledge of the Soviet zone, the replies were just as dismaying.

Only three out of twelve raised their hands when the TV reporter asked them to name the leaders of the DDR, their political parties, and their aims and objectives. Of the three, two were East German

[8] The trial of Wilhelm Schubert and Gustav Sorge. See page 22, Chapter II.

refugees and gave answers which indicated they knew what the Communist aims were.

The same questions also were posed to students in vocational schools, those, in other words, between fifteen and eighteen, already serving out apprenticeships. They knew very little more than the *Volksschule* pupils.

"The vocational school may dispense a great deal of knowledge," the narrator interjected, "but they do not have a real history curriculum. Ask about Hitler, the Hitler régime, or about the DDR, and you get virtually the same responses as in the elementary school. What they have not already learned before, they will not learn here, either. They start out in life [politically unprepared], the great mass of our students, the voters of tomorrow."

And what do the parents say to all this?

Some 95 per cent considered it essential, important, or good that their children be fully informed about what has happened in Germany since 1933. Only 5 per cent were opposed to an effective modern history program. The students were nearly 100 per cent in favor of more instruction on the subject.

"I want to know more," said one youth, "because there was a Jewish synagogue near here and I want to know why Hitler had it destroyed and why he had such hatred for the Jews."

"We Germans are always accused of persecuting the Jews and others. And we really don't know anything about it," a girl enjoined.

"As we read and heard about the concentration camp trial of Schubert and Sorge, many of us young people asked ourselves why they had done those things," explained a teenage boy. "They must have been delirious. In the English press there is so much criticism of us and we have to defend ourselves against that. That's why I would like to know more."

Of a dozen or so who appeared on the screen, all wanted to know more about Nazism, about communism, about what had transpired in their early childhood and why their country had been destroyed and divided.

"I'll admit that I haven't concerned myself with all this too much privately," one youth confessed. "But I'd like to say that perhaps the schools ought to go into this a little deeper. I don't want to blame the schools, but I think it's their responsibility to teach us."

There it was. A young German student had placed the blame where most Germans put it, where they feel the major responsibility rests.

Leading German education officials insist that curricular programs include recent history, in particular that of the Nazi régime. But, they admit, if over the years, German youths still have not formed a clear picture of the situation, still don't know the truth, and in many cases know hardly anything at all, then the schools have indeed failed on certain levels. They attribute this to several causes. They maintain, first of all, that there is an insufficient demand on the part of the parents for more extensive information and emphasis on the subject. Second, educators point to a distinct lack of interest and enthusiasm on the part of the teachers to delve into these problems. Third, there is no encouragement in textbooks to go into the matter deeply.

One high-school teacher interviewed on Neven-DuMont's show said he had taken his senior history class through the start of World War II. Then time ran out. Another high-school instructor who teaches both history and social science explained that the latter course was the most adaptable to the problem of Nazism. But, he asserted, it was scheduled for one hour per week and that hour was infringed upon frequently by other school activities and absences, making it difficult to analyze and discuss the Nazi problem effectively.

A teacher at a *Mittelschule* (middle school)[9] for girls in Frankfurt insisted that the only way he could "squeeze" modern events, particularly the developments following World War I, into the history program would be by reducing the time he devoted to the Middle Ages. He suggested a complete reorganization of the history curriculum.

A *Volksschule* teacher disagreed with this contention saying each instructor had sufficient leeway in which he could make his own changes. Any teacher who wanted to discuss Nazism and the war in class could do so, he said, as the class outlines are quite flexible.

[9] Actually an upper, or secondary school classification, accounting for approximately 10 per cent of the total population's educational experience. Students graduate from middle schools at age sixteen and are then qualified for the lower and middle strata civil service positions, white-collar jobs, and as skilled and semi-skilled labor.

Yet the most common argument is still that the curricular schedules do not provide the time to devote to the problem of the Third Reich and World War II.

Another frequently heard postulate is that the history texts are inadequate for very recent or current developments.

Some teachers maintain that parents don't want their children drilled in these matters.

Others argue that events which have occurred in the past fifty years are too recent to be viewed with historical objectivity. One teacher in this category, for example, feels that even World War I is too recent a subject matter for a history course. In fact he takes his classes only up to the founding of the united German Empire in 1870–1871. Many are so systematic that they delve into earlier periods with such detail and consume so much class time they really can discuss modern events in only cursory generalities.

Thousands of teachers are still trying to untangle their own murky notions about the twelve-year Reich and the turbulent political period preceding it. Thus, they feel they are unqualified to attempt objective instruction. Instead they avoid the topic or circumvent it with brief and indefinite allusions. Many high- and middle-school students have been heard to say that teachers fear being ridiculed by their own pupils. To explain objectively Hitler's rise to power teachers would have to point out how the mass of the German people had been duped by the dictator. But they would appear ludicrous in front of their classes should a student happen to ask: "Teacher, what did you do during the period?"

Then some feel as one Hessian high-school instructor.

"I'm careful about criticizing the Third Reich during the Fourth Reich, for I don't know yet what sort of government will take over the Fifth Reich."

Is it true that many ex-Nazis including those who were barred from teaching positions by Allied occupation authorities have been reinstated by way of the "131 Law"?

"Yes, many ex-Nazis are back in our schools," admitted Dr. Wolfgang Bobke, a spokesman for the Hessian ministry of culture and education, "but I'm certain that the really dangerous Nazis have not returned and there are still many ex-Nazi teachers who have not and will not be reemployed. Those who were rehired first of all are not all history teachers and secondly the great mass of them were fellow travelers or minor party members. I don't think that's the problem."

"The problem is more that the average teacher is too indifferent to the problem to make the extra effort needed to instruct in detail," said another Hessian educator. "He has to do research, pick out extra textbooks or other works which will present the problem dramatically to his students. That requires effort and the average teacher is too lazy to do that. It's easier and more convenient just to glide over subject matter which is controversial and brings back unpleasant memories and pangs of consciousness for the teacher."

The Zind, Fernau, Venatier, and Stielau cases prove, however, that those few teachers who are still ideologically attached to the Third Reich will find a way to give vent to their ideas, even if only by means of slight, barely perceptible inflections, side comments, or such adverbs as "allegedly" 6 million Jews were killed.

Fortunately, for each Zind or Venatier there are thousands of democratically oriented teachers, especially in the younger ranks. Even before Neven-DuMont's TV documentary, positive steps in the right direction were being taken. Thus, for instance, a Bavarian state agency has prepared a set of records of Nazi speeches which unmask the party leaders in all their fanaticism and absurdity. They were made available to schools. Student reaction to them has been universally good. They hear the speeches of Hitler, Goebbels, and Goering and laugh. They asked how their parents could have been so foolish as to have believed all that. And they ask their embarrassed teachers: "How could you have believed it?"

The official textbooks that are in use in German schools have met with considerably more criticism than the teaching plans and the efforts of individual teachers. Although this is a pressing problem one must keep in mind that in the final analysis, no matter how good the textbook is, it is the use which the teacher makes of the book that determines the quantity and quality of modern history instruction.

Several large textbook publishers dominate the scene in Germany. Leading among them are Ernst Klett Verlag in Stuttgart, Moritz Diesterweg Verlag in Frankfurt, Hirschgraben Verlag, Frankfurt,

Georg Westermann Verlag in Braunschweig and Darmstadt, and Mundas Verlag in Stuttgart. Although all history books have come under fire in recent years, extremely severe criticism has been heaped on the titles of two of the largest publishers, Klett and Westermann.

Most state cultural ministries prepare a list of approved texts which is made available to teachers, principals, and school superintendents in the state. Theoretically, each teacher has the right to select from this list the textbook he wishes for his class. For reasons of practicality, however, school officials in any given city usually attempt to standardize the texts. Approval of the list of books is left to a committee of experts in each of the individual state education and culture ministries.[10]

Although it would be unfair to generalize about all the books, there are certain generalities which do apply to them all. They are characterized by a relatively brief and superficial treatment of the period from World War I until the present. All the books tend to gloss over the injustices of the Hitler régime but become more detailed when they discuss the unfortunate lot of Germans in the occupation periods after the Second and First World Wars.

All display nationalistic attitudes in their discussion of the lost eastern territories such as Silesia, East Prussia, and Pomerania. All have an accusatory tone when dealing with the plight of the expellees from these eastern territories and the Czechoslovakian Sudetenland.

The books tend to gloss over the war-crimes tribunals, and what little they say has an anti-Allied ring. In one book the term "war criminal" appears consistently in quotation marks, indicating the authors questioned the theory that the defendants in the military tribunals were criminals.

Not one book drives home the real horrors and brutality of the Nazi system. None of them draws clear connecting lines between the injustice of the Nazi régime, the blindness of the German people in allowing the Nazis to come to power, and the subsequent German fate during and after the war. There is a distinct break in what

[10] The autonomy of the states in matters of education and culture is a postwar development designed to prevent central federal control. It is a right guarded jealously and considered one of the most important safeguards of democracy.

ought to be a line of logic and reasoning. One is struck by the absence of a "cause and effect" interpretation of recent history.

While a great deal of space is devoted to the plight of the Germans during the early occupation period, only a few of the texts make any mention of the Marshall Plan and how it aided ruined, starving Germany.

There is also a marked tendency toward glorifying the victorious actions of the German army and minimizing the injustice of the invasion of Poland, France, Belgium, the Netherlands, the Scandinavian countries, Greece, and Russia. While most of the texts describe in great detail the horror of the Allied bombing missions over Germany, only a few explain that these were the result of Germany's air attacks on Britain and the Nazi call for total war.

The students simply are not confronted with the whys and wherefores of the occupation, Germany's defeat, and Germany's defamation in the eyes of the world. A pupil completely unfamiliar with the era will never understand why there were war-crimes trials, why a resistance movement, why Germany was destroyed, and why it was occupied. He may know that all this happened, but his conception will be a twisted one encompassing resentment, not toward the Nazi perpetrators whose misdeeds threw Germany into defeat and divided her, but resentment toward the victors of World War II.

Although each book [11] makes at least some mention of the brutalities and atrocities committed by the Nazis, these are treated in such generalities and so superficially that they leave no marked impression on the student whatever. No attempt is made really to explain the dictatorial system by describing how it operated and terrorized, not only the people of the occupied nations, but the Germans themselves.

While most texts are liberally supplied with illustrations and photographs which describe battle scenes, German soldiers freezing in the snows of Russia, German cities bombed and destroyed, not a single textbook of the dozen has one picture depicting Nazi atrocities. One book does contain a picture of the exercise yard of Oranienburg concentration camp near Berlin, but Oranienburg, one of the first concentration camps, was more like an ordinary prison than any

[11] The author examined twelve of the most widely used texts, ranging from *Volksschule* through *Gymnasium* level.

other. There are no pictures of such liquidation camps as Auschwitz or of near-starving inmates of Buchenwald or Dachau, no photos of mass graves in Poland or Russia.

Only a small percentage of the books provide accurate figures on the number of concentration and liquidation camps and special extermination squad victims. Usually these are passed off in generalities, such as "many," "millions," or "hundreds of thousands." It is easy to argue that school children do not have a proper conception of figures in the millions. Yet even the *Volksschule* students interviewed by Neven-DuMont knew exactly the number of unemployed Germans who were provided work by Hitler.

There is in these German history books a clear trend, not toward changing the facts, but toward twisting their implications to suit German ends, a distinct attempt to minimize unpleasant facts, and a very noticeable omission of the lesson which Nazi history *should* present to the new generation.

It is only fair, however, to point out that a few texts are very positive in these directions and others are being rewritten to bring them up to standard. Nor are the schools limited to these history books. Supplementary literature is available to every teacher when he begins to broach the subject of modern events. Most school libraries are well stocked with such informative works as Walther Hofer's *National Socialism—Documents from 1933 to 1945*, and Harry Pross's *The Destruction of German Politics, Documents 1871 to 1933*, Eugen Kogon's *The SS State*, and Hans Rothfels' *The German Opposition to Hitler*.

But putting the generalities aside, some of the textbooks contain passages that merit closer scrutiny. Following are selections from books on the approved list of numerous states for the school year of 1959 to 1960.

Der Mensch im Wandel der Zeiten (Man in the Changing Times) by Ida Maria Bauer and Otto Heinrich Mueller, edition of 1958, published by Georg Westermann Verlag, Braunschweig and Darmstadt, consists of two volumes, designed to be used in series over a period of three years, that is, in the fifth, sixth, and seventh grades of elementary and middle schools. The texts have been criticized extensively in and out of Germany. They are used widely in Hessian schools.

Volume A, written for fifth and sixth grade students, is in the form of a "history reader." The approach, through the use of stories and situations, is pedagogically well prepared. The book opens by introducing a little boy named Manfred Krause who is just starting to study history in school. History is made dramatic for him by the story of his own family. Through this arbitrary family situation the pupil is told of Manfred's life, how his mother's first husband was killed in the war, how she was expelled from Silesia, how she met her second husband, Manfred's own father, where the grandparents, aunts, and uncles live.

It continues by describing the terrible postwar period which Manfred, being born in 1948, cannot remember, how everybody had lost everything, how there was no food, and how his father was in an American prisoner-of-war camp.

Manfred, as the little story unfolds, asks his father how he happened to have become a traveling salesman. In the course of this interchange the father tells Manfred how fortunate he had been to get a job in 1932, when, after all, 7 million people were unemployed.

Throughout this first chapter, which deals exclusively with the history of Manfred's family, there is undue emphasis on the expellee problem. Although the chapter has certain positive aspects, created by the "fact" that Manfred's mother was driven from her home in Silesia, no attempt is made to explain why she had to endure this exodus.

There is, however, a strong antimilitaristic passage which deserves mention. The stage for this is set by relating that Manfred has started a family photo album on one page of which he has pasted pictures of his great-grandfather, grandfather, and father, all in military uniform.

"Manfred's father didn't feel quite right about his son having pasted the three pictures next to each other," the book explains. "The pictures brought to mind three wars in which three generations of the Krause family had been forced to participate. And these three wars had brought suffering and misfortune to the entire family as well as all the German people, other people, and the entire world."

Although the passage fails to place the blame for the war on the Germans, it is certainly antimilitaristic. A much more forceful position is taken in relating what has happened to Manfred's relatives.

One aunt, it is explained, married an American soldier and now lives in far-off Chicago. Another aunt, according to the little story, has lived in Brazil since 1935. This "biography" of Aunt Rosel represents the most effective attack on the Nazi régime in any of the twelve texts.

The Brazil aunt, so the story goes, was engaged to a young man in Silesia who was the leader of a religious youth group in 1934. He refused to join the Hitler Youth. He was arrested by the SA, eventually released from prison, and then escaped to Brazil. Rosel followed him there and they were married.

". . . Even Aunt Rosel wants to come and visit her fatherland which she hasn't seen for so long," the narrative continues. "She probably won't be able to see her Silesian homeland, though. . . . Just as her husband did, in those days, she left a country in which people were arrested and jailed merely because they had a different opinion about things from that of the government."

So much for the opening chapter.

Modern history is not discussed again in this book [12] until, on page 200, Chapter XVII, *Auf dem Wege zur Demokratie*, one finds the following interesting passages about the period and events leading up to World War I:

The European industrial states were inconvenienced by the successes of the German businessmen in foreign markets. In addition to that, there were other tensions. . . .

Germany's alliance with Austria was a thorn in the side of the Russians. . . .

The English considered themselves hemmed in in the expansion of their empire by German colonial possessions.

From pages 208 to 217 the book discusses the Hitler régime in pure chronological order, then starts to relate about the bombed cities, the expulsion of the ethnic Germans from the eastern territories, and the occupation. Some enlightening phrases from the paragraphs covering the postwar period are:

[12] It is a joint venture, by the way, on the part of several contributing authors.

The war cost 30 million lives . . . and in the land [Germany] there was the hard, unrelenting victor. . . .

In commenting on the de-Nazification and war-crimes tribunals, the book said that Germans were haled before these boards "by the foreign gentlemen."

In a chronological table of historic events in an appendix, the period between 1939 and 1945 is covered only in these words: "Second World War, 12 million Germans were expelled from their homes."

Volume B of *Der Mensch im Wandel der Zeiten*, directed toward seventh and eight grade students in elementary and middle schools, has this to say on the subject of the persecution of the Jews:

They were deported by the thousands and ten thousands to concentration camps, ghettos, and liquidation camps where the furnaces smoked day and night.

Einst und Jetzt (Then and Now) is the title of a two-part history book issued by Moritz Diesterweg Verlag in Frankfurt. Its authors are Dr. Waldemar Hoffmann and Georg Mueller. This work, like the Westermann title, is also divided into a first volume for fifth and sixth graders in the form of a "historical reader," while the second part is chronologically arranged for seventh and eighth graders. *Einst und Jetzt* is approved in six of Germany's ten states plus West Berlin.

In Volume I there is a short story about Hitler, appearing on page 108, which states, among other things:

Hitler forced weapons into the hands of the German people and led his forces of millions toward the West, South, North and East. . . . In his mistaken judgment he also declared war on the U.S. But they had tremendous reserves and air flotillas.

On page 248 of Volume II one can read:

. . . With the help of his Gestapo, Hitler locked Communists, Social Democrats, and opposing politicians in so-called concentration camps. There they had to work hard behind barbed wire, were grilled, tortured, and beaten. Many died. Hitler's hate toward the Jews was limitless. In the course of the years he took away their property, their livelihoods, tore apart their families, and finally had countless ones killed. . . .

No figures, no details, no dates, no explanations as to why Hitler did all that. On page 267:

Because of their rapid advance, Hitler's concentration camps fell undestroyed into the hands of the Allied troops in the East and the West. In these camps Hitler had driven together the enemies of his inhuman dictatorship, above all Jews, but also Poles, Russians, Czechs, French, and, not least, Germans of all parties, Protestant and Catholic priests, officers and intellectuals. Extermination squads of the SS gassed men, women, and children. Thus Hitler and his helpers brought shame to the entire German people.

The German people had to atone. . . . Millions [of Germans] fled fearfully from the East before the victoriously advancing Russians. Those left behind had to suffer indescribable things. Whoever withstood the invasion of the Red Army was forcefully expelled from his homeland: for the Russians, Poles, and Czechs took possession of the German land. The Germans trekked out of East Prussia, Pomerania, Silesia, the Sudetenland, Bohemia, and Moravia. Supplied only with the barest necessities, they wandered despairingly westward from one village to the next . . . plagued by hunger and disease.

This volume devotes generous space to the *Wehrmacht*'s early victories and is marked by a distinct undertone of pride. Part of the story of the war is told in the form of a German soldier's diary. Some 113 words are devoted to his description of the bombing of Dresden. However, none of the other brutalities of the war, those committed by Germans, are described in any detail or with any drama.

Lebendige Vergangenheit (*The Living Past, History for Middle Schools*), published by Ernst Klett Verlag of Stuttgart, is a six-volume work, the first volume being a history reader. Its 1957 edition is in wide use. Volume 5, covering the period from 1850 until the present, was written by Fritz Simonsen, a school superintendent.

On page 132 one finds the following concerning the invasion of Russia:

. . . Hitler feared a Russian attack while German troops were still fighting on the Western Front. He wanted to get the jump [on the Russians].

On page 144, this about the Allied occupation: ". . . Morgenthau developed a plan which would have eliminated the Reich for all time. Germany was supposed to become grazing land for goats. . . ." Simonsen wrote, explaining that this program, however, was disapproved because it would have meant starvation for millions of Germans. Instead, it was decided to allow Germany light, peaceful industry. "Nevertheless," he continued, "the manufacture of synthetic gasoline, rubber, and other industrial products was forbidden. . . . Cartels and trusts were supposed to be 'decentralized.' In many of the laws the desire to destroy German competition on the world market became apparent."

This book, too, is very sympathetic to expellees, devoting considerable space to the great injustice of the enforced exodus from the eastern territories but failing to explain the causes. Such terms as "militarists" and "war criminals" are in quotes.

Spiegel der Zeiten (Mirror of the Times) is a five-volume set for middle schools by Diesterweg Verlag. The fifth volume, entitled *Die Neueste Zeit*, deals with modern history. The period from 1900 to 1945 is covered in a hundred pages. A half page is devoted to the expulsion and extermination of the Jews.

Books used in *Gymnasien* are equally sketchy. The chief difference is that they use more sophisticated language and go into more detail on subjects other than the Third Reich. Thus we find that fifty-four pages are devoted to the period from 1933 to 1945 in the modern history volume of Klett Verlag's high-school series, *Geschichtliches Unterrichtswerk für Mittelklassen, Ausgabe B.* This is considerably more than in other textbooks, but the basic question once more is how the Nazi period is interpreted. This volume, entitled, *Um Volksstaat und Völkergemeinschaft*, by Dr. Hermann Pinnow and Dr. Fritz Textor, takes an unduly conciliatory attitude, highlighted by frequent insinuative additions to interpretations of facts which must leave a deep mark on impressionable youths. In discussing the advent and progress of World War II, the authors concern themselves with the invasion of Russia. On page 185 they state:

The war with Russia began on June 22, 1941 [Germany being] supported by Finns, Romanians, and Hungarians, later also by small units of volunteers from Spain, France, Belgium, and Norway.[13]

On page 186, in a discussion of Hitler's tactical mistakes, it says: "Above all, his senseless political methods in the occupied eastern territories drove the population toward sharp resistance."

America's entry into the war is discussed on page 187 with these remarks:

WAR IN THE PACIFIC: The danger of war breaking out between Japan and the Americans became increasingly imminent during 1941. To force Japan to call a halt to its war against China, Roosevelt made use of the most serious economic pressures, designed to cause the collapse of Japan's economy. Months-long negotiations broke up on America's intentionally tough demands. Therefore, the military party in Japan, which would rather take up the bitter battle than knuckle under the American pressure without a fight, gained control.

The air war over Germany is described thus on pages 190–191:

From the end of 1942 large air raids by the British, later by the Americans, brought death and ruin to the Reich. The number, effectiveness, and flying radii of the Anglo-Saxon bombers increased steadily. Their attacks were directed, not so much against the militarily important war industries and transportation centers, but they destroyed millions of homes, thereby killing hundreds of thousands of people, and destroyed countless cultural monuments, libraries, churches, research and education facilities. Eventually not even the farmer in his fields or the pedestrians on the open country highways were safe from the attacks.

All Nazi crimes are wrapped into several brief paragraphs on pages 191–192, the only mention of what took place in concentration camps:

The more the military situation in Germany worsened, the more hope in victory declined, the more harshly did the rulers pull in the reins. More

[13] The original German text appears consistently in the present tense. For purposes of clarity and fluency I have used the past tense in the translation.

people than ever before were sent to concentration camps. The battle against Christianity and the Church was intensified. Besides that, mass murders of the most gruesome sort took place.

A campaign against the helpless inmates of insane asylums was hidden under the code name "Destruction of Life Not Worthy of Living." Organizations of the National Socialist party determined which of these unfortunate people would be allowed to live and decreed that the rest would be sent to their death. It went even worse for the Jews in Hitler's realm of power. Ever stricter measures were employed as the war progressed. Hitler ordered the "Final Solution of the Jewish Question." In the Reich and in the occupied territories several million Jews were arrested. Most of them met a horrible death in the gas chambers of special "liquidation squads."

The grisly liquidation program progressed with the greatest secrecy. Only a few people knew about it. Many suspected that terrible things were going on but no one had any proof, no one dared to raise his voice. Death for him would have been certain and his death wouldn't have had the slightest external effect.

This book, on the other hand, is sharply critical of war-crimes trials and the de-Nazification program. It is very detailed on the expulsion of the ethnic Germans from the eastern territories, giving exact figures on the number of refugees, just as it gave exact figures on the number of unemployed who were put to work by Hitler when he came to power.

Grundriss der Geschichte, Klett Verlag's history book for *Gymnasium* seniors (Volume 3 by Dr. Hans Herzfeld, Dr. Jochen Dittrich and Dr. Edeltraud Dittrich-Gallmeister), portrays in detail an extermination squad's work in a ghetto. The place was not identified but the description was sufficiently impressionable to last in a teenager's mind for many years. *However, in the example cited, the atrocities were committed not by German SS men, but Ukrainian volunteers.*

Grundzüge der Geschichte (Outline of History), another upper-school book, is published by Moritz Diesterweg Verlag. Its Volume VII *From the Beginning of the French Revolution 1789 Until the Present,* by Dr. Ernst Busch, discusses the rise of the Nazi régime, the war, and the occupation, in fifteen pages; the Hitler atrocities in a few lines.

For the Western world, the Second World War stood under the sign of a crusade: the democratic states against the totalitarian dictatorships. The atrocities committed by National Socialism in the occupied territories were terrible. The executions of politically suspect persons and hostages were countless. The countries were plundered and their workers dragged to Germany. Millions of Jews were exterminated in the concentration camps.

Certainly history books in other nations are no more critical of their own countrymen than the Germans are of theirs. For all practical purposes, only the English, the Indians, and the Southerners perform the role of villains in American schoolbooks. British histories present a view and interpretation of the American Revolution completely different from those of United States texts. And Napoleon Bonaparte fares better in French books than he does in English or German ones. Although this trend is explicable, it is far from desirable, at any rate not in Germany, where the "villains" of history are still (and again) politically active. German school children should not be spared the facts, for only through a direct encounter with the mistakes of their fathers can they chart a new course and learn to defend themselves against a possible recurrence of the past.

Fortunately, not only foreigners, but German observers agree with this principle. The call for improvement in the textbooks and the modern history program has come from all quarters. Most cultural and educational ministers have demanded revised texts from the publishers. "This will come," said Hesse's Dr. Bobke. "It will come through sheer pressure of public opinion and competition. For as things are developing at the present time,[14] culture ministries all over the country will be forced to become more heedful of domestic and foreign attitudes, thus more demanding and critical of the texts they permit in the schools. As this occurs, certain publishers whose books do not meet the increasingly rigid standards, will find themselves excluded from the approval list. They will have no choice but to rewrite the chapters in question. The pure element of competition, I feel, will result in steady improvement."

The course of official action to revise and expand the modern history program predates the post-Christmas anti-Semitic wave by

[14] Following the anti-Semitic wave after Christmas Eve, 1959.

nearly two years. The first echoes of public dissatisfaction were heard early in 1958. They gained impetus in midyear through the publication of the *Süddeutsche Zeitung*'s exposé. In February, 1959, Chancellor Adenauer, speaking to representatives of the Central Association of Democratic Resistance Fighters and organizations of victims of Nazi persecution, criticized the lack of political education in the schools. He blamed inadequate schoolbooks and the absence of aggressive political instruction for anti-Semitic and neo-Nazi activities.

On March 12, 1959, federal President Theodor Heuss [15] sent a letter to the standing conference of German cultural ministers,[16] asking them to investigate the modern history curriculum. His letter was read into the minutes of the April 23 and 24 conference. The ministers voted to have their "school committee" research the problem in greater detail. Five days after this conference, Neven-DuMont's TV documentary was telecast across the country. Many newspapers and magazines in and outside Germany published stinging excerpts from the program. By midsummer, 1959, most of the cultural ministries had taken or planned some concrete steps.

The topic of political education as well as reform plans calling for a ninth elementary school year remained in the news haphazardly until Christmas Eve, 1959. Since then, the educational policies and their potential responsibility for the wave of neo-Nazi incidents have been in the limelight. In fact, to a large degree, the educational system has become the scapegoat. This sweeping generalization, however, simplifies the problem too much and is, in truth, unfair to German educators. There *has* been what the Germans have termed a "lack of courage" to discuss Hitler and Nazism in the schools, but it must be remembered that efforts to improve the situation had been under way in varying degrees in the different states for more than one year prior to the Cologne incident.

[15] Heuss served as the Federal Republic's first president until September, 1959, when his second and final term expired. He was succeeded by Heinrich Luebke, former federal minister of agriculture.

[16] The ministers of culture and education from each of the ten German states and Berlin meet periodically to discuss mutual problems. Although there is no federal ministry of education or culture, there is close state integration through this standing conference. The chief civil servants in each ministry, heading such departments as education, radio, and theater, have formed standing committees which meet even more frequently than the ministers.

Because the individual states are completely autonomous in their educational and cultural policies, no over-all view of the situation and proposals to improve it is possible. However, an examination of the programs of two states, representing diametrically opposite poles in postwar German politics, will provide a cursory, cross-sectioned glimpse of current problems and developments.

Hesse, one of the states originally established by United States occupation authorities, has had a predominantly Social Democratic administration since January 6, 1947. Its present minister president (governor), Georg Zinn, has been in office continually since January 10, 1951, with two elections in between. Its cultural minister since January 28, 1959, following the last election, has been Professor Dr. Ernst Schuette, Social Democrat and educator by profession.

The Rhineland Palatinate, on the other hand, originally French occupation territory, in the area west of the Rhine, is predominantly Christian Democrat. It has had a CDU government since its establishment. The state is primarily agrarian and has a huge Catholic majority. Its cultural minister is Dr. Eduard Orth, head of a large furniture factory whose sales to state agencies implicated him in a political scandal in early 1959. Dr. Orth has been in office since September 1, 1956. The Rhineland Palatinate, which encompasses such cities as Mainz, Trier, Worms, Speyer, Coblenz, Kaiserslautern, and Bad Kreuznach, is the only state in which the German Reich party (DRP), represented by one member in the legislature, was outlawed following the Cologne synagogue desecration.

While Hesse, considerably more industrial, cosmopolitan, and largely Protestant, has had its share of anti-Semitic incidents, including the Kurt Sumpf case in Koeppern, the Rhineland Palatinate has served up two teachers linked with neo-Nazistic activities. One was Venatier, who committed suicide, the other a young high-school instructor who was active in the German Reich party.

As early as April, 1959, less than three months after his ministerial appointment, Hesse's Dr. Schuette held a press conference at which he expressed his dissatisfaction with the scope of political and modern history education in Hesse and promised to take decisive remedial action. He told newsmen that he felt the facts about the Hitler régime were being taught too sketchily and too late.

In the spring of 1959 he ordered an extensive survey of the modern history and social science program in upper schools. It revealed that the majority of instructors were approaching history in a purely chronological fashion. As a result, 60 per cent of the senior class courses usually began with the French Revolution or the Age of Reason; 30 per cent with the demise of Napoleon or the Revolution of 1848; some 10 per cent with the 1870–1871 unification of the German Empire.

In classes where the instructors had started with the French Revolutionary period, the survey showed, students rarely were taken past the end of World War I by graduation time. This was in direct violation of ministerial degrees which called for special emphasis in graduation classes on the post-1917 period. Of the 60 per cent which had begun with the French Revolution, the report explained, some one fourth, or 15 per cent of all students, had not yet reached the twentieth century.

In the over-all picture, the survey indicated, by graduation 17 per cent of all *Gymnasium* students had studied history only up to the turn of the nineteenth century; another 18 per cent had reached the end of World War I, 22 per cent were in the period of the Weimar Republic, and less than half had started learning about the Third Reich. The report stated that it had been impossible to determine to what extent the Hitler period had been discussed in weekly social science courses. The ministry survey had determined, moreover, that the post-World War II period had not been covered in any of the upper classes.

On June 22, 1959, Professor Schuette issued another decree to improve the situation. Directed to all principals of public and private *Gymnasien* and the leaders of study seminars for teachers, it said tersely: "I expect that in the future, no later than the end of the summer vacation, major emphasis will be placed in all graduating classes, on the epoch after 1917. One of the main objectives in teaching history is to explain to our youth its position and future responsibilities in relationship to historical developments. A history course which does not include developments since 1917, in particular since 1933, fails to accomplish this purpose. . . ."

The education minister ordered that other eras be dealt with more superficially to leave time in the curricular schedule for detailed discussion of the post-World War I developments. In addition, Hessian authorities called for more emphasis on modern history in *Volks-schulen*; teacher seminars were started; and the Hessian *Landeszen-trale für Heimatdienst* [17] launched a program to bring its books, films, and pamphlets to the schools.

On August 26, 1959, Schuette reiterated his policies and demands in an article in a Hessian teachers' trade journal. Then little more was heard of the issue until the synagogue smearing in Cologne. Again German newspapers editorialized that the inadequate history program was chiefly responsible for the wave of anti-Semitic outbursts. Their lack of knowledge about the Third Reich, it was theorized, made young people susceptible to racist and nationalist propaganda from extremist groups.

Hessian cultural authorities issued a second decree, similar in principle to that of June 22, but directed instead at elementary and middle schools. Professor Schuette ordered that the full facts of the Hitler Reich and the meaning of Nazi ideology be emphasized with no punches pulled in all state schools, starting with the fifth grade. He also called for the distribution of four thousand copies of Thomas Gnielka's booklet, *Falschspiel mit der Vergangenheit*,[18] to the teachers' libraries in all Hessian schools.

In Rhineland Palatinate the problem of history and political education was first aired publicly at a July 3, 1959, conference of high-school rectors and principals. The meeting had been called expressly for the purpose of discussing this matter. Dr. Orth, the state's cultural and education minister, praised the principals for their efforts in the past and expressed his appreciation and understanding for the difficulties they faced.

The [recent] remonstrances by the press are disturbing [he stated]. Since they are not entirely unfounded, we cannot just pass over them without comment. Undoubtedly, some of the reports were greatly exaggerated. Without a doubt, the facts in some cases were blurred by generalizations, and without a doubt, some of the articles were sensationalized, but there is also little doubt about the fact that some of the allegations are true, and that one or the other journalist lodged his criticism with the feeling that one of his responsibilities is to act as a seismograph of our democracy. . . .

[17] A state agency for political education. See page 224.
[18] See page 90.

. . . What have we done so far? What can be done in the future? The following:

1. It is essential that our youth receive a penetrating picture of the period after 1917, that the phenomenon of Hitler become clear in its causes and effects, and that an all-encompassing knowledge of modern history be guaranteed. Likewise, the fundamentals of our democracy must be taught.

2. But learning and knowledge do not suffice. . . . The learning must become understanding, and knowledge must be turned into evaluation. Deeds and facts must be impregnated with a viewpoint and understood, not by condemning or praising them, but by careful weighing and balancing of the various aspects.

Dr. Orth stated that knowledge and understanding of the Nazi period must be evaluated so that students come to realize their responsibility for the maintenance of a free and democratic state.

On July 14, he issued a decree concerning modern history and civics education in the state's upper schools. Sent to all high-school principals, it set exact guidelines for instructors. It prescribed two instead of one hour per week for civics courses in all senior classes, and that history hours be increased to three a week. Since the two subjects supplement and complement each other, Dr. Orth ordered that the same teacher instruct both courses.

The decree established a minimum of forty-five hours per semester to be devoted to the post-1917 period and to the problem of Nazism and communism in civics courses. Examiners at the testing sessions, which all German seniors must undergo before being graduated, were instructed to question students about their knowledge of recent history and current events. The decree ordered further that at least twenty hours be devoted in the second semester of the tenth grade to the Nazi régime and recent history and that school principals question tenth-graders on their knowledge of the subject before passing them into the eleventh grade. The ministry also promised to make topical bibliographies and teachers' aides available. It organized three-day conferences and seminars to acquaint history and civics instructors with the newest education methods.

Dr. Orth announced a contest for all schools. As a prize, a book dealing with the problem of citizenship and democracy and a certificate would be awarded to the senior in each school who had been selected by the student council as the most active in history and civics courses. Following the Cologne incident, this program was expanded to encompass elementary, vocational, and middle schools as well. A ministry official pointed out that in addition to expanding the formal curriculum, the state has had a long-standing practice of regularly inviting high-school classes to attend sessions of the state legislature, followed by a lunch in the official cafeteria with Dr. Orth.

The Rhineland Palatinate's civics course has been a mandatory part of the educational program since 1952. It is taught in all classes from the seventh grade upward. Teachers colleges now have special courses in civics (called *Politische Gemeinschaftskunde* in the Rhineland, *Sozialkunde* in Hesse) and besides being a separate course, curricular programs prescribe that civics serve as an underlying principle in geography, history, science, and religion classes. "But there is only so much which can be done," the ministry official declared. "If you push the subject too often and too long, the children would rebel."

Encouraging as these developments in Hesse and the Rhineland sound, the political education picture, generally speaking, is as yet a dismal one. The new policies result from crash programs. They are stopgap remedies, adopted in the majority of cases in the wake of foreign and domestic criticism which could no longer be ignored. Whereas educators should have taken a position of leadership, they are instead on the defensive, busily apologizing for inaction and scurrying around in search of fast solutions.

Although there has been consistent criticism of the schoolbooks, it was not until February, 1960, that a subcommittee of the standing conference of cultural ministers initiated a full-scale investigation of the texts. The probe was not launched by a desire of the conference to effect potential improvements but to determine whether "press and public allegations" concerning the contents of the histories were "justified or not." Steps were taken in all states, but not until an entire postwar school generation, those children born between 1939 and 1945, had left the classrooms without a clear knowledge of recent events in their country's history or an understanding of how the Nazis came to power, what their aims were, and how they affected world history.

As a defense, many teachers contend that their efforts to delve deeper into the problem of Nazism has met with adverse reaction on the part of parents. But it is inescapable that the major share of the responsibility lies with the school system. This attempt to shift the blame to the parents simply does not ring true in Germany, where the teacher is a highly respected authority of the state. There is great awe for learning in the German society, considerably more, for example, than in our own country. Most German parents would rather support the teacher's viewpoint than criticize him or side with their own child. The teacher has prestige and authority. He is considered an arm of the state's discipline, and so long as he retains that position he, not parents, will determine what school children are taught. The responsibility rests with the nation's teachers to use this power for good, for rooting out the remains of a twisted way of thinking rather than avoiding the issue because it might be embarrassing.

True, this is not an easy task, for the German teacher attempting to accomplish it finds himself in a uniquely paradoxical position. He has great power and authority, he enjoys unusual amounts of respect and prestige, yet if he tackles the problem of Nazism in the most logical way he must use that influence to show Germany's youth that unbridled might and authority are the basic attributes of a dictatorship like Hitler's. He must teach that the government also has responsibilities and that it should derive its powers from the will of the majority, that discipline is a legitimate tool only of a state based on right, justice, and equality. If he attempts to assign a role to the resistance movement, he must even teach that the individual has a moral right to flaunt the authority of the state if the state has misused its might and privileges. In assigning the opposition to Nazism its proper place in German history, the teacher must even sanction breach of discipline when obedience would result in ignoring the dictates of the individual conscience.

This is a tightrope situation even in a society where the principles of democracy are virtually ingrained in the youth. In Germany, where democracy has been an oft-interrupted experiment, the perils are even greater, and the teacher's task seems monumental. It certainly cannot be accomplished by those educators who have not severed their bonds with the Nazi ideology.

Notable progress in this direction can be attributed to the efforts of several little known institutions in the sphere of political information. Their contributions are vital to both journalism and education. One is the *Bundeszentrale für Heimatdienst*, which literally translated means Federal Center for Home Service. Its objectives are the cultivation of political education and democratic thinking in Germany.

The center, in existence since 1952, is an agency of the ministry of interior. A committee of *Bundestag* members, representing all parliamentary parties, supervises its activities. The center is modeled after a Reich Center for Home Service, which was active along similar lines during the Weimar Republic. Its work is multifold. As an example, it has subsidized numerous books on the persecution of the Jews under the Nazi régime. In 1959 it distributed a mass-circulation magazine insert on the history of the Jews, another insert entitled "Prejudice," and a supplement on the events of the Crystal Night in November, 1938. The center also distributed eighty thousand copies of an eyewitness concentration camp report to all German schools and other interested circles. In the fall of 1959 a copy of Alan Bullock's Hitler biography was sent to all high-school history teachers.

The center also produces and circulates documentary and entertainment films which foster democratic principles and tolerance. Its two most important periodicals are a weekly newspaper called *Das Parlament*, which reports in detail the activities of the *Bundestag* and *Bundesrat* as well as the important pan-European legislative bodies. Another periodical with a circulation of eight hundred thousand is an information bulletin for political education which provides class and program material for social science courses and sociopolitical study programs in industry. Its budget in the fiscal year of 1958 was 7.3 million DM.

Every year more than 1 million German school children participate in the center's essay contest, writing compositions on topics of political education. Annually the center sponsors nearly seven hundred conferences and seminars with a total participation of thirty thousand, and some one thousand individual lecture evenings. In 1958 approximately three hundred fifty thousand books and pamphlets, including some topical novels, were distributed free. More than two thousand copies of various films—some of them popular entertainment pictures

with a political moral or a plot outlining strong democratic responsibilities—are in circulation constantly.

Another federal agency is the Munich *Institut für Zeitgeschichte*
(Institute of Modern History), which has become Germany's most
important research center on National Socialism. In the ten years
since its establishment, the institute has published twenty-five major
studies on Nazi persecution. It makes available suitable publications
on the topic to schools, adult education centers, and commercial
periodicals. It answers inquiries, provides visual aids, sponsors exhibi-
tions, gives advice on the publication of textbooks, and helps formulate broadcasting material for children's and school hours on the
state networks.

The various states also maintain "Centers for Home Service." That
of Hesse is representative. Its director is a member of the Social
Democratic party (since the Social Democrats are the majority party
in that state). The director of its film division is a Christian Democrat, and so on down the line, representing the parties which in turn
are represented in the Hessian state legislature. In addition to the
free distribution of important books on Nazism and German politics,
including Paul Schallueck's novel, *Engelbert Reinecke*, the Hessian
center's program includes the publication of special newspaper and
magazine inserts, circulation of films and recordings to schools, unions, industries, clubs, and discussion groups. Radio plays such as Max
Frisch's *Herr Biedermann und die Brandstifter*; Walter Jens's *Ahas-
ver*, and Stefan Andres' *Sperrzonen* have been reprinted in attractive
pocket book editions and are available to amateur theater groups,
school reading clubs, and drama societies.

During 1959 the center produced four special newspaper inserts
which were published in numerous Hessian dailies. Later made available on a reprint basis, they are: "It Started on January 30" (selections from a radio series of the North German network), a four-page
newspaper insert; "A Look Backwards," facts and personal experiences about the fate of the Jews in Germany, sixteen pages; "The
End of a Stubborn Legend," a one-page critical analysis of Hitler's
economic policies; "July 20, Forgotten or Living Heritage?" a one-
page newspaper insert.

Films available on a check-out basis from the center include a ninety-minute movie called *Stresemann* another ninety-minute film entitled *Marriage in the Shadow,* the story of actor Joachim Gottschalk and his Jewish wife who committed suicide under the Nazi régime.

Shorter documentaries, compiled from wartime newsreels, include films about the People's Court trial of the resistance leaders, Hitler's rise to power, Hitler's fiftieth birthday and others. All the films are 16 mm. with sound track. It is interesting to note that demand for the films is so great that lending periods are limited to one week.

Chapter XII

Press
Literature
and Film

Aspiring dictators, no matter how powerful their military or paramilitary forces, cannot succeed in their aims without either the help or the subjugation of a nation's press, its writers, and motion picture and radio industries.

Hitler and Goebbels had learned this axiom well, and with it they mastered Germany. The press was controlled, the democratic journalists were driven from their desks, the "dangerous" books were burned and their authors banned and exiled. Movies which posed a threat to Hitler were outlawed, the directors and producers compelled to use their talents for the Nazi cause. Eventually the entire motion picture industry was state owned. The nation's radio service was put under the strict control of Goebbels' propaganda ministry, finally subjected to his complete direction and domination. It became a serious crime in Germany to listen to foreign broadcasts, to read the works of authors who had been banned. No journalist dared to speak out against the régime. When the war ended, the German people subsisted in an intellectual vacuum.

But, just as press, radio, film, and literature are essential to a dictator's success, likewise they are decisive in the formation and maintenance of a democratic state. Of all the revolutions that have taken

227

place in the German way of life since 1945, none has been so complete, none has been so successful as this changed position of the press and its allied fields. There are still weak spots, but generally speaking Germany's strongest bulwark for democracy is its press, its radio system, now state, not nationally controlled, its vast publishing industry, and its crop of promising young postwar authors.

The press has become solidly entrenched. It has become an aggressive watchdog of democracy. It fights vigorously against any infringement of its freedom. And the states are currently engaged in a bitter quarrel with the Federal Government which seeks more control over the radio and television networks, and the major publishers and writers have successfully kept rabid former Nazis from their ranks.

Unfortunately, however, there are still Nazi and Fascist elements on hand who have launched their own publishing ventures. These are limited to slightly more than a dozen book publishing houses and a handful of extremist magazines and newspapers, most of them associated with or supported by neo-Nazi or right radical parties and political interest groups. Nevertheless, their activities are sufficiently disconcerting.

During 1958, 1959, and early 1960, there was a marked reversal in the development of the neo-Nazi publishing industry. Two of its leading writers died, some of the publications were banned, several publishers were tried and convicted of libel and subversive activities. Others have been forced out of business or so successfully ignored by the major publishing associations that they will be compelled to fold eventually.

Of some thirty antidemocratic book publishing houses, some of them so insignificant that their inclusion in the list is of debatable fairness, only twelve exhibit at the annual Frankfurt Book Fairs, sponsored by the all-powerful Market Association of the German Book Trade. Of the twelve, only six can be considered really antidemocratic. The other half dozen have published only one or two books of questionable content and attitude during the past three years.

Whereas there were some forty-five in 1956, in 1960 there are only eighteen nationalistic, militaristic, or neo-Nazi weekly and monthly periodicals, with a total paid circulation (by their own admission) of 150,000. Most of them are closely associated with right radical political parties or political pressure groups. More than two dozen have either shut up shop for lack of readership, have been gobbled up by more powerful publications and organizations, or have been banned for subversive activities.

One of those which has been banned, for example, is *Die Anklage*, an organ for "victims of de-Nazification," published by Robert Kremer.[1] Its highest circulation figure was 3,000 and it included among its contributors Johannes von Leers.[2] Among the theories espoused by *Die Anklage* was that figures about atrocities in the concentration camps had been widely exaggerated. A quote typical of the publication's attitude is this from the June 1, 1956 edition:

The German people know that the claim of 6 million murdered Jews is pure propaganda. They also know that certain Jewish and Christian circles want to heap an inhuman blame on the German people to keep them spiritually broken and enslaved.

Successor to *Die Anklage* was a publication called *Der Ring*. It was the organ of the now outlawed Federal League of former internees and victims of de-Nazification. It had its editorial offices in Duesseldorf, and by April, 1959, when the league was disbanded, *Der Ring*'s circulation had risen to 24,000 monthly. *Der Ring* became infamous for comments such as these:

There is still a lot of talk and a lot written about the crimes committed in the concentration camps. Aside from the fact that the figures have long since been proved as exaggerated, in the interest of fairness and humanity we must protest against covering up the injustices committed in the [Allied] internment camps.

There are, after all, still three men confined at Spandau—Hess, Speer, and Schirach—who served their Fatherland in the way they believed was best.

Another among the list of extremist publications is *Der Reichsruf*, official organ of the German Reich party.[3] Its publisher is Adolf von

[1] See page 59.
[2] *Ibid.*
[3] See page 99.

Thadden, the executive secretary of the party. Issued weekly, its circulation is estimated to be 20,000.

Der Freiwillige (The Volunteer) is the official mouthpiece of the HIAG, mutual assistance association of former members of the *Waffen SS*.[4] It gives no circulation figures, but the distribution is considered extensive because of the organization's size.

Deutsche Soldatenzeitung (German Soldiers' Newspaper) is issued by Schild Verlag, Munich, a nationalistic publishing house. The paper, with a circulation of 27,500, is the official organ of the *Verband deutscher Soldaten* (VdS).[5] Its subtitle is "independent publication for honor, right, freedom, European security, and comradeship." The *Soldatenzeitung* even received a 13,000 DM monthly subsidy from the Federal Government for some time, but this was revoked in the wake of a heated parliamentary debate.

Nation Europa, published in Coburg, is considered one of the most extreme Fascist voices in Europe. It is supported by various right-radical organizations from all over the Continent and even the United States. It has been the subject of endless press and parliamentary controversy for years. A monthly, its circulation is approximately 6,000.

Die Deutsche Gemeinschaft (The German Association), "fighting organ of the German freedom movement and the national opposition," is published on a biweekly basis by a similarly named right radical association.[6] August Haussleiter, former Adenauer cohort-turned-rightist, heads the organization and the publication's editorial staff. Its circulation is 15,000.

Der Quell, issued by the High Watch publishing company, lists as its editor Franz von Bebenburg, Mathilde Ludendorff's son-in-law.[7] *Der Quell* is one of several Ludendorff periodicals. Its attitude has been termed "nationalistic" and "anti-Semitic." The circulation is 7,500.

Der Stahlhelm, official organ of the Stahlhelm League of front line soldiers,[8] like *Deutsche Soldatenzeitung*, is published by Schild Verlag in Munich. Its circulation is approximately 9,000.

---

[4] See page 111.   [5] See page 115.
[6] See page 106.   [7] See pages 104–106.
[8] See pages 116–118.

Others are *Deutsche Freiheit,* official organ of Dr. Otto Strasser's German Social Union; [9] *Junger Beobachter (Young Observer),* official publication of numerous right radical youth organizations, circulation 12,000; *Der Luftwaeffen Ring,* newspaper for German air force vets,[10] circulation 5,000; *Deutscher Aufbruch,* organ of Karl Meissner's German Bloc Movement,[11] and last but not least, the *Nordische Zeitung (Nordic Paper),* organ of the Circle of Friends for the Maintenance of Nordic Cultural Heritage.

Of all of them, two merit more detailed examination. One of these is *Nation Europa,* until recently involved in several legal suits. The other is the *Deutsche Soldatenzeitung,* whose rabid nationalistic and militaristic attitude has occupied many a parliamentary session and provided grist for the mills of editorial writers.

The *Soldatenzeitung* is published by Schild Verlag which has made a name for itself with nationalistic and militaristic nonfiction books. It lists among its authors former *Waffen SS* Major General Kurt (Panzer) Meyer,[12] rightist Erich Kernmayer; ex-field marshals Albert Kesselring and Erich von Manstein; ex-Grand Admiral Erich Raeder; former vice chancellor Franz von Papen; teacher Hans Venatier,[13] former SS Colonel Otto Skorzeny, and many others. The newspaper received a monthly 13,000 DM ($3,000) subsidy from the Federal Press and Information Office for several years until December 31, 1954. It was not until October 22, 1958, however, that the federal government and the *Bundeswehr* made a clean break with the *Soldatenzeitung* and officially disassociated themselves from the publication. It had become uncomfortably blunt in its attacks on the federal government, particularly the "citizen in uniform" ideology which Colonel Wolf von Baudissin had pioneered in the new army.

The leadership of the *Bundeswehr* disassociates itself distinctly from the so-called *Deutsche Soldatenzeitung* [a defense ministry spokesman announced]. The soldiers of the *Bundeswehr* have nothing to do with this publication and will not have anything to do with it in the future, so long as the periodical's present attitude continues.

It is calamitous, but apparently unavoidable, that this publication is

[9] See page 108.   [10] See page 115.
[11] See page 107.   [12] See page 112.
[13] See page 196.

entitled *Deutsche Soldatenzeitung*, thus creating the impression here and abroad that it represents the thinking of German soldiers. In reality, however, only a small group of individuals hides behind this presumptuous title. This publication's principles are rejected categorically by the officers, noncoms, and enlisted men.

Some six months later, public pressure was still on and a defense ministry spokesman was compelled to reiterate the ministry position regarding the *Soldatenzeitung*, describing it as "a sheet for incorrigibles who have failed to learn from the past." According to reliable reports, however, the paper is still read and distributed among the *Bundeswehr* personnel and some members of the German forces are by-line contributors.

In its ninth year, the *Soldatenzeitung's* original purpose was to propagate the democratic principles of the Federal Republic among World War II veterans. More and more, however, the trend in the paper was toward defamation of the new Germany's democratic principles and institutions.

Its attitudes emerge clearly in just a few quotes taken from random issues. In the June, 1957, edition, before the paper went on a semimonthly publishing schedule, the following comments appeared about West Germany's radio programming:

> The unusual attractions of the Nation Socialist broadcasting activities . . . lay in the inflexible sequence of the daily program, and in the exceptional radio qualities of certain men, such as Joseph Goebbels, unsurpassed anywhere in the world.

In the March, 1958, edition, about the Jews in Germany, the *Soldatenzeitung* said: "Apparently certain circles are trying to accomplish just the opposite of what was practiced under Hitler: instead of racial defamation we now face attempts at establishing racial priority. . . ."

In the same issue, concerning Colonel von Baudissin, the paper stated: "Here is the enemy of genuine German soldiering, a man who should be excluded for all future times from the internal guidance of the *Bundeswehr*."

In the April, 1958, issue, there was the following: "The days are over [concerning the immediate postwar period] when any snot-nosed brat could besmirch the reputation of the German people and their history, and heap upon the German military profession garbage pails full of words. . . ."

In the September, 1958, issue an angrily-worded article criticized the trial and conviction of former Field Marshal Ferdinand Schoerner [14] and lauded Schoerner's military achievements. One month later the paper took the same attitude toward Sepp Dietrich [15] when he stood trial for manslaughter in the Roehm purge. The *Soldatenzeitung* described Dietrich as a "commander respected by all of us —a soldier who never acted other than in the interest of his fatherland."

A monthly publication, *Nation Europa*, has long been considered the central organ of all neo-Fascist elements in Europe and Germany. The stockholders in its corporation include a Swede, a couple of Swiss, two Chicagoans, a Canadian, and many Germans. Its principal stockholder, editor, and publisher, is Arthur Ehrhardt. Its contributors include England's Fascist leader Sir Oswald Mosely; Einar Aberg of Sweden; Maurice Bardeche of France, as well as leading right radicals and Fascists from Spain, Italy, South America, South Africa, and the Near and Middle East. Publisher Ehrhardt, sixty-one, was sentenced December 5, 1957, to a three-month suspended jail term and three-year probation for defamation of the Federal Republic's form of government and comparing it unfavorably with that of the Third Reich. A second charge of advocating the overthrow of the democratic and constitutional order could not be substantiated.

Germans were afforded a close-up view of *Nation Europa* in an unusual labor dispute which has been wending its way in and out of the German courts since 1957. The case is that of typesetter Helmuth Schammberger, employed in the plant where the magazine is printed. One day, in the fall of 1957, while setting type for *Nation Europa*, Schammberger came across an article which contended that anyone who had been interned in a Nazi concentration camp had been there probably for justifiable reasons. Schammberger, whose father had been whipped, beaten, and tortured in a camp, refused to continue work on the publication. Fired without notice, he took his case to a German labor court in Coburg and demanded severance

[14] See page 33.
[15] See page 35.

pay. Most German newspapers covered the trial and blasted with stinging editorials the labor tribunal's decision that Schammberger had no right to refuse to work. His suit for severance pay was rejected, and Schammberger was ordered to pay court costs. Not a man to take things lying down, he appealed his case up through the state labor court and finally the federal tribunal for labor disputes in Kassel which decided in his favor on February 5, 1960.

Although such publications as *Nation Europa, Der Quell, Der Reichsruf*, and so forth, present a potential danger to the democratic future of West Germany, the degree is relatively slight. Many are very insignificant. None of them has a large circulation. It is doubtful whether they have any noticeable impact on the German public as a whole. The greater number are house organs for various right-radical associations. They circulate among the membership, rarely outside. The problem of the right-radical book publishers, however, is quite different. The possibility that their literary products will find wider circulation is more imminent. Sentimental war memoirs, military adventure books, pseudohistorical apologies for the Nazi régime and atrocities are finding their way into the nation's bookshops.

The preponderance of these publishing houses with their revived Fascist and neo-Nazi authors utilizes book clubs, book mail-order plans, and book subscription services operated by political soul mates. Despite this apparently restrictive means of distribution, some of the titles have scored disconcerting successes. One such book service is maintained by the Schild Verlag of *Soldatenzeitung* fame. Among the authors whom it recommends for every German home and every family where the "spirit of the fatherland still survives," are air aces Adolf Galland and Ulrich Rudel; ex-SS generals Paul Hausser and Panzermeyer; Papen, Skorzeny, Venatier, Manstein, and Kesselring.

The following advertising blurbs excerpted from several Schild Verlag insertions in 1958 and 1959 explain, in the publisher's own words, the firm's political principles.

Die Wahrheit über Malmédy (The Truth About Malmédy) by Lothar Greil is an eighty-page book with an orientation sketch which sells for 3.40 DM. In it, according to the advertisement, "actual military events are described and documented accurately. . . . The truth about Malmédy and the most shameless of all the so-called war-crimes trials are laid bare here with the help of documents and statements."

Für Tapferkeit und Verdienst (For Bravery and Merit), a seventy-two-page book with colored plates is described by the publisher as "an almanac of the medals and citations awarded Germany and its allies in the First and Second World Wars."

Kurt (Panzer) Meyer is represented in the Schild portfolio by the second edition of his illustrated 416-page linen-bound book, *Grenadiere (Grenadiers)*. Advertisements describe "Panzermeyer," ex-major general of the *Waffen SS*, as "the youngest division commander of the *Wehrmacht*," who, "although innocent, was first sentenced to death by the Allies after the war, then pardoned after nearly ten years."

Schild Verlag has also published a book on the "Article 131 Law" which gives advice on how to apply for pensions under its provisions.

Prager Totentanz (Prague's Dance of Death), by Olga Barenyi, "a novel about the *days of the revolution of 1945*," is described, among other things, as "a monument to the hundred thousand Germans and Czechs senselessly murdered in the Prague inferno of May, 1945. While the grisly voice of Radio Frequency 418 incited to organized murder and threatened death to anyone who might have compassion with German women, children, or wounded German soldiers, . . . the internal struggles of the new rulers were battled out."

Although Schild Verlag has not been represented at the Frankfurt Book Fairs for some time, it does advertise in the *Börsenblatt*, the publication of the German book trade which sponsors the fair.

One right-wing publisher's books were thrown out of an exhibition hall at the 1955 fair. The publisher, Waldemar Schuetz, former SS leader, at that time press chief for the German Reich party, and until 1958 DRP member of the Lower Saxony state legislature, had introduced a volume called *Die Ritterkreuzträger der Waffen SS (The Ritterkreuz Wearers of the Army SS)* and *Letzte Aufzeichnungen, (Last Notes)* of Alfred Rosenberg, the Nazi party's ideological chieftain. Schuetz already had published works by such authors as Hans Grimm, Hans Ulrich Rudel, Paul Hausser (of HIAG fame), and Maurice Bardeche, the French Fascist leader.

When his latest two titles appeared on his Plesse Verlag stand at the 1955 Book Fair, leading German publishers petitioned the fair management to force Schuetz into removing objectionable titles from his booth. When nothing was done, the publishers helped themselves. Just before Federal President Theodor Heuss was to make his rounds of the exhibition, they threw the display and its books outside. Herr Schuetz spent the rest of the fair day at the nearby Leopold Stocker Verlag stand. Schuetz is also director of the Reichsruf Verlag which publishes the German Reich party organ.

The case of Schuetz brings to mind that of his friend, Leonhard Schlueter, former culture minister of Lower Saxony, former German Reich party crony, later a member of the Free Democratic party (FDP) which vaulted him into his ministerial post. Schlueter owns the Goettinger Verlagsanstalt (Goettingen Publishing Institute), and his wife was one of the founders of Schuetz's Plesse Verlag. Schlueter has published the works of Rudolf Diels, first head of the Gestapo under Goering; Franz von Papen; Rudolf Klagges, former Nazi minister president of Brunswick; and Hugo Backhaus, alias Dr. Herbert Grabert, who wrote a book called *Volk ohne Führung (A People Without Leadership)*. The book was labeled as subversive in 1958 and both Grabert and Schlueter were convicted by the German federal supreme court on April 30, 1960, of defaming the state and distributing unconstitutional literature. Schlueter was fined 1,200 marks in lieu of two months in jail. Grabert was sentenced to a nine-month suspended jail term. All thirty-six hundred copies of the book which have been sold are to be confiscated and unsold volumes destroyed.

The Druffel Verlag, located in Leoni on Lake Starnberg, is influenced principally by Helmut Suendermann, ex-press chief of the Reich propaganda ministry and assistant to Joseph Goebbels. In addition to Suendermann's own books, Druffel Verlag has published the works of Mrs. Rudolf Hess, Ribbentrop, and other Nazi greats. Munich's district attorney attempted to file a criminal charge against Suendermann and the Druffel Verlag in 1957 with the ultimate aim of banning its books, but a district court rejected the case. The DA appealed to the Bavarian state supreme court, but the case was turned down there, too. In 1958, on the other hand, Druffel Verlag sought a court order to force the book fair management into letting display space to the Suendermann firm. A Frankfurt district court, however, ruled against the petition.

Even more numerous than the right-wing publishers are those who produce militaristic literature. Most of them are accepted by the *Börsenverein* (the book trade association) and regularly display their titles at the fair.

Prominent among them is Kurt Vowinckel Verlag, which offers an entire shelf full of military titles. In its series *The* Wehrmacht *in Battle*, Vowinckel has published *Angriff einer Infantrie-Division (Attack by an Infantry Division)*, a chronicle of the 101st Infantry Division's battlefield activities; *Partisanenkrieg (Partisan War)*, a treatise on the partisans and the underground movement in the central sector of the Eastern Front.

Vowinckel's series of personal military reports, each costing 9.80 DM, includes a book by Hermann Frank about fighting the guerrilla bands in Albania, and A. E. von Ernsthausen's experiences as a mountain artillerist in the Caucasus.

One of the firm's prize offerings is a three-volume effort on the *History of the Armored Corps* Grossdeutschland. There are other gems, such as *Witebsk—Battles and Defeat of the 3d Armored Army; Mountain Troops at Uman; The Final Battle in the Balkans,* and *48 Kilometers to Stalingrad.*

Koehler's Verlagsgesellschaft features military, naval, and science fiction books as well as chronicles about famous composers. Some of its titles are: *Battleship "Admiral Graf Spee"—Battles, Victory, and Sinking,* by Commander (Ret.) D. F. Rasenack, with an introduction by Vice Admiral Krancke. *Hunters and Hunted—German Submarines 1939/1945,* by Jochen Brennecke, which the publisher describes as "the most informative work about the action of the submarines in the Second World War."

Even Carl Roehrig Verlag, who specializes in technical books for railway workers, has published two "militaristic" volumes which "present a picture of the sacrifice, courage, and accomplishments of German railwaymen in World War II." One of them, *Bahnhof Russkinaja Meldet Sich Nicht (Russkinaja Station Doesn't Answer),* is the story of the advance in Russia, the *Schienenwolf (Track Wolf)* deals with the eastern retreat. Each book sells for 13.80 DM.

Considerably more dangerous than the publishers who distribute hard-cover, linen-bound editions through book clubs and the like are the publishers of dime novels who reportedly sell as many as 15 million copies of militaristic literature each year. Ranging in price from

50 Pfennig to 1 DM, these cheap novels are popular with teen-agers and subteen-agers. They all glorify war, some to the extent that there is no longer any question of neo-Nazi leanings.

An excellent study of the problem has been made by Gerhard Halberstadt, an official of the *Deutsche Angestellten Gewerkschaft* (DAG), the German white-collar workers' union in Hamburg. For almost six months, beginning in the summer of 1959, Halberstadt spent his free evenings reading these dime novels, available at newsstands, railway station kiosks, and in stationery stores. The result of this half-year pastime is a 163-page report which the DAG has filed with the Hamburg state senate. The union hopes that the German federal censorship board for "literature dangerous to the moral training of youth" will examine the report and take action against further distribution. Halberstadt stated that the majority of dime novel publishers undoubtedly were less interested in the political aspects of their products than the financial results. War stories sell because they are brutal and exciting, he surmised.

However, many of the right-radical authors who write hard-cover war stories for the adult market have also found a medium in pulp. Prominent among the authors is air ace Hans Ulrich Rudel, who even went so far as to quote Hitler in one of these dime novels. The youth censorship board chairman Robert Schilling agreed to investigate two titles: Rudel's *Trotzdem* and SS General Papa Hausser's book *The SS in Battle*, and on May 6, 1960, decided to ban them.

In addition to the dime novel and hard-cover publishers, there are many other right-wing, militaristic works being printed each day. However, the great majority of them stem from publishers so insignificant that they print their works on mimeograph machines.

Although they pose a potential danger to Germany's democratic future, neither the extremist publishing houses nor the extremist periodicals have attained sufficient success or public acceptance to constitute a significant threat at the present time. Fortunately, there is the opposite pole—the hundreds of democratic newspapers, magazines, authors, and book publishers who form a solid front against the incorrigibles.

Considering the mass brainwashing, the terror and censorship that prevailed during the Nazi régime, German newspapermen deserve nothing but credit for the speed with which they have accepted the principles, responsibilities, and objectives of freedom of the press. Although many German newspapers are notoriously unreliable, and all but the most conservative and those trying to adopt American journalistic techniques have a marked tendency toward editorialized news reporting, they do form an impressive and uncompromising bulwark against any suggestions of autocracy or relapse into dictatorship. Some newspapers stand in the foreground of the fight against neo-Nazistic, nationalistic, and militaristic developments. Others have avoided a controversial position in these matters, adhering to an editorial policy of "we'll follow but won't lead." Still others, and unfortunately some of the mass-circulation tabloids are among them, have consistently shied away from their responsibilities of helping to reorientate and reeducate the German public.

While some papers are practically obsessed with the problem of accounting for and preventing a recurrence of the past, others have skirted the crucial issues. Generally speaking, all the major metropolitan dailies have contributed their share by reporting the major war-crimes trials, the serious anti-Semitic and antidemocratic incidents. The only area in which there is a noticeable reluctance to take these issues by the horns is in the provincial press.

Among the leaders in the field are papers from all over the country. In listing just a few of them, first place goes to the *Frankfurter Rundschau*, a daily with 114,000 circulation and a reputation of extremely liberal politics. It was one of the first newspapers to be licensed by the United States Military Government. In fact, the *Rundschau* was published daily shortly after American troops occupied Frankfurt and before World War II had ended officially. Although accused of being pro-Communist in the early years, it has undergone a complete change in policy and today is unequivocally opposed to dictatorship from the left as well as the right.

In southern Germany, Munich's *Süddeutsche Zeitung* is the major spokesman against antidemocratic tendencies. This publication is the largest of the city's three dailies with a circulation of 211,000. The Süddeutscher Verlag (South German Publishing Company) also houses a liberal tabloid called the *Abendzeitung*, with a circulation of 92,000.

In Berlin two dailies, both published by Ullstein Verlag, dominate the free city's newspaper activities. One is the *Berliner Morgenpost* with a circulation of 202,000, the other is the *Berliner Zeitung* (BZ), circulation 286,000.

In Bremen, the *Weser Kurier*, with a circulation of 110,000 daily, the city's largest, is also the official organ of the Bremen state government. It is liberally oriented.

In Bielefeld, the second largest daily is the Social Democratic *Freie Presse*, circulation 96,000.

In Mannheim, the *Mannheimer Morgen* leads with a total circulation of 123,000. The *Allgemeine Zeitung*, with a circulation of only 25,000, is also considered very liberal.

In Frankfurt, another liberal voice is the *Abendpost*, a national tabloid with a circulation of 180,000.

Germany's mass-circulation newspaper, the ten-pfennig *Bild Zeitung*, with daily sales of more than 3 million, is virtually unpolitical. It carries only sketchy reports of national and international news, concentrating instead on sensational treatment of less significant news events.

But regardless of their political tendencies and their attitude toward Chancellor Adenauer, the *Bundeswehr*, the war-crimes trials, the anti-Semitic incidents, all German papers stand united in their defense of expression and opinion. Two recent government attempts to curtail that freedom met with tenacious resistance from newspapermen.

One of these proposals was the so-called "Lex Soraya," designed to protect the honor of the individual. The bill was initiated when the Iranian Shah complained of overly sensational and tasteless publicity when he and Soraya, then his wife, toured Germany. The other legislative measure against the press was the so-called "muzzle law," intended to protect the *Bundeswehr* from slander and libel.

Lex Soraya, which ran aground on bitter press opposition, was to protect heads of foreign states and members of their families from "degrading" newspaper claims. The bill was directed primarily against German illustrated magazines and sugary pulp newspapers which base their large circulation on so-called "intimate, unimpeachable reports" about the private lives of Queen Elizabeth, Princess Margaret, Peter Townsend, Antony Armstrong-Jones, the Shah of Iran, and most other European and Middle Eastern notables.

Failing to enlist support for Lex Soraya, the government has drafted a reform of the German criminal code which, though still several years from becoming a law, would impose extensive restrictions on press freedom. One clause which has been subjected to vehement criticism provides up to two years in jail for anyone who, "in a public gathering, by distribution of written material, records, or the reproduction of pictures, makes assertions about the private and family life of another person so as to touch upon that individual's honor and personal dignity, regardless of whether the claim is true or not."

The highly controversial "muzzle laws," introduced in 1957 and purported to protect the *Bundeswehr* from defamation, were influenced greatly by the antirearmament manifestations. Two of the bills merely called for a change of existing paragraphs in the criminal code which already protect government agencies and civil servants, including policemen, firemen, streetcar conductors, and mail carriers from insult, slander, and libel. A third bill, however, provided prison terms for "anyone who makes or spreads false or grossly exaggerated statements in order to hinder others from entering military service or to hinder the Federal Armed Forces from fulfilling their mission." The government's explanation for the muzzle bills was that the new army required protection in the wild battle of ideas.

Regardless of their political leanings, most papers have one failing in common: editorializing news copy. It is actually considered bad reporting to treat a news story in the terms of cold hard facts. Many German papers do not run editorials, the majority have no editorial pages and there are no syndicated political columnists. Of course, there are exceptions to this. Some of the larger dailies are starting editorial pages, others have had them for quite some time. A number feature daily editorials on the first, second, or third news pages. Still others are making a valiant attempt to divorce themselves from opinion in the news columns. However, the provincial press—and it serves the bulk of German newspaper readers—still points with pride to the editorialized news reports.

Very few of the papers in southern Germany are friendly toward the Americans. Incident news, such as crimes, accident and maneuver damages caused by GI's generally are treated with undue sensationalism and are garnished with considerable editorial comment. Strange as it may seem, most of these newspapers are at the same time receptive to the sheaves of publicity material handed out to them by U.S. Army and Air Force public information officers. It is only in rare instances, however, that military officials have been able to convince local newsmen to treat misbehavior of American soldiers with the fairness and restraint which they grant German wrongdoers.

Cities such as Mannheim, Augsburg, Stuttgart, Frankfurt, and Berlin are excellent examples of good cooperation between the German press and the United States Forces. There crime stories involving American soldiers are treated objectively. The military's public relations troubles stem from the smaller communities, such as Bamberg, Kaiserslautern, Wuerzburg, Aschaffenburg, Darmstadt, and Nuremberg. Part of this can be attributed to the size relationship between United States and German communities. The smaller the town and the larger the military contingent, the greater the chance of trouble and disagreement.

Despite their frequent criticism of the behavior of American troops, most German newspapers are quick to defend the NATO alliance and would probably be the first to complain if American troops were withdrawn from German soil. In the meantime, carping about the behavior of American soldiers—and it is far from good—helps to fill the news columns of the more sensationally-minded dailies.

Certainly the majority of newspapers are aware of their responsibilities in a democratic society as well as their rights and privileges. The reeducation of the nation's press corps was an easier task than the reeducation of the entire German population. There were hundreds of newsmen after the war who were glad to go to work and defend democratic principles. Many had kept silent during the Hitler régime, had tried to write noncontroversial stories, or had worked on publications of a noncontroversial nature. Others had been imprisoned or exiled. Whether today they are leaders in the fight against neo-Nazism, militarism, and nationalism, or whether they ride the fence in the anonymity of the provinces or behind the façade of editorial conservatism, I am convinced that the majority of them are at least aware of their position and their responsibilities and thus form a major safeguard for democracy in Germany.

Unfortunately, the same cannot be said for Germany's mass circulation general magazines. There are no equivalents to American "picture" and "slick" publications. The German publishing industry

has developed instead the so-called *Illustrierten,* or illustrated magazines, a crossbreed between the two United States formats. Although
they feature large photo-picture sections, cartoons, and nonfiction
reports, they also carry serialized novels or "documentary reports,"
and occasional short stories. A guarded approach to sex, gossip, scandal, particularly concerning movie stars and royalty, is their stock
in trade.

These mass circulation sheets have a virtual monopoly on the
magazine market. The ten major publications score newsstand and
subscription sales of about 9 million weekly. In addition they reach
millions through "readers' circles," lending subscription services
which deliver a selection of illustrated publications by messenger
each week to cafés, restaurants, barbershops, beauty parlors, medical
and business offices. Stapled into sturdy folders, they are read there
by patients, clients, and customers, then picked up again at the
end of the week and replaced by new issues.

The largest and most successful is *Stern (Star),* published in Hamburg, with a 1960 circulation of 1,300,000. The smallest is the
Münchner Illustrierte, which sells 444,000 copies, according to 1960
reports.[16]

Their covers, with a few exceptions, are patterned after that of
Life magazine insofar as they use the solid red rectangle in the upper
left-hand corner for their flag and have a red band running across
the bottom of the page for price listings. A pretty girl is usually the
subject of the cover picture. Featured generally are several pages of
photo-journalistic reports about major news developments in and
outside Germany. Then starts the text portion with serials, nonfiction
reports, and the like.

Revue and *Münchner Illustrierte* [17] are liberally inclined.

Revue took a strong stand on the anti-Semitic outbreaks which
followed the Cologne synagogue desecration and once it got hold of
the topic held on to it for several issues with hard-hitting picture
stories. It also has embarked on a campaign to expose former Nazi
judges.

What characterizes all the other publications is a type of serialized

[16] However it stopped publishing in September, 1960, and has been incorporated into the *Bunte Illustrierte.*
[17] *Ibid.*

"documentary novel" or "documentary report" which tends to glorify militarism and nationalism, bolster the standing and reputation of German "doughboys" during World War II, and minimize the Nazi crimes while drawing attention to the injustices committed by the Allies. This type of serial has placed the illustrateds in the spotlight of criticism from educators and government officials. However, the attacks have had no noticeable effect on either the editorial policies or the circulation figures.

These "novels," "documentaries," and serials are not openly nationalistic, militaristic, or apologetic. Their chauvinistic trends are coated with readable excitement, love, and drama. There are the "now-it-can-be-told" stories which reveal alleged secrets of the Hitler era. Under this heading fall stories about secret weapons developments; battles that were lost because the *Führer* was a demagogue or the general in charge of the division was a coward; reports of intrigue behind the *Führer's* back. The group includes stories of secret marine and U-boat operations which, had they been given a chance, might have turned the tide of the war. The majority of these reports make it appear that everything was not quite as bad as the Germans have been led to believe. They are apologetic, rationalizing reports, exploiting drama and excitement while failing to tell the entire story.

Popular, too, are the "I was Hitler's chambermaid" memoirs. This category includes reports on Goebbels, the intimate life of Hitler and Eva Braun, how Goering became an air ace, that Rudolf Hess was in reality a misguided idealist, and so on.

Yet another group comprises the "not all Germans were bad"— reports which usually glorify the simple soldier and the man on the street. These epics frequently are sugar-coated with French-German, Russian-German, Dutch-German romances in Nazi-occupied countries. They establish the theory that many German soldiers felt an affinity for the local population (which they did) and tried to help them. By featuring a popular, sympathetic protagonist who fights against unbelievable odds of Gestapo cruelty and Nazi stupidity, the character becomes a hero whose attributes appeal to each and every reader.

There are the "last stand at Tunis" chronicles: documentary reports of important battles or military operational theaters. Generally these are strong on German heroism and approach the German side of the story from a human interest point of view while writing off the Allies statistically. They usually carp about the numerical and material superiority of the Allies and praise Germany's excellently trained legions for fighting a heroic battle to the end until they were submerged by a flood of Allied men, guns, and tanks.

The "capitulation and catastrophe" documentaries spotlight the misery and misfortune of the Germans in the waning days of the war and in the immediate postwar period.

A clear picture can be obtained from an analysis of some of the magazines. The January 2, 1960, issue of *Bunte Deutsche Illustrierte (Colored German Illustrated)*, 915,000 circulation, consisted of a four-page picture story on New Year's in Burma and Japan; a two-page picture story on German ski champion Toni Sailer's visit to Tokyo; a two-page interview story with members of the federal cabinet on predictions for the year to come; another two-page story on an interview with a famous German fortuneteller who made her predictions for 1960; a two-page spread on Brigitte Bardot and her husband's brief military career; a four-page continuation of a novel; two pages of a contest; fourteen pages on President Eisenhower's tour of India, Pakistan, and Afghanistan; a one-page color picture; another three-page serial novel; three pages of an installment of a detective story.

In addition the magazine featured a four-page picture story on Otto von Hapsburg, pretender to the throne of Austria. This article dealt with Otto's exile and the lobby which wants the ex-monarch to return to his "fatherland." A loose translation of the title would be "The Homesick Emperor." A one-and-one-half page picture showed a smiling emperor with his five children. The caption read: "He's a good father. He just can't offer his children a fatherland of their own so long as he is banned from his homeland." (The head of the House of Hapsburg now lives in Passau in southern Germany, near the Austrian border. His exile was ordered after World War I.) Deck headlines on the story read, "Austria is waiting for him: . . . Every person has a homeland, even a Kaiser." The magazine interviewed people on the streets of Vienna. All of them expressed the hope that the emperor would be allowed to resettle in Austria (without taking the throne, of course).

The same issue of *Bunte Deutsche* carried an installment of a serial on the life and loves of Joseph Goebbels, Reich propaganda minister. Entitled, "The Great Seducer," it was subtitled, "the most dangerous man in the Third Reich. A documentary report about Dr. Joseph Goebbels." Although Goebbels doesn't come out exactly a hero, it's impossible to read the story without gaining a little sympathy for the man, particularly for his love life.

The January 9, 1960, edition of *Revue*, in addition to eight pages on the wedding of the Shah of Iran and Farah Diba, two pages on Nevil Shute's *On the Beach*, novels, short stories, and an "inside" story about Maria Callas' private life, featured an installment of "the great novel of peace in war," *Etappe Paris*, which was described as follows in a brief summary of that week's installment: "Germans and French girls find their destiny in the shadow of the invasion. For First Lieutenant Klink and his armored company, H-hour has struck in Normandy. But in Paris there's still love, life, and laughter. . . ." The installment deals with a *Wehrmacht* captain's one-man battle against Nazi terror. He is pictured as a "good German" who has fallen in love with a French girl whose father hates *les Boches* so intensely that he even refuses to thank the captain for a good deed he performed.

The January issue of *Quick* (circulation approximately 1,220,000) devoted seven pages to a report on the Shah's wedding and ran three-page installments of a serial on Evita Perón, the fate of German war brides in the United States, and a German secret agent's love affairs during the war.

The story of Evita Perón is very favorable to her and her dictator husband, that about the war brides describes their life in the States as very perilous, while the secret agent is another "good German."

Neue Illustrierte, of January 9, 1960 (circulation 845,000), brought the usual run of stories about the Shah, a report of a *Life* magazine article on "jumpology," a four-page picture spread on aircraft accidents, and a four-page installment of a serial about wartime espionage and propaganda work described as "an unknown chapter from the invisible war." There was a four-page "inside" story on Kaiser Wilhelm entitled, "Now I Can Tell ALL," and a three-page story about the fate of a German girl in the United States, headlined "Little Woman from Germany."

Stern, the largest of the illustrated periodicals, devoted three pages to the Nevil Shute film, four pages to the Shah's wedding, and a documentary entitled, "The Lights Went Out in Europe," describing the political developments just at the start of the war.

Kristall, an illustrated with 478,000 circulation, has been in the public spotlight for quite some time. Published by Axel Springer Verlag in Hamburg, the same firm that issues the 10-pfennig *Bild Zeitung* and the *Hamburger Welt, Kristall* was the subject of many newspaper headlines in August, 1959, when a number of its top editors walked off the job in protest against the hiring of a former Nazi. The publisher had planned to put Dr. Paul Schmitt, erstwhile press chief of Joachim von Ribbentrop's foreign office, into the job of running *Kristall's* "Political and Current Events" section.

Schmitt had written for *Kristall* and other German illustrated magazines under a variety of pseudonyms for several years. He has established a reputation for wartime documentaries. The *Kristall* editors who staged the walkout objected to his employment in an important salaried position on grounds that they would no longer be able to influence Schmitt and edit out what they called militaristic and nationalistic tendencies in his stories. The publishing house gave in and so did Schmitt. He withdrew from further association with the magazine, and Axel Springer Verlag explained that there had been no plans to put Schmitt into a position where he could influence tendencies of any of the company's publications and that the entire incident had resulted from a misunderstanding at an editorial conference. The four editors apparently returned to work.

In the January 2, 1960, edition *Kristall* published an installment of a documentary serial on the Normandy invasion entitled "They're Coming." Following is an excerpt:

. . . This encounter near Villers Bocage on June 13 is one of the great adventurous episodes of the battle of Normandy: five "Tiger Tanks" against an entire British brigade of the 7th Armored Division, the élite of the famous desert rat, Montgomery. In British war history, the exchange is described as the Battle of Villers Bocage. The British chroniclers claim their forces shot up seven Tiger tanks. But since only five entered the battle and four returned undamaged, the figures cannot be correct. No wonder, because in defeats and retreats the tabulations are generally wrong, on both sides! Losses here, losses there—at any rate, Montgomery's armored offensive was stopped by Michel Wittmann's five Tigers. Five Tigers won the battle. Five Tigers caused the chaos of Villers Bocage.

. . . Street fighting in Villers Bocage lasted until the evening of June 13. Then the English left the battlefield and retreated toward Livry with the rest of their decimated units. There wasn't much they could save. The entire staff of their A Company with twenty-seven tanks and all track and wheeled vehicles of the brigade had been lost. The brigade general, fifteen officers, and seventy-six men had been killed. The first rifle brigade left four officers and sixty men on the field. . . .

. . . But Montgomery didn't fight with just one brigade. . . .

. . . Twilight comes. The ruins of Tilly stand eerily in the sunset of June 16. The 50th and 49th British divisions storm the cornerstones of the front without pause, as if there were nothing more important in the world than the capture of these bombed-out, burned-out hamlets.

And concerning another war development, the unidentified author goes on:

. . . In Great Britain's capital, all hell breaks loose. The air-raid sirens howl uninterrupted. Mysterious, unmanned flying objects race with 600-kilometer speed from the area of Calais and Dunkirk through the air and explode before, in, and around London. The V-1 is there! The Age of Rockets has started. . . . For the first time in their history the Britons experience an artillery attack on the metropolis. . . . The first firing of the V-1 had actually been planned for December, 1943. But the British learned of the plan through treason. They discovered the firing pads and bombed them. The next date was set for February 15, 1944. Again the ramps were destroyed by bomber attacks. Then, in the night of June 15 to 16, it was finally time. . . .

On the topic of Germany's capitulation in the skies:

. . . This was the surrender in the air. This was the German *Luftwaffe* on the Western Front: a neglected, badly beaten instrument. Those are the roots for Germany's defeat on the invasion front. . . .

The *Frankfurter Illustrierte*, with a circulation of 574,000, has serialized a documentary entitled, "They Won the War but Lost the Peace," a critical analysis of Allied postwar plans and tactics. The January 9, 1960, edition also carried a report on the uprising against the Germans in Prague entitled: "Beat Them, Kill Them,

Don't Let Any of Them Live." This installment pictured the
Czechs as a band of insane, revenge-seeking barbarians. It told little
of the atrocities the Germans had committed in Czechoslovakia but
delved into a bloody, detailed description of the uprising and how
Germans had suffered during the Prague revolt.

> . . . In German barracks and hospitals everyone breathes with a sigh
> of relief: the Americans in Prague—if that's so, then there is no need
> to be afraid [the article read in part]. Even though Prague has been
> declared a hospital city—fifty thousand wounded German soldiers lie
> in eighteen army hospitals—one can never be quite certain whether the
> Russians will respect the sign of the Red Cross or not. . . .
> . . . The Germans are dragged from their homes, beaten on the streets,
> driven into the prisons. . . . Neither women nor children are spared.
> One doesn't ask them for their political opinions, whether they were
> fighters against fascism, whether they themselves may have been interned
> in concentration camps for fighting the battle which the Czech people
> have just started to fight against Hitler's régime of terror. It suffices that
> they are Germans.

The article went on to explain briefly, in a passage about twelve
column lines long, the German atrocities in Lidice and the deportation of Czech citizens. The rest of the article again dealt with the
crimes committed by the Czechs in this moment of their revolt and
liberation.

> . . . This is the hour of the Czech triumph, and the proud represen-
> tatives of the Czech resistance movement enjoy every minute of it. . . .
> . . . Now the Germans will capitulate. The Czechs look coolly and
> arrogantly toward Toussaint, under whose eyes deep shadows have formed
> from the sleepless nights he has spent. . . .

Those are the illustrated magazines with their stories of the war,
the hierarchy of the Nazi régime, the monarchy. Is it any wonder that
the Germans are beginning to view the dismal recent past as the
"good old days"?

Two magazines—directed at a more discriminating, considerably
smaller audience—help stem the tide with some degree of effectiveness. One is the weekly news magazine *Der Spiegel (The Mirror)*,
now in its fourteenth year of publication, with a paid circulation of

merely 400,000; the other being the Munich satirical magazine *Simplicissimus* with a circulation of 50,000. Particularly the *Spiegel*, modeled on the format of *Time*, has done a creditable job of holding aloft the banner of journalistic liberalism in Germany. Not only does the *Spiegel* cover the news behind the headlines, but it does so with such unbelievable irony and acidity that the effect is long-lasting. It is widely respected, and to an extent even feared in government. It has exposed many injustices and aired numerous political skeletons. It stands unequivocally in the foreground of the battle against neo-Nazism.

The current version of *Simplicissimus* is a postwar revival of the widely popular satirical magazine, banned when Hitler came to power. Its make-up, attitude, and approach to politics are basically the same as during the days of the Weimar Republic. Unfortunately, its circulation is small and its sphere of influence limited, due partly to its sophistication.

Contrary to the way the Nazis had established it, Germany does not have a centralized state radio system. German radio is not a private enterprise, as in the United States. Neither is it a nationally owned medium as in Great Britain. Instead, there are ten stations which, if one chooses, can also be called small networks, each operated on a state, not federal level. But even in this decentralized form, state control is limited. The stations are not owned by the *Land* governments, but are *Anstallten des öffentlichen Rechts*, that is, "institutes of the public domain," being owned directly by the listeners. The state government acts only in an advisory, middleman capacity. Each station is governed by a board of directors, made up of representatives from the government, church, schools, labor, industry, political parties, and so on. The board in turn hires a superintendent on a time contract to manage the station. The federal government enters the picture at two levels only. Federal mailmen collect the monthly listening fees of 2 DM for radio, 5 DM for TV receivers. And the postal ministry is responsible for assigning frequencies and giving technical assistance in laying long-distance transmission cables and establishing TV relay stations.

The ten stations, or junior networks, are virtually independent of one another, in fact, competitors so far as radio is concerned. They do, however, cooperate on certain TV programs for cost-saving reasons. The major television shows are staged and produced in the studios of respective stations, then broadcast over the entire country. Responsibility for the production of various programs rotates. In between these nationally telecast shows, emanating from various stations, the local stations still broadcast certain of their own programs, particularly newscasts.

The stations are: RIAS (Radio in the American Sector) Berlin; Radio Free Berlin; Radio Bremen; the Hessian Network; the Bavarian Network; the South German Network; the Southwest Network in Baden-Baden, shared jointly by the states of Baden-Wuerttemberg and Rhineland Palatinate; the North German Network in Hamburg; the West German Network in Cologne, and a Saarland Network. This diversified establishment results from the German constitutional provision guaranteeing the individual states complete cultural and educational autonomy. It is considered one of the vital safeguards against potential autocratic control of the educational system.

A bitter political fight raged in the last half of 1959 through the late summer of 1960 concerning the establishment of a second television program. Much as in Great Britain, the individual German stations broadcast "first" and "second" radio programs, differing from each other in timing and intellectual appeal. TV, however, had been operating on a single-program basis since it was inaugurated. For some time the federal government had tried to initiate a second program. In 1959 a bill calling for its establishment under central government control was introduced by the federal cabinet.

The proposal met with stiff resistance in the *Bundesrat*, the upper house of parliament which, similar to the United States Senate, was established to represent the states, not the population as a whole. Even the CDU states opposed the measure, although it was sponsored by Adenauer, on the contention that it infringed on states' rights and paved the way for federal control of all radio and TV activities. Social Democrats and Christian Democrats in the *Bundesrat* teamed up to oppose the bill, arguing that decentralized radio and TV on a state level cannot be controlled by a strong, propaganda-minded federal government as it was under the dictatorship and directorship of Josef Goebbels.

In July, 1960, it appeared as if a compromise solution was possible in the form of a limited corporation in which the Federal Government would have 51 per cent, the states, 49 per cent control. But before the measure could be approved, Adenauer rammed through a federal TV channel on a legal technicality.

The states were incensed at this infringement of their rights and threatened to launch a third program which would compete with the federal channel.

What the states guard so jealously is an extremely liberal program of public entertainment and education. More has been accomplished toward the democratic orientation of the German people by radio and television—with 10 million receivers—than by any other mass communications medium. Several outstanding productions which come to mind are Juergen Neven-DuMont's TV documentary on education; a 1956 TV program on the *Bundeswehr*; a 1954 Northwest German Network show about the senseless defense by German paratroopers of the French city of Brest, and a 1959 TV program called "The Best Years of My Life?"

German radio and television are in the forefront of efforts toward developing human understanding, religious and racial tolerance, and in defending democracy. The radio networks produce hundreds of programs annually which demonstrate the Jewish contribution to German culture, point out the atrocities of the Nazis, warn against nationalism and militarism, and plead for understanding among all peoples.

Although news commentators have no scheduled programs as they do in the United States, nearly every German station presents ten-minute news commentaries following the several daily newscasts. The commentators are not always radio personalities, though. Frequently they are respected educators, newspapermen, or political experts who divulge their views on important developments. These brief but informative lecture-editorials have added immeasurably to the German understanding of government, democracy, and daily world events.

Occasionally the aggressive enthusiasm of German radio men backfires. Such was the case in the TV program about the city of Brest. Entitled, "Nothing but Smoking Ruins—The End of Bastion Brest," its script had been written by Erich Kuby, successful novelist, screen, radio, and TV writer. Kuby, once a seaman in the German navy, criticized the "last-ditch stand" tactics at Brest following the Normandy invasion. According to him, this fanatic defense had unnecessarily cost the lives of ten thousand German soldiers. In his documentary TV dramatization, Kuby had made frequent references to former paratroop General Bernhard Ramcke, who had commanded the bastion. The general, feeling he had been libeled and slandered in several passages of the script, preferred criminal defamation of character charges against Kuby and station official Ruediger Proske. The case came to trial in February, 1959, and after some 270 witnesses had testified, most of them substantiating Kuby's allegations, the two radio men were acquitted.

In a more recent TV program, produced by Radio Free Berlin, TV reporters scoured the country, interviewing German war veterans, workers, mothers of sons killed in the war, ex-generals, and organizers of veterans' groups. The documentary show "The Best Years of My Life?" fired away at rightist and militarist elements which were seeking to establish chauvinism, nationalism, militarism, and powerful central government theories as ideals for Germany's new generation.

Following the Cologne synagogue incident, which was publicized extensively on radio and television, a German current events show staged interviews with three convicted swastika and slogan smearers. One of the interviews took place in jail. More than any other journalistic effort during the period following the Cologne desecration, this TV program brought home to the German people how little the perpetrators knew of Nazism and Judaism, how sketchy had been their education on these matters.

American motion pictures still predominate as German box-office hits. Westerns are popular, musicals go well, grade-B thrillers rarely reach German shores, and the top United States productions are just as successful in Germany as in the United States.

However, in addition to movie imports—the Germans draw most of their foreign films from the United States, Great Britain, Italy, and France—Germany's own once imposing film industry has made a substantial comeback. Widely criticized for their inability to make good musicals or thrillers, but their seemingly fathomless capacity for mass-producing *heimat* or homeland films with such insipid titles as "The Forester of Echo Valley," "The Pink-Cheeked Milkmaid of Dinkelsbuehl," or "The Happy, Heroic Cowherd," some German movie makers have finally turned toward more profound themes.

Although the German motion-picture industry has self-censorship principles which rule out "subjects or situations suited to the promotion of National Socialist, militaristic, imperialistic, or racially inflammatory tendencies," a few such films nevertheless have been produced. War pictures have been criticized most extensively in recent years. Despite this there are many movies with uncompromising antiwar and anti-Nazi themes.

By no means the cinematic masterpiece which advance publicity had described it, Frank Wisbar's Stalingrad film, *Hunde Wollt Ihr Ewig Leben,* took bitter cracks at militarism. It exposed the German general staff's blind obedience to Hitler and demonstrated dramatically how an entire army of German soldiers fell victim to the mad "victory or death" philosophy which sparked the *Führer*'s war plans.

The three films based on Hans Helmut Kirst's best-selling trilogy *08/15* were pragmatic if jocular assaults on Prussian military doctrine.

The Devil's General, based on the play by Carl Zuckmayer, was a smash success in Germany as well as the United States. No moviegoer, knowing that such a *Luftwaffe* general had really existed, could leave the theater unmoved or unimpressed by the principles for which the hero died. The film showed in palatable but convincing terms how powerful the dictatorship had been and how it had poisoned the minds of German youth.

There have been two films on the resistance movement and the July 20, 1944, bomb plot against Hitler.

A number of foreign productions have registered overwhelming success in Germany, foremost among them *The Diary of Anne Frank* and the original Lew Ayres version of *All Quiet on the Western Front,* which is still making the rounds of German cinemas.

Several films, however, should be discussed in detail. They are a cynical epic about the "typical" German, called *Wir Wunderkinder (We Wonderful People);* a bitter antiwar film entitled *Die Brücke (The Bridge);* an even more brutal war picture called *Strafbatallion 999 (Disciplinary Battalion 999)* and the film version of Albrecht Goes's book, *Unruhige Nacht (Restless Night).*

We Wonderful People is the story of Hans Boeckel, an upstanding young man, and Bruno Tisches, an opportunist. The two grew up together in the same town, lived through the Kaiser Reich, the Weimar Republic, the rise of the Nazi party, the Third Reich, the war, and the economic miracle of postwar days. The picture is rib-tickling and rib-punching simultaneously. It is actually a film within a film. The lives and times of Hans and Bruno are related partly by two music-hall characters, one of whom narrates on the side as in the days of silent flickers, while his assistant plinks and plunks appropriate music on an upright piano. According to advance publicity material, "the heroes of this story have one thing in common: they aren't heroes."

During the inflation Hans Boeckel sold newspapers so he could study right and wrong. He didn't know whether the papers were left or right. Bruno Tisches sold stocks and bonds and joined the Nazi party. He earned a lot because his right hand didn't know what the left was doing. "After the war Hans managed to make out once more. That's the German miracle. After the war, Bruno managed to make out once more. That is also a German miracle."

The movie opens with a view of Hans's and Bruno's home town, Neustadt on the Nitze. The Nitze turns out to be an irrigation ditch and Neustadt is anything but new. The narrator points out the city's tired tourist attractions such as the gasworks. The time is 1913, and Neustadt is in the midst of celebrating the anniversary of a battle because, as the narrator explains, with piano accompaniment, the people haven't had a war for a long time, so they want to commemorate an old one.

In that early scene the basic difference between Hans and Bruno already becomes apparent. While Hans is an easygoing, good-natured fellow who wants to get ahead with hard work, Bruno seeks the easy way out. The film, with a good joke at almost every turn of the reel, rolls on through the years.

At the end of World War I the narrator sings, to the tune laid down by the ever-present piano, "Enjoy the postwar period before it turns into the prewar period." Bruno joins the up-and-coming Nazi party and rises with it. One hilarious scene shows him in the men's toilet of a restaurant after he and his political comrades have just wound up an evening. Used to heiling everyone, he raises his arm to say goodbye to the washroom attendant with a Nazi salute.

"Heil Hitler. With a towel that's 50 pfennigs," the attendant quips. Bruno pays up and says, "Next year everything'll be different."

After he leaves, the attendant mutters, "What'll be different? They'll always come to pee."

Bruno moves up in the world as a Nazi, Hans moves steadily downward as he's forced to quit his newspaper job because of his un-Nazilike ideas. As war finally comes, Hans moves to the front as a draftee, Bruno stays back home as a well-fed party functionary who soothes the fears of soldiers' wives with promises of victory. In the middle of one of his patriotic declarations, there's an air raid and the screen goes blank. The narrator jumps in and tells the pianist the film broke. "Darn it," replies the piano player. "We never get to see the final victory."

After the war, Hans is lifted from his ragged existence with his wife and children by an American officer, a former German Jew whom Hans had helped to escape the Nazis. Bruno, however, has gotten on his feet all by himself in black market dealings. They meet. Bruno has changed his name from Tisches to Anders, which in German means "different." Herr Bruno Different tells Hans he wasn't really a Nazi, that he had realized Hitler was crazy, "but I went along with him to prevent the worst from happening."

Eventually, Hans moves up the ladder, becomes a respected newspaper editor. Bruno, though, has laid the cornerstone for his fantastic rise in the miracle economy with his black market activities. He becomes director of a big company. One day, Hans refers to Bruno in an editorial as an old-time Nazi. Bruno tries to get Hans fired.

In a dramatic scene in the publisher's office, Bruno insists he fought the Nazis all his life and asks Hans, "What did you do?"

Hans warns that Germany must look out for men like Bruno and see to it that they don't get back in power again. In a rage, Bruno rushes out of the office and steps into an open elevator shaft under repair, his final and most dramatic exit.

"There are many more like him," the narrator explains. "Unfortunately not every elevator is broken."

Bruno's funeral is another mockery. He is lauded as a great man by a tear-stained orator.

The film played in most major German cinemas, received excellent reviews, and is making the rounds of the neighborhood theaters. There have been reports of occasional mumblings of indignation among the audience. One American who saw the picture in Frankfurt said a large, hulking man arose in the middle of the film and stomped out of a downtown theater angrily. But for the most part *We Wonderful People* scored a tremendous success, bringing out, for the first time, the real issues of recent German history in a light, comical, yet hard-hitting fashion to a mass audience.

Die Brücke, on the other hand, is anything but light or comical. Based on a novel by Manfred Gregor, it portrays war in all its horror. The *Berliner Zeitung*, in a review, described it as a movie in which the last war, Hitler's war, becomes a star in front of a camera, that has no filter on its lens.

The action takes place during the last desperate days of the war in a small south German town. The Americans have crossed the Rhine and are heading to meet the Russians. Seven schoolboys, aged sixteen, are drafted into the *Wehrmacht* and, with only a few days' training, ordered to defend the bridge outside their home town. The bridge has no military value and defending it is useless.

When the sergeant in charge of the boys, a veteran of four years' fighting on the Russian front, is shot by a fanatical People's Storm member, the boys, alone, without leadership, decide to follow their orders and try to prevent the Americans from taking the bridge. The film depicts how six of the seven children are killed a few days before the end of the war.

What is so striking is the manner in which the child soldiers and the Americans die. Not as Western heroes, who spin around, then drop dead, these actors scream, instead, in agony with horrible wounds. One particular scene shows an American sergeant approach the boys on the bridge and tell them to go home. They can't understand a word he says. He doesn't understand them. But they have one word in common. Through the confusion and talk the boys hear him say the word "kindergarten." That angers them and the American is shot down. His screen death consumes several torturous minutes.

Considered by many critics as equally forceful in its approach is *Strabatallion 999*, the story of thousands of German soldiers who

were forced to serve in special disciplinary units in lieu of imprisonment for everything ranging from minor infractions of military discipline to serious felonies. Not even the most hardened, inhuman
criminal deserved the fate which awaited him in these battalions.

With the aid of four cases, the film depicts for what reasons men
were sentenced to serve in the disciplinary units. One is a doctor
who had failed to report for induction because he had been incapac-
itated from the effects of an experiment he had performed upon
himself. The purpose of the experiment had been to save the lives
of thousands of wounded soldiers from tetanus. Another man is a
farmer who overstayed his pass. There is a colonel, holder of the
Ritterkreuz, but convicted of disobeying a lawful order by evacuating
his wounded troops from a surrounded bastion, and finally a common
thief who committed a burglary during an air raid. All serve in the
same company, suffer the same inhumane treatment, then are pressed,
under tactically senseless circumstances, into the midst of a Soviet
offensive where they meet ignominious deaths. The picture is un-
mercifully realistic, sparing the viewer no cruelty, no viciousness or
savagery. Very few men survived in these outfits and other soldiers
had only hazy notions of conditions in them.

Far less ferocious, and more introspective, is *Unruhige Nacht*, a
film based on the short novel by Albrecht Goes. It deals with a
Wehrmacht chaplain's experiences one night during the war just
before he is to prepare a young soldier for his dawn execution. The
film opens in the pastor's study, some time in the later 1950's, when
he is approached by a government representative and asked whether
he would care to join the *Bundeswehr* as a chaplain. The story of his
most terrifying war experience—the restless night before meeting the
soldier to be executed for a minor offense—flashes back in his mind
as he rejects the offer.

Germany's legitimate theaters have also contributed to the general
reorientation of the country. The Anne Frank play has run in practically every major house, as have the plays of Berthold Brecht, in
particular *Mother Courage* and *Schweyk in the Second World War*.

Of particular importance, too, are Germany's political cabarets.
Most major cities have at least one such group, varying in dramatic
competence. Several, such as the *Schmiere* in Frankfurt, the Duesseldorf *Kommödschen*, and Berlin's *Insulaner*, are well known all over

the country. However, their audience capacity is small, with the exception of the *Insulaner* whose shows are broadcast nation-wide.

The intellectual vacuum created by the Hitler dictatorship affected modern literature more than any other sphere of endeavor in Germany. The works of important German authors who had contributed to the formation of democratic thought in the post-World War I period were banned and burned. Many writers were in exile, and those who remained were either imprisoned or terrorized into silence. Refilling the vacuum after the war was not an easy task. Although Germans were interested in the works of their refugee authors, there were only a handful of writers in devastated Germany itself who began to speak out in behalf of the future they invisioned. Nearly five years passed before the new generation made any significant domestic or foreign impact.

Foremost among them is Heinrich Boell, an unusually literate social critic. Of his early efforts, two works in particular stand out as vital contributions to Germany's reorientation and democratization. Both have had measurable success in Europe. One, *The Train Was on Time,* concerned a young German soldier, returning from leave to the front. He senses that death awaits him and even determines the time and location of his fate. He spends his last days letting life rush by.

Another early success was scored with his unusual novel *Adam, Where Art Thou?* In reality a collection of individual experiences, *Adam* is classified as a novel because the individual tales actually make up loosely connected chapters, linked together by a single thread that runs through the entire book. In the closing scene, the protagonist sees his parental home displaying a white flag of surrender. He rushes to the house, and just as he reaches it artillery fire from his own lines destroys the house and kills him. The shot had been fired by a *Wehrmacht* officer who wanted to fight to the last man and objected to the white surrender flag on the house.

Boell's most recent effort is *Billiards at 9:30,* the strange chronicle of an architect's family in a city on the Rhine. The senior member of the family had designed an abbey as his first major project. During the war his son, a demolition expert, destroyed the abbey. The grandson, however, plans to rebuild it.

Boell's advent was generaly hailed as a literary renaissance in Germany. He was only twenty-eight when the war ended, having lived through most of it as an infantryman. Since then his stature has grown steadily.

There are many others, too, who in the years since 1948 have made an impact on the German literary scene. Albrecht Goes has contributed materially with *Restless Night* and *The Burnt Offering*, two works which concern themselves with the past in terms of individual conscience.

Paul Schallueck's 1958 novel, *Engelbert Reinecke*, spotlights a teacher in a West German city who must face up to his country's past. His father was killed in a concentration camp, but the people who sent him there are today Engelbert's own colleagues. He must decide between avoiding the memory of the past or identifying himself with his father.

Peter Bamm, in his *Invisible Flag*, effectively brought out the human equation of war.

Hans Helmut Kirst's rollicking trilogy *08/15* aims at the heart of Prussianism and German militarism. It was read by millions, seen by millions on the screen, and has formed postwar German attitudes toward the army.

Ernst Juenger in his wartime and postwar diaries has made a substantial contribution to the Germans' understanding of their own past. Juenger, a very intellectual, unemotional author, is widely respected because of his heroism as an officer during World War I. His protest against the Nazi terror carried considerable weight during and after the Hitler régime.

One of the most important postwar authors, although he gave his countrymen and the world a total of only 300 printed pages before he died, was Wolfgang Borchert. A native of Hamburg, he wrote one important radio play, *The Man Outside*, which had a short-lived but powerful impact. In addition he became noted for his poems and short stories, written in a style so radically different that a virtual cult was established around him. Borchert died in 1947 in Switzerland at twenty-six from a disease he had contracted in a Nazi prison. But even in his last days he wrote feverishly, crying out with almost fanatical passion against dictatorship, war, militarism, and all the twisted principles the Germans had cherished during his youth.

Borchert's demands for a new lease on life for a new generation are almost unheard today except by a small minority of Germans. Perhaps, if it had not been for Ernst Rohwolt, the Hamburg publisher, Borchert's works would never have appeared. Rohwolt produced Borchert's efforts in pulp paper pocket books, and soon the young rebel was known all over war-torn Germany. After his death, Rohwolt published a complete hard-cover collection of Borchert's writings, including his youth and childhood attempts. This volume since has been reissued in a special reduced-price edition.

The high cost of books in Germany is one of the obstacles to gaining a mass audience. The average linen-bound novel or nonfiction work sells at approximately 15 DM. Considering that the average German income is still only between 400 and 500 DM per month, the greater part of the population cannot afford to purchase books. However, the major publishers have joined in a cooperative venture to issue certain titles in "people's editions" which generally retail at less than half the price of the original. Thus, Borchert's complete works; 08/15; Theodor Plevier's trilogy, *Moscow-Stalingrad-Berlin*; Friedrich Sieburg's *God in France*; and numerous others have been published in hard-cover editions at approximately 7 DM.

It was Ernst Rohwolt who introduced the pocket book to Germany. These postwar pulp paper editions which carried advertising (and still do) were a revolutionary development in Germany. The German concept of the pocket book was quite different from America's. At a time when Westerns and detective thrillers still made up the basic paperback production in the United States, only important works, certain classics, vital best sellers, and important nonfiction books found their way into German pocket editions. Although some publishers do have detective story issues, all shun Westerns, sex novels, and the like.

Following in Rohwolt's footsteps, three other major German publishing houses soon entered the pocket book field, all selling at approximately the same price. The books are very durable, the covers exceptionally well designed, the selections extensive, and the price within the reach of even an apprentice. Leading in the field today are Rohwolt of Hamburg, Fischer Books of Frankfurt, Ullstein of Berlin, and List Books of Munich.

The pocket books, selling from 1.90 to 3.30 DM, depending on the publisher and, in some cases, the number of pages, include not only German authors such as Bamm, Boell, and Borchert, but also the exiled and banned Germans as, for example, Stefan Zweig, Franz Werfel, Kurt Tucholsky, Erich Maria Remarque, and Thomas Mann. American, British, French, and Italian writers are also well represented in the pocket book lists.

In addition, *The Diary of Anne Frank* is in pocket book form, the Fischer paperback having sold nearly seven hundred fifty thousand copies. Walther Hofer's documentary on the Third Reich has sold seventy-five thousand copies as a pocket book. Also available as paperbacks are Hans Rothfels' *The German Opposition Against Hitler*, and Fabian von Schlabrendorff's *Officers Against Hitler*.

The Germans are avid readers. There are, for example, nearly a hundred bookshops in Frankfurt am Main, a city of six hundred thousand population. Young people are well acquainted with the foreign and German contemporary writers. This widespread interest is demonstrated over and over again at the annual Frankfurt Book Fairs, when all German and many foreign publishers display their new titles and the bulk of their previous production. The fair, although established as a buyers' market for book dealers, draws tens of thousands of visitors from all over the country who browse through the gigantic, sprawling Frankfurt fairgrounds and select their reading matter for the coming winter.

Of special importance in the postwar literary development is a small Frankfurt publishing house which specializes in offset editions of satirical cartoon books. Baermaeier and Nikel Verlag's inexpensive, hard-cover cartoon volumes have aroused wide interest and comment. One of the first and most effective was Kurt Halbritter's biting cartoon commentary on militarism entitled *Discipline Is Everything*.

Undoubtedly the most unusual book to come out of Germany since the war is *Denk Ich an Deutschland (When I Think of Germany)*, a collection of stock news and agency photographs, cleverly juxtaposed with skillfully thought-out captions to form a highly controversial political commentary.

The first volume, published in 1956 by Juergen Neven-DuMont and Michael Mansfeld, created a storm of protest and indignation in official circles. By unearthing quotations from German and Allied leaders and using them in the picture captions, the authors compiled a razor-sharp criticism of postwar Germany. As an example, underneath a closeup of a herd of sheep, Neven and Mansfeld wrote: "The truth of yesterday. . . . The truth of today." The picture covered two facing pages. On the left-hand side ran quotations from Eisenhower, Churchill, Molotov, Theodor Heuss, and Adenauer dating from 1945 to 1949. On the facing page the authors quoted the same statements on the same topics in speeches made anywhere from three to ten years later. Thus, in 1945 General Dwight Eisenhower was reported as saying that German militarism had to be abolished at all costs. In 1954, as President, Eisenhower was quoted as saying that a measurable contribution to the defense of Europe would be accomplished by the establishment of a German army.

A second, equally biting volume of *Denk Ich an Deutschland* was published by Mansfeld alone in 1959, leaning more toward a critical historical analysis of Germany than the current political barbs which had sold three press runs of the first volume as if they were free samples at a diamond mine.

Chapter XIII *The People Speak*

Germany, 1960, is a puzzling, complex melting pot of political attitudes, an aggregate of vastly divergent concepts, plagued by the undercurrent of its unsurmounted, unvanquished past. The poles of thought and ideology are far apart. They range from such embittered resistance fighters as Otto John, who see the Nazi menace around every corner, to the incorrigibles and their neo-Nazi protégés. In between are the Hans Schmidts.

Of the ones I know and have met, a few live on the funereal side of the Iron Curtain, the East zone. The majority are inhabitants of that economic miracle, the Federal Republic. It would be presumptuous to say that they reflect in any way a cross section of postwar German life. They are merely unsystematically picked samplings. Some I know intimately. Others I have met only in passing. Many are chance acquaintances who were lured or lured me into a discussion. They are quoted at random. They do not represent any particular categories or classes or trends of German thought. But they do, in their conversations, give deep insight into the numerous attitudes rampant in Germany today.

For example, there is Mr. H. B., who died in the spring of 1959. He had been a Nazi all his adult life. He was a National Socialist

264

before the Nazi party existed and remained a Nazi long after the Hitler régime had crumbled into ruin and ashes. For his efforts and for his loyalty to the Nazi party, B. rose to the rank of captain in the SS, was imprisoned by the French after the war, was sentenced to death by a French military court, then released after nearly six years in jail, de-Nazified and classified as a major offender. He was ordered to work only as a common laborer, and finally died of lung cancer. For his forty years of loyalty to the principles of Nazism, he had no more rewards than a few pictures of himself in SS uniform and the Iron Cross he had won in World War I.

B. had been born the son of German parents in the French part of Switzerland where his father worked as a brewery director. He enlisted in the German army as a teenager during World War I because "more than anything else, I wanted to identify myself with the German fatherland. Being a German in a foreign country, I always felt somewhat detached and abandoned." The greatest moment of his life, he used to say proudly, was when Kaiser Wilhelm had visited his regiment on the Western Front and he was introduced personally to the Emperor.

After the armistice, B., violently anti-Social Democrat, became a member of the Black *Reichswehr,* and soon joined the fledgling National Socialist German Workers' party. As late as 1958 he boasted of the party's hectic early days when "I used to clean out the Communist and Socialist meeting halls. They'd have some speaker on the platform and my boys would walk in and stand at the back of the hall for a few minutes. If the fellow on stage didn't stop speaking immediately, why we'd just start working our way forward with billy clubs. Cleared 'em all out. They were all afraid of me. All someone had to say at one of those meetings was 'B. is here,' and the place was in panic. Nothing brutal, you know, just good fights. But we sure cleaned the Reds out of town."

By the time Hitler came to power, B. was a full-time, paid member of the SS. He came up through the ranks, attaining a captaincy by 1945. He was one of the Nazi bosses of Stuttgart. His faith in Nazism, pan-Germanism and Germany's destiny to rule the world was unshakable. Fourteen years after the régime had collapsed, B. still believed stanchly that the British and the French had been responsible for World War II, that the unfairest treaty ever written had been drafted at Versailles, that Hitler had been betrayed by his generals, and that, if it had not been for this betrayal, Germany would have won the war.

The SS, he insisted, was nowhere near as bad as "postwar Allied propaganda made us out to be." As far as the Russians were concerned, he frequently said, "well, if you Americans had listened to us and joined us in an offensive toward the East, instead of demanding our unconditional surrender, you wouldn't be in the fix you're in now."

B. was convinced, right up to the day he died, that the Jews in Germany had owned all the property, controlled all the press, and would have ruined Germany economically if Hitler had not appeared on the scene. When confronted with the atrocities committed by the Nazis, his standard retort was:

I would never have subscribed to anything like that had I known about it. I never harmed a single Jew. But, after all, you must realize that much so-called atrocity propaganda was put out by the Allies after the war to demoralize the German people. I refuse to believe that all those things really happened. And, don't forget, there were thousands of criminals, antisocial individuals, homosexuals, and saboteurs in the camps. Of course there were a few sadists in SS uniform, but not as many as you have been led to believe.

B. had his own version of history and was able to reel it off perfectly. Interpretations that would seem fantastically inaccurate to others appeared perfectly logical to him. He had an unflagging faith in his convictions, even when all the facts proved him wrong. Despite his long association with the Nazi party and his rowdy activities in the 1920's and 1930's, he was not a cruel man, and within the circle of his family he was as kind a husband and father as one could find. Strangely, he enjoyed the respect even of his enemies, simply because he had the courage to stand up for what he thought, even under the threat of death, poverty, and social ostracism. His belief may have been blind, but it was certainly firm.

His wife swore allegiance to all his principles—until the war ended. She had ridden high on his prestige and power. Then, when times became tough, she deemed it appropriate to think differently about the régime to which her husband still paid homage. She even sought to counteract his theories and teachings in their home. Though by no means a religious woman herself, she scoured the city of Stuttgart to find a pastor who would consent to conduct her notorious husband's funeral.

The pastor came in civilian clothes [she said a few weeks after B.'s death]. He made no allusions to my husband's past, but gave a wonderful sermon. I suppose my husband twisted in his coffin when he realized there was a minister standing over him, but I just couldn't send him under the ground without that. It would not seem right. Perhaps he'll know, wherever he is, that all his fanaticism was for naught and that the answer, after all, lay with God, the God in whom he refused to believe.

In the strictest sense of the term, B. was one of the *alte Kämpfer*, one of the old fighters. Not all old fighters remained as stanch in their convictions once the fight was finished as he did. Many of them, such as Herr S. L., are bitterly disillusioned today, although still in agreement with many of the theories espoused by the Hitler régime. S. L. is only fifty-nine, but an aging man, suffering from the after-effects of a stroke. He lives in a small city in the Soviet zone.

Although he joined the NSDAP shortly after its founding, he never reaped any of the benefits of membership. He was not in the SA or the SS. He enjoyed no commercial or economic advantages from the Hitler régime or its persecution of the Jews and the confiscation of Jewish property. During the prewar period he continued to work his way upward as a junior executive in a wholesale electrical company. He believed in the party, in Germany, in the supremacy of the German race, and was certain, until he returned in rags from the Eastern Front, that his fatherland would win a glorious victory. His family followed him loyally. His three oldest children all belonged to the Hitler Youth.

He sacrificed everything—and it was pitifully little—for his convictions. When he was on the Russian Front—as an ordinary private —he wrote his wife telling her to donate all his civilian suits to the German Winter Aid program. "Our victory is as certain as the fact that day follows night," he once wrote his family from a front-line post which was under heavy Soviet fire. When, instead of victory, the régime for which he had fought ended with an ignominious defeat, S. L. dragged his way home on foot in borrowed, tattered civilian clothes. Waiting for him was his cold, starving, and war-weary family of six.

Not an active believer as H. B. had been, S. L. also clung to his ideas. When Allied news broadcasts told of German atrocities, L. rejected them as "preposterous lies." He was de-Nazified, deprived of his right to go back to the job he had left, and became, instead, a traveling salesman. Today he leads a hand-to-mouth existence, trying to be an independent in a socialized economy.

Although he still clings to many of his old beliefs and theories, his ideals are gone and he has become apathetic to political developments. When his eldest daughter married a Jew in 1956, he said to her in a letter, "I hope you won't have any children. After all, it's a racially mixed marriage and they're likely to be defective." But when a baby, a perfectly healthy little boy, was born and he saw it for the first time, L. became as doting a grandfather as any other. S. L.'s world has crumbled around him, and at his age, he'll never find a new one.

That eldest daughter broke from the family tradition completely. After receiving nearly all her formal education under the Nazis, she fled to the West in 1950. A year later she went to England to learn the language. She learned more than that. For the first time she got a glimpse of Germany as others saw it. She met men and women of different races, nationalities, and religious beliefs. Already converted to democracy and the principles of tolerance as a result of her exposure to numerous influences in the United Kingdom, she went to France and studied in Paris. She supported herself by baby-sitting for American families. Two of them were Jewish.

She met Negroes, Jews, Arabs, Americans, Russians, Irishmen, Englishmen, Frenchmen, and many of her own countrymen, all of them the intellectuals and pseudo intellectuals who populate the Left Bank. Her experiences in two foreign countries turned her into a dedicated opponent of any form of dictatorship, but it was not until she was twenty-six years old, five years after she was eligible to vote, that she cast her first ballot in a political election. "I hate parties and politics," she explained in self-defense. "I hate anything connected or associated with government. There is nothing we can do about it anyway, and if we vote one way, and the system turns out wrong, we are to blame afterwards. I just want to live for my family."

As a member of the Hitler Youth, fiery in his naïve, juvenile adoration of the Nazi régime that ruled his country, young G. S. was fifteen years old when he was drafted into the *Wehrmacht* to help defend, to the last man, the decaying Thousand-Year Reich. His mother still recalls her shock at seeing him in a helmet that came down almost to his nose. His uniform jacket in those waning days of the war, when supplies were short, reached nearly to his knees, and the sleeves extended past his finger tips.

Young S. spent only a few days in the war, then his unit was disbanded and he returned home. It was not long before he began to see the Hitler régime for what it had really been. But the only substitute he had was the Communist government that ruled the East zone where he lived. He held out until 1955, then fled to the Federal Republic.

With his training as a mechanical engineer, he found an excellent position in Stuttgart, and after being with his company for two years, was sent on an exchange program to the United States. Since his return from America, S. has become a severe critic of everything German.

There is no hope for Germany so long as we are mired in the old traditions of order, system, discipline, and loyalty to superiors [he lamented in one conversation].

After one year in the United States I'll never be happy here again. It's not just that I have to work less in the States to earn four times as much as I do in Germany, but it is the working climate, the attitude of the people, the way they treat you, and the way they expect to be treated, that is so different.

In the States you can get to the top if you're good and know something. Here you can reach the top only after you've been on the bottom long enough for those on the top to die.

So long as we cling to the idea of unquestioning loyalty to superiors and insist that "discipline means everything," we Germans will never change. We'll continue to make the same mistakes over and over again. We must change the structure of our social system. We must yank out the roots of traditionalism before we can begin to hope for a new Germany.

Much like S. in his attitude is a waiter in Stuttgart, Egon. His last name, if I ever knew it, has long escaped me. He also joined the *Wehrmacht* when only fifteen.

At the time I thought it was wonderful [he confided]. Meanwhile I have changed my mind. I was enthusiastic then. How else should I have been? I knew nothing else. We believed in victory until the last minute. The *Führer* and the fatherland were our highest ideals. That's the way we learned it in school.

My parents were opposed to the Nazis, but I was so fanatically in favor that, had my parents been any more vociferous in their opposition I wouldn't have hesitated for a moment to turn them in and report them to the Gestapo.

My father hated the régime. He always swore he'd come home from the war as a civilian. "I'll never enter this house as a soldier in uniform," he used to say.

I was so ashamed of my father for talking like that, but I've learned something since those days. Today I am proud of the fact that my father had the courage to say such things at a time when it could have cost him his life. And I'm ashamed of myself for having had such crazy ideas. But we all learn the hard way.

Then there is the taxi driver whose one-time faith in Nazi principles has turned into a bitter, cynical rejection of all political ideals. His father had been a prominent member of the Gestapo and "I attended the Adolf Hitler School."

But today he asks:

Why did Hitler kill all the Jews? Why did he first make life so good for us, then start the war and destroy everything? Why is it the little man always has to suffer in the end?

We Germans still haven't learned anything from the past. Look at all those people in the East zone running around with Socialist Unity party (SED) badges. Yesterday they sang *Deutschland über Alles*, today they sing the *International*.

As for me, I hate communism, Nazism, dictatorship, and any other kind of ism. Why can't human beings just live and let live, so there won't be any more wars and dictators and mass executions and what have you? Who gains by it all?

One can meet many different trends of thought in Germany. There are those who fought the Nazis, those who tolerated them, and those who fought for them. One can find the suspicious, cynical ones such as one journalist who views every development in his country with a pessimistic eye, convinced that history will repeat itself as surely as the seasons do. There are the trusting, unsuspecting ones, such as W. M. and W. E., also newspapermen, who are convinced that most people have a phobia about Nazis today.

One meets the many hundreds who feel neither one way nor the other, remaining content to reap the benefits of postwar Germany's miracle economy. They live on the crest of the boom and shudder at being reminded of the recent past. Such a woman, for example, is Frau W., only twenty-one, mother of two happy, healthy children, wife of a once-divorced, middle-aged businessman. Her apartment is equipped with the latest and newest electrical appliances and kitchen gimmicks; she wears flowery dresses because they are the latest style, though hardly becoming to her somewhat buxom contours. When her husband's radio repair business expanded from a one-man to a ten-man operation, she felt that a Volkswagen was too ordinary a vehicle for her and traded it in for a posher Borgward.

When *The Shop Around the Corner*, a prewar American film criticizing the Nazi régime, played in a Frankfurt theater in 1958, Frau W., unaware of its subject matter, happened to see it. Asked by another German woman what she thought of the picture, Frau W. replied,

It's terrible. I just can't understand why we are continually fed that sort of thing. I'm so tired of hearing about the Nazis. Why is someone always trying to remind us of that period? I think it's an affront to our dignity. After all, we have the hardest currency in Europe now.

One German journalist, working on a small paper in the southwest German city of Kaiserslautern is a dedicated anti-Nazi but is convinced that most of his professional colleagues tend to exaggerate the problem today. When, in July, 1959, the chief of the Rhineland Palatinate bureau of criminal investigations, formerly police chief of Kaiserslautern, was arrested and charged with war crimes, the newsman refused to believe the allegations were true. "He just doesn't look the type," the reporter said to his friends. "I know the man, I've worked with him. He's an excellent policeman and if he was a Nazi or committed war crimes, why, so did I."

Herr J. H., a free-lance writer, considers himself a stanch defender of the opposition movement.

We Germans are proud of our resistance movement to Hitler, for it operated under the most difficult circumstances [he said in reply to an American soldier's contention that the officers who had plotted the July 20, 1944, uprising were, in reality, traitors and should be treated as such, instead of being honored].

Only someone who has lived under a dictatorship and experienced the fear it generates, only someone who has lived under tyranny and tried to revolt against it can understand how difficult it was for the "traitors" of July 20. To those of us in Germany who look back with shame on the years from 1933 to 1945, the resistance movement, the plotters, if you wish to call them that, will always remain as heroes, as shining examples of men with courage and principles.

Herr K., an ex-prize fighter, operates a small, but high-priced, all-night restaurant in downtown Frankfurt, famed not only for its excellent food but for its congenial atmosphere as well. K., a hulking man who could never hide his former profession, is also known for his outspoken political beliefs.

Since K.'s successful restaurant is almost a private club, the patrons must agree with him on political issues or they are asked to take their business elsewhere. One of K.'s basic beliefs is that Nazism was the rottenest system ever to rule a European country. Being big and beefy enough to defend his concepts with action, K. has established a reputation for tossing ex- and neo-Nazis and Nazi sympathizers right out on their ears.

During one such encounter, a customer who had bent his elbow on the bar for the better part of an evening expressed the mild comment that "Hilter wasn't all that bad, you know. After all, he built the *Autobahnen,* gave us employment and good wages."

"Out," shouted K., then removed the man's beer glass, refunded him the price of the beer, and moved around from behind the bar to show the gentleman the door. No one would be so foolish as to argue with K. The customer left.

After twelve long years of that Nazi nonsense [K. said when his temper had simmered down], I don't have to put up with that kind of talk. I just can't understand those people. You'd think that with all that has happened, they'd have learned something. At any rate, if they haven't they're too stupid to rub elbows with my regular customers. I won't have them in my place, and fortunately I can afford to throw them out.

I think we're entitled to a few years of peace and quiet before those idiots decide to start the Fourth Reich. I plan to make the most of the intermission.

Mrs. L. G., married to an American, but still a German citizen, believes that reports of ex- and neo-Nazis activities in government and of an organized Nazi underground are highly exaggerated, attributable to leftist propaganda. When the *Frankfurter Rundschau* published Thomas Gnielka's exposé on right-radical youth organizations, she passed it off by saying that the paper had once been Communist and is still "certainly very sympathetic to the left." Mrs. G. comes from a very conservative and propertied family and cannot escape from the belief that the *status quo*, whatever it may be, is ideal.

Herr K. M. is a sixty-seven-year-old carpenter who opposed the Nazis from the day they gained power until the day in March, 1945, when American troops marched into Frankfurt.

I embraced the first GI I saw [M. explained], and tried to tell him how glad I was that he had come. I saw my countrymen do things that I thought not even barbarians would do. Hitler established the cruelest dictatorship the world has ever known.

Now that you Americans have conquered some of us and liberated those of us who looked upon you as liberators, the responsibility rests with us to prevent the past from repeating itself. I hope I'm not too old to help.

The vice president of a German shoe company, who served as a highly-decorated first lieutenant and tank platoon leader in World War II, is today a bitter opponent of rearmament.

I am convinced that from a purely military point of view there is nothing to be gained by the establishment of a West German army. And, if we really want a democratic Germany, rearmament was started fifteen years too soon. The people who are reenlisting today are the same old Nazis who left the army in 1945. They have learned nothing new since then. Manstein is in the defense ministry and former SS officers are being permitted to join the *Bundeswehr*. This, to me, is incredible.

But a *Bundeswehr* captain insisted that the situation is nowhere near the critical point which the shoe company executive implied.

Those of us who are officers today are the "young Turks" of yesterday. We were the potential reformers in those days. We just did not get the opportunity to reform. Back in 1941, most of my officer buddies thought as I did, that if we ever got to the top in the army, we'd change things. Now we have our chance and we plan to take advantage of it.

There are only a few of the Prussian types still around. Those who are back in uniform, are too old for cadre or training positions. We keep them on desk jobs.

Among both the older and the younger generation there are many whose attitudes toward both the Nazi régime and today's democracy are completely apathetic. They feel that "we have no say in government anyway. What can we do about the actions of our leaders? If we did vote, our one ballot would not change the course of events."

And there are those who, instead of humility, carry resentment in their hearts. No incident represents them more dramatically than that experienced by a German-born American soldier, riding in uniform on a Stuttgart streetcar some years ago.

The car was fairly well crowded, and the soldier sat down on a two-seat bench, already occupied by one passenger. Facing him on the opposite seat were two more Germans. The three men, although it was a weekday noon, were under the influence of alcohol.

No sooner had the soldier taken his place, when one of the Germans remarked, "They have their jeeps, their tanks, their airplanes and even their private trains. Why do these Amis have to muscle in on our streetcars, too?"

"You know, my son was killed on the Western Front and I was wounded by the Americans," another of the trio chimed in.

"I'm still waiting for compensation payments on the damage their bombers did to my house," the third commented.

"All this business about sovereignty is just a lie," said the first one. "So long as the Amis are here, we'll never be sovereign, it'll always be an occupation."

The entire conversation was in German. Suddenly, the soldier reached into his Ike jacket pocket, pulled out his streetcar ticket stub, and said in a Saxonian dialect: "Gentlemen, my 30 pfennigs are as good as your 30 pfennigs, and I venture to say I worked just as hard for mine as you did for yours." A tense silence descended on the crowd in the car. The only sound was the hum of the electric motor and the clacking of the wheels. Then started a political argument between the soldier and the Germans that lasted for a good half hour. The debate drew in most bystanders on the car.

"You talk about your losses in the air raids," the soldier said, "but what about the millions of innocent people who were killed in your concentration camps, the millions of innocent people whom you separated from their families and deported to Germany as slave laborers, the millions of homes your armies destroyed? What about them?

"Exaggerations," said one of the three.

"There may have been individual cases of executions in the concentration camps, but most of the inmates were criminals or enemies of the state, traitors, if you will," said one of the more sober members of the group.

Through the long interchange, although both sides were evenly represented among the passengers, the GI won out in popularity.

Fortunately, for Germany and the Western world, there are others such as a twenty-five-year-old youth whose parents rode on the crest of the Nazi régime. He occasionally tells of arguments and heated political discussions in his home, then sighs, shakes his head, and laments, "My parents will never change." He is, in a sense, typical of a vast group of young Germans between twenty-one and thirty years old. Though born during or shortly before the heyday of the Nazi régime, their most vivid recollections of it are of the régime's decay. They remember little of the good times, of the benefits for which their parents yearn, but their teenage minds were impressed by the hunger, chaos, destruction, and unhappiness that reigned over the last year of the war and the early occupation period.

They are too young to remember the economic advantages of the Third Reich, but old enough to recall the misfortunes that befell Germany because of the régime.

Today they are the young men and women who, as children, stood wide-eyed watching American soldiers throw away surplus food for which they later scavenged in garbage cans. They were the knock-kneed, goggle-eyed kids who thankfully accepted gifts of chocolate and chewing gum, who in later years attended the American-sponsored German Youth Authority dances, hungered for jazz, and wore blue jeans and bobby socks.

It is with them that the hope for Germany's future lies.

Chapter XIV

Will Democracy Triumph?

How long will it take the Germans to free themselves completely from the legacy of the Hitler dictatorship? Can they, in fact, sever the remaining bonds entirely? What guarantees are there that Germany is immune from any resurgence of Nazism?

Such questions puzzle not only foreign observers but thousands of responsible Germans as well. One man who has grappled with the problem repeatedly over the past decade and a half is Walter Kampe, Catholic bishop of Limburg. His thoughts and comments on the complex aspects of postwar Germany's development merit extensive consideration.

The greatest difficulty facing the resistance to the Nazi influence [states Bishop Kampe], lies in the fact that our German people have not overcome National Socialism spiritually. A military defeat, no matter what its catastrophical dimensions, is no proof of the righteousness or wrongness of an ideology. We did not reject Nazism as the result of an inner perception of the rottenness of its morality, but because of its fateful outward results. In the meantime this has all been forgotten, but it keeps on smoldering subconsciously.

We're still too close to the years between 1933 and 1945 to conquer

277

this problem easily [Bishop Kampe said on another occasion]. Understandably, at first many people considered that the easiest and best way was simply to forget and let grass grow over the past. But we realize today that this simply won't do. . . . We must understand the past, whether we welcome the obligation or not. Until we do this, as we know from experience, strange things will have a way of happening—events that may actually confront us like ghosts. In whatever way one chooses to interpret the phenomenon of Hitler, it cannot be denied that he has invaded our national history. We need to come to grips with him, however painful and humiliating, however harassing and depressing this may be for us. We owe this . . . to ourselves. We have to have patience with ourselves. We also need to ask for the world's patience, so that we can quietly get on with our task. We should neither try to hush over anything nor exaggerate. Rather, we should unravel objectively what still lingers in our memories as an entangled skein. Perhaps we ourselves shall not quite reach our goal, but at least we shall have cleared the way for the young people.

On another occasion, early in 1959, Bishop Kampe, writing in *Der Sonntag* the diocesan paper of Limburg, was more militant:

. . . What we lack here is an organized fusion of all anti-Nazi forces to build a sturdy dam against the secret and underground attacks which undermine our as yet not too solidly established democratic society.

The bishop touches on the core of what is really an intricate, puzzling, and paradoxical state of affairs.

Germany's repudiation of Hitler was not internal, but an external renunciation forced upon it in defeat. We knew this full well at the time it happened. As a consequence, the Germans were charged with collective guilt for the crimes committed during the Third Reich and collective responsibility for the war which Hitler started. Yet, after only ten years, while many of the war criminals were still in prison, while the physical and spiritual aftermath of war was still everywhere apparent, West Germany was restored its full sovereignty as a political and military equal in the Western community of nations.

The result, unfortunately, is that Germany is encumbered with an independence granted too fast and a democracy based on too shaky a foundation. Germany must cope with an armed force established too soon after the last war, but too late to take advantage of the professional military skill which German soldiers had acquired. Germany is still flailing in the wake of an occupation that was once too harsh and then too lax, an economic catastrophe that was turned into a miracle of economic reconstruction too quickly, and a program of reorientation that failed to reorient.

American policy toward Germany was dictated by the exigencies of postwar developments in our relations with the Soviet Union. It is of no consequence here whether that policy was right or wrong, for history cannot be rolled backward and the past cannot be undone. Even if this were possible, it is probable that, despite knowing the consequences and the results, we would, under the pressure of the East-West conflict, implement the same policy over again.

Although many of the faults which can be found with Germany today are traceable to this policy of meeting exigencies, numerous problems have their origin in the military government of Germany up to 1949 and even in the presurrender planning, such as there was.

At the outset, our occupation was hard and harsh. We demanded unconditional surrender and that is what we got. We imposed an often uncompromising rule over the defeated Germans. Yet in less than five years our policy was in reverse, geared to the all-important theme which still dictates most of the actions of our military forces in Germany today: improving German-American relations. This in itself may be admirable, but it also encompassed the objective on our part to forget the war and Germany's role in it as quickly as possible. This policy in many instances has been refined to the point of the ridiculous and ludicrous. Among our military officialdom in Germany, the subject of World War II is taboo.

Just as an example, in May, 1960, an American newspaperman in Frankfurt asked for army cooperation in arranging interviews with soldiers for a story on the fifteenth anniversary of VE Day. He wanted to ask veterans as well as young draftees what they remembered and what they were doing when the surrender was announced. His request was turned down by military officials on the grounds that such an article would open up old wounds and would not be in keeping with the principles of fostering better German-American relations. Yet when the Germans are equally quick to forget the past we accuse them of failing to take responsibility for their mistakes of yesteryear.

In many instances our occupation was haphazardly carried out. Although we conducted a witch hunt for Nazis and an extensive purge, many Nazis successfully pulled the wool over military government officials' eyes, gaining their confidence. They moved into positions of political and economic power. Yet, paradoxical as it may sound, at times our occupation was unduly harsh, creating resentments which still linger among various elements of the German people. It is upon these resentments that neo-Nazi agitators can play their propaganda tunes and win substantial audiences.

Our reversal in attitude was too complete and too rapid. While as late as 1948 and 1949 we were still screening and sifting the population for Nazi elements, within a year the issue of a Nazi past had become inconsequential. The predominant question became: has he ever been a Communist? A classic example is that of a former Army employee, screened several times and cleared of any possible Nazi associations. After a few years service with a United States Army agency, he resigned and applied for work with Radio Free Europe.

"Yes," said an RFE official, "we'll take you but you'll have to get a political clearance."

"Why?" asked the German, explaining he had been cleared frequently.

"Oh," said the official, "that was for Nazi associations. We are no longer interested in that. For all we care you could have been a bigshot Nazi. We're interested now in finding out whether you have ever been a Communist."

Faced with such enigmatic American attitudes, who can blame the Germans for suggesting—as many still do—that the United States should have signed an armistice with Hitler and joined forces in an eastward march to fight the Russians.

The Germans are still bitter and resentful over other aspects of the occupation. Many still believe that the war-crimes trails were merely a front for exercising the victor's privilege of revenge and they accuse us of hypocrisy and melodramatics for giving the defendants fair and just trials with every opportunity to present their side of the case.

"You knew the war criminals were guilty," Germans often say. "Why did you go through that big act?"

The de-Nazification program was one of the most unpopular of the postwar era, and resentment over it still lingers today, nearly ten years after the last de-Nazification board outside of Berlin filed its cases away forever.

In our effort to reorient German political thinking, we brought over the blessings of democracy. Although the framework of Germany's government and its legal foundation—the basic law, or constitution as we would call it—are of German origin, both were greatly influenced by occupation authorities. Final approval of the basic law lay with military government officials.

Once the government was established, the constitution approved and the first elections held, Germany, we assumed, was on its way. It is impossible, however, to don democracy like a coat. Democracy is not merely a form of government laid down in a set of documents and principles. It is the result of political evolution, and more than anything else, a frame of mind.

In practice and in a formal sense, Western Germany is a democracy. The people vote for their representatives in free and secret elections; the governmental machinery is equipped with a certain check and balance system; the decisions of the cabinet and the laws passed by the parliament are subject to interpretation by the constitutional court; there are basic guarantees of individual rights and good safeguards against the establishment of a dictatorship. What is lacking, however, is a real understanding of the nature of a democracy. The Germans are going through the motions of living in a democratic society without really knowing what it is supposed to be.

Since the Federal Republic was established, now a period of eleven years, it has been governed, not only by the same party, but the same man. This is due to more than just the normal political fortunes which periodically befall a party in other, older, more mature parliamentary democracies. In Germany there is more than merely a good platform, good administration, or political "personality cult" behind the Christian Democratic Union's and Chancellor Konrad Adenauer's success all these years. Certainly the CDU has not been as victorious in state and local elections as it has been in federal contests. In considering this, one must ask: How much is the CDU's national popularity due to the fact that Adenauer is a democratic version of the strong leader, the *Führer* who dominates a powerful central government and assumes final responsibility for his administration's policy and actions?

Many observers attribute The Old One's record of electoral triumphs to the theory that he is an extension of the *Führer* idea to which most Germans still conciously or unconsciously subscribe. The theory may be correct and the real test of German democracy may not come until the day Adenauer dies or relinquishes political power to a younger, more energetic successor.

True, the election turnout in Germany is far greater than in the United States and surpasses that of many other European democracies. But there is less direct personal participation, less individual interest in political campaigns on the part of the German voters than in the United States or other European countries. This is due, to some extent, to the nature of the electoral machinery and constitutional framework, but more than anything else to the dominant position and centralized structure of the political parties as vast, impersonal organizations in German life. There is an apparent lack of direct contact between individual candidate or parliamentary deputy and his constitutents. The candidate subordinates himself to the party organization and its policy, functioning more as a representative of the party which seeks his election to office.

This trend is visible in the daily functioning of the *Bundestag*. Deviation from the party line in the parliament is virtually unheard of. Reports of CDU deputies voting the SPD way on any given bill are rare indeed. The party in parliament and at the polls is a political entity to which individuals subscribe their loyalty. With the exception of a few outstanding personalities who move forward to party leadership positions, German legislators are mostly nameless individuals who fade into an anonymous group called the governing party, the opposition, or minority faction. It is not so much the question of Gustav Schultz, deputy in the *Bundestag* from Bavaria, who happens to be a member of the CDU/CSU, but more "a CDU deputy from Bavaria" who happens, incidentally, to be named Schultz.

A major barrier to more direct personal contact between representative and voter is the proportional representation system used to a greater or lesser degree in elections throughout West Germany.

Under this plan, certain candidates need not be residents of the district they represent. In fact, a number of candidates are on a party reserve list. When all the votes are tabulated, each party is awarded a certain number of "list seats," distributed in proportion to the popular vote. If a party gains, say for example, fifty seats which come from the list, the first fifty names on it, selected of course by the party leadership in advance of the elections, will become members of parliament. If the party wins enough votes to seat fifty-one, the fifty-first name on the list also becomes a representative. Although the proportional representation system is not used exclusively in Germany, there are no states in which there is only a simple majority vote decision. The Federal Republic's electoral system is a compromise between the two concepts of representation.

For all practical purposes, however, when a German goes to the polls he does so to elect a party ticket, not an individual. His only real choice of individuals is between the party leaders or those personalities designated by the party directorate to become chancellor should the party win a majority or gain enough seats to form a governing coalition.

Although a creditable effort has been made both by the parties and the press to create a more direct, more personal relationship between voter and candidate, there is still, for American concepts, a wide cleft and wall of formality that separates them. Just as an example, a spot survey in a Frankfurt newspaper office of some twenty-five Germans, all of them (except for clerical help) professional people with an above-average education and interest in politics, revealed that only three could name their representative in the *Bundestag*.

This, of course, manifests itself in the day-to-day operation of Germany's democracy and is evident in German attitudes toward the government. Most Germans still do not really believe that their *Bundestag* representative is responsible to them. They see in him not so much an elected delegate whose duty it is to carry out their wishes, but a "public official" who is to be treated with respect and distant formality because he "governs." Instead of shouting, "let's throw the rascals out of office," Germans treat unpopular decisions of the parliament with the attitude, "well, that's the government. What can we little people do about it?" Despite the democratic framework, universal suffrage, and the guarantees of basic human rights, the average West German today still considers the government as "The Government," an authoritative force far removed from his personal life over which, he feels, he exercises little real control.

The hopeful signs for a change in this attitude are reflected on the local level where there is a much greater degree of personal, man-on-the-street interest and participation. It is, of course, easy to attribute this situation to the so-called "lack of a democratic tradition in Germany." That, however, is only a partial explanation. Democratic tradition, at least formally, is not all *that* lacking in German history. Democracy did not just begin with the Weimar Republic and end with the Third Reich. There was a popular assembly, the *Reichstag,* even in the imperial days from 1871 until 1918, a period of nearly fifty years. Although Bismarck was the real ruler until 1890 and Wilhelm II was an almost absolute monarch, neither Bismarck nor the Kaiser could rule freely without answering to some extent to the people. There were political parties and they were becoming increasingly powerful. The middle-class revolution of 1848 saw the first, though short-lived effort at parliamentary government. But even since the Middle Ages, certain free cities of the Reich had always had a degree, at least, of representation and self-determination in managing their affairs.

However, during these various, often limited democratic experiments, including the Weimar Republic, one factor of government has remained unchanged: the civil service. It is a dominant force in German political life, for upon the civil service falls the major responsibility for enforcing, administering, and interpreting the law. Until the Federal Republic was founded in the postwar years, civil servants even had a say in making the law because professional public officials were permitted to hold seats in parliament.

Democratic development is by necessity hampered in a state where the police, judges, district attorneys, teachers, public health, postal, railway, telephone, and telegraphic officials are public servants and virtually all phases of administration are in the hands of a civil service so autonomous, so traditionally established, that its members form a social class all by themselves.

In few societies do civil servants enjoy as many privileges and as much respect as in Germany. The position of the *Beamter* is still revered by the public. His word is law and foolish or revolutionary is the individual who would question it. The public servants assume their positions for life. When they reach retirement age, they are paid liberal pensions by the state for which they have not had to make a single contribution during their working years. Their powerful position in the government stems from the fact that they are more than merely administrators of the law: they are virtually arbiters of the law. Many of the higher ranking officials are almost autonomous, and on the federal and state governmental levels, they are influential in molding government policy. Under such circumstances, where the great mass of the public has its only contact with government through such powerful professional civil servants, it is easy to understand how democratic development can suffer.

Some of the obstacles to a really practicing democracy are written into the constitution or basic law. There is, for example, no provision in this document for a referendum. But manifold as the causes may be, it is an inescapable fact that although the Germans have a democratic framework, although they go through the motions, they still do not understand what really makes a democracy tick. All too often one hears the comment: "That isn't done in a democracy," and the reply, "Oh, it isn't? I didn't know." What is drastically needed is not so much a real understanding of the outward principles and mechanics but the nature of the democratic process. All too many Germans have merely resigned themselves to the pleasant fact that they now "live in a democracy," consequently they "have become democrats."

Although Germany's loyalty to the Western camp is unchallenged, and for the present the United States and the Free World allies have virtually nothing to fear from its remilitarization, the Germans themselves face a great number of problems in dealing with their new army. Disregarding the international needs for the *Bundeswehr* or the purely strategic advantages which NATO may derive from it, the army, in terms of Germany's democratization, came too soon, and, at the same time, too late.

Rearmament was launched too soon in the sense that too many of the old militarists, the *Komissköpfe* as they are called in German, were still available and eligible for reenlistment. The *Bundeswehr* was organized too late, however, to take full advantage of the practical military training most Germans had received during the war. Army planners were forced to rely on a larger-than-desirable number of *Komissköpfe* to form the cadre.

Although Helmut von Grolman, the special parliamentary commissioner for defense matters, praised the attitude of officers toward the new democratic state in his first annual report, he admitted that many officers and noncoms still lacked a sense of familiarity with and trust in the democratic form of government. Above all, Grolman emphasized, the *Bundeswehr* had been built up too rapidly, resulting in undue pressure and demands on troop unit leaders, a lack of experienced officers, particularly company commanders, and too few young officers and noncoms.

Rearmament has been effected too fast and initiated too soon to guarantee that the *Bundeswehr* will mesh into the new German democratic order. For the time being one can adopt only a wait-and-see attitude and hope for the best. Certainly, from an emotional point of view, a generation or more should have passed before Germany was permitted to rearm, if at all. Rearmament is not popular among Germany's European allies, although they recognize the strategic need for a West German army. Neither is rearmament popular among many of the Germans who still feel the sting of the last war. It appeared for a while as if the traditional German military spirit was broken. It is unfortunate that international pressures have forced a reawakening of that spirit from outside Germany.

As the military spirit is being reawakened, almost artificially, so is the spirit of nationalism. This is bolstered by Germany's spectacular economic renaissance. Although the miraculous recovery and reconstruction are a tribute to German ingenuity and industriousness, they are also an unfortunate prick to the ego of Germany's European neighbors and a potentially dangerous shot in the arm for German attitudes of superiority. Not only has the miracle economy enabled former war profiteers to make their startling comebacks, but it has also made it possible for most Germans to fall back on their beliefs of supremacy. They see the rise of new buildings, new industries, new demands for German products, resentment toward German competition from their former enemies-turned-allies, and it is logical for them to say, "we're wonderful people."

"Well, we are wonderful people," said one German who knows his country well. "The only trouble with so many of us is that we are too aware of it and once aware, believe that fact entitles us to special privileges and rights."

As the Germans bask in the complacency of a job well done, they not only forget to give credit where credit is due for their fabulous economic recovery and their high standard of living, but they also fail to take proper responsibility for their past mistakes and crimes. The German miracle economy is a purely German achievement to a great cross section of the population. The help they received from the United States through the Marshall Plan has long been forgotten. Curiously many Americans who look with awe upon the new Germany have also forgotten how many of their tax dollars went into helping establish the current German crystal palace.

Unfortunately, many Germans have been so preoccupied with meeting the day-to-day pressures and needs of their booming, bustling economy, that they have forgotten to come to grips with their history. It is not only that they have suppressed the facts of the Hitler régime because they are too shocking, too strenuous on the average conscience to think about, but many millions have simply been too busy to give it any thought. Once they had amassed enough of the good new things of life to have the leisure to think, those thoughts were too disturbing and unpleasant.

Except for the political division of Germany, there are virtually no remnants of the war, no sources of remorse, no visible signs of punishment for past mistakes which affect any large segment of the population. Even the quest for unity and spiritual association with the East Zone must be fired up artificially through various devious means of propaganda. Only a small proportion of the West Germans have any real ties with the Soviet-occupied German Democratic Republic.

For that majority which has no such ties, the remnants of war have practically disappeared. They must, in fact, be reminded that there was a war and that Germany lost it. True, there are still many homeless, still many impoverished, still thousands who are missing and hundreds of thousands of war widows and wounded, but even for many of them, time has healed the wounds. Under the circumstances, it is obvious that there is little remorse, little desire for self-flagellation because of crimes committed by "the Nazis, but not by me."

Furthermore, many Germans still have not been able to face up to their own responsibility for the past which is so terrible they suppress it into the subconscious. When they are reminded, they react with indignation, attempting to rid themselves of the collective moral blame ascribed to them.

Yet the Germany of 1960 *is* a different Germany from that of the Hitler and pre-Nazi days. Although there are many developments to criticize, there are many more to praise. There can, in fact, be no real comparison with the Germany of the past, and an attempt to draw parallels between the negative aspects apparent today and those of the past is both unfair and alarmist. Although there are neo-Nazis, there is no danger of a Nazi resurgence or of neo-Nazism. Although there are Nazis in government and private life, to say that the Nazis are back in power is exaggeration of the crassest sort. Although there are nationalistic elements and the democratic development of the *Bundeswehr* leaves a lot to be desired, there is no imminent threat of excesssive militarism or nationalism. Anti-Semitism, although a factor, is relatively speaking and in consideration of past history, not much more prevalent in Germany than elsewhere.

Although former Nazis are receiving pensions, the Germans are paying their restitution and reparations debts. While the Germans may gripe and complain about this and that, they are keeping their contractual promises to their allies. There are pressure groups demanding a general amnesty for Nazi criminals, but the official position is that all vestiges of Nazism must be stamped out and Nazis must be punished. It may have taken fifteen years to bring to light the failings of the educational system, but once public pressure was brought to bear on responsible authorities, remedial action was and is being taken. And, while there is a nationalist and neo-Nazi press, it is overshadowed by democratic literature and journalism.

Above all, though it may appear hypocritical and insincere, the Germans are exceedingly sensitive to foreign opinion of them. In fact, many of their actions, many of their statements, and a good deal of their official and private behavior are dictated by one rule of thumb: "What will the Americans, or the British, or the French, or the Danes think of this?" They have been criticized severely from without and within for this attitude, but let's be frank: one of history's frequent complaints of the Germans has been their apathy, their complete disregard for foreign attitudes and opinions.

The real determination as to whether the new Germany is a fact or fable can only be made in the future.

Is the German democracy solid enough to withstand the test of economic recession or depression? Can it weather a political onslaught from either the left or the right? How will it fare once it has to contend with its first change of top leadership?

These are the real problems that confront the Germans and the West and they cannot be answered yet.

Index